SIMON SHERIDAN

The Initiation of Nietzsche

Wagner's Disciple

Copyright © 2025 by Simon Sheridan

All rights reserved. No part of this publication may be reproduced, stored or transmitted in any form or by any means, electronic, mechanical, photocopying, recording, scanning, or otherwise without written permission from the publisher. It is illegal to copy this book, post it to a website, or distribute it by any other means without permission.

First edition

This book was professionally typeset on Reedsy.
Find out more at reedsy.com

Contents

Introduction	1
Part 1: Preliminaries	7
Why Wagner and Nietzsche Were Never Friends	7
A Model of Human Development	16
Nietzsche's Childhood and Adolescence	19
The Upheaval in 19th Century Germany	24
Why Appearances Deceive: The Dionysian and Apollonian	39
Why Wagner was Primarily a Storyteller	42
The Orphan Story Template	47
Why Stories are Real	56
The Journey into the Sacred	68
Part 2: The Orphan Story of Nietzsche and Wagner	75
The Hero Meets the Elder	75
The Call to Adventure	82
Initiation Begins	96
The Confrontation with the Shadow Elder	129
Wagner's Betrayal	162
Fighting the Elder	190
Wagner's Apology	220
About the Author	251
Also by Simon Sheridan	252

Introduction

About one hundred and fifty years after their deaths, why should we in the modern West care about the relationship between Richard Wagner and Friedrich Nietzsche? This question is worth asking at the outset since many commentators have sensed something special in the bond between the two, and yet very little in the way of satisfactory explanations has been forthcoming. What's more, as time has gone on, the influence of Nietzsche has arguably now surpassed that of Wagner in the broader culture. This has had the result of adding a further layer of confusion due to the fact that most analysts approach the subject through the prism of Nietzsche's mature works, all of which are vehemently anti-Wagner. It could be argued that these have served to subdue interest in Wagner. The story is more complex and much more interesting than that, however.

Although the composer retains a hardcore following who gather each year at the Mecca of the *Festspielhaus* in Bayreuth to pay homage to his works, and although many of those works still form part of the canon of classical music, Wagner's influence on modern culture is limited. In many respects, this is deeply unfair since Wagner can be seen as the forerunner to a number of modern trends. The *Gesamtkunstwerk*, his modification to the operatic art form, had anticipated almost all of the qualities of modern film. Like film, Wagner had insisted that the story be the centrepoint of the work. Like film, Wagner made use of music to highlight and accentuate the story. He also paid great attention to acting, costume, props, sets, and all the rest. A Wagner opera required a small army to put into production, something that is also true of a modern film.

The parallels do not end there. Wagner also presaged the rise of modern pop culture by demanding that his *Gesamtkunstwerk* be a true expression of the culture of a people (a Volk) and not just a frivolous amusement for the elites of society. Furthermore, in order to break the dependence on aristocratic money, Wagner experimented with modes of fundraising that bear an uncanny resemblance to modern crowdfunding. Thus, a very strong argument can be made that Wagner laid the groundwork for both modern film and modern pop culture. That is true not just in theory, but in practice. At the height of his popularity, he really had turned the art of opera into something very similar to the modern blockbuster.

A final correlation between Wagner's work and more modern counterparts is that his use of grand quasi-mythological narratives and characters can also be seen as the precursor to the modern genres of fantasy and science fiction. Consider how popular *Lord of the Rings* and the original *Star Wars* trilogy are in modern culture, and then consider that Wagner had explored very similar motifs in his *Ring Cycle* and final opera, *Parsifal*.

Bearing in mind how much Wagner seemed to be ahead of his time and had anticipated many of the artistic innovations of the twentieth century, it is an irony that he is now put in a nice neat little box with the label "Opera Composer" on the front. In his own time, he had explicitly tried to distance himself from that world by stating that his art should not be called opera at all. He wanted to call it "Drama" and he wanted it to be popular outside of the snobbish and cloistered world of classical music.

We could find all kinds of ad hoc reasons why this happened, including technological changes, social and political ructions, or the fact that history tends to simplify reality down into easily memorable categories and it's simply easier to remember Wagner as a composer of operas. What we will see in this book, however, is that there is some justice to the way in which Wagner has been treated by history because, despite the successes he had, he really did fail to achieve the vision he set out earlier in his life. He did so by quite explicitly betraying that vision. His posthumous punishment is therefore to be included with the group of people who he despised and who despised him in return. He is now thought of as *just a composer*, when he had always wanted to be so much more.

That is only half of the story, however. The other half is that there was one, and seemingly only one, man who realised that Wagner had betrayed his ideals, and that man was none other than Friedrich Nietzsche. The historical misunderstandings that surround Wagner are only amplified when we add Nietzsche into the mix. If we assume that Wagner was *just a composer* and Nietzsche was *just a philosopher*, then the relationship between the two seems rather strange since these are seemingly discrete fields of endeavour with little to do with each other. Things get even weirder when we understand that Nietzsche was not even a philosopher when the two men first met; he was a university student studying philology, a discipline that doesn't even exist anymore.

Therein lies the secret to the story because Nietzsche was not a philosopher when he first met Wagner, but he would become one just a few years later as a direct result of the influence of the composer. Furthermore, what is regarded as Nietzsche's mature philosophy began immediately after the break with Wagner and was, in fact, predicated on that break. We might even go a step further and argue that it was Wagner's betrayal of his ideals that saw Nietzsche become the philosopher he is remembered as by history. In other words, it was Wagner who turned Nietzsche from a philology student into a philosopher, one of the greatest in the Western canon.

How on earth could an opera composer train a philosopher? Well, again, this comes back to the confusion around Wagner. He always considered himself more than *just a composer*. Although Wagner's art was in many ways the precursor to modern film and modern pop culture, we have to remember that he was advocating for these ideas at a time when it was genuinely dangerous to do so. 19th century Germany, and Europe more generally, was a hotbed of competing ideologies and a time of major uncertainty where different visions for the future were all competing with each other for prominence and power. Wagner had dabbled in political revolution as a young man, but he would later channel his energy into what he believed was a revolutionary form of art and culture. It was Wagner's thrilling and passionate avowal of these ideals that attracted Nietzsche and Nietzsche's first published books were essentially co-written with Wagner in that the ideas they contained were jointly developed during the intimate discussions the two men shared over a three year period at Wagner's house in Lucerne, a time which served as Nietzsche's philosophical apprenticeship.

In answer to the question of why we should care about the relationship between Nietzsche and Wagner, the first answer is that it's a hell of a story in and of itself. Wagner was a grand visionary, a dangerous revolutionary who had been exiled from Germany for ten years, and then returned like the prodigal son to realise the vision he had laid out in his younger years. Nietzsche was a brilliant young scholar who got swept up in the composer's vision for the future and then, miraculously, met his hero and found himself a regular guest at Wagner's house idyllic mansion on the shores of Lake Lucerne. The series of events that made all that possible are incredible, and the entire relationship is as full of extraordinary coincidences and symbolic resonances as any of Wagner's operas. Thus, the story of their relationship is worth telling just because it's a great story.

The break between the two men would also be as dramatic as a Wagner opera, revolving around the betrayal of the younger man by the older. We said earlier that Wagner had sold out his ideals; well, Nietzsche was perhaps the only one at the time who realised that fact. Why this affected him so profoundly was because he had come to believe those ideals. He did so because Wagner taught them to him.

This leads us to the second reason why we should care about the story of Nietzsche and Wagner: because the ideals and ideas the two men explored are worth understanding in more detail. One of the main planks in Wagner's thought was that art was the supreme metaphysical task of life. In his language, he wanted art to be fundamentally connected to Life and Nature. But Wagner was never interested in ideas for their own sake. He wanted to put them into practice. He genuinely dedicated his life to art, and he made that decision not while sitting in a comfortable chair by the fire but at a time when he was faced with complete ruin. As a result of this dedication, the differences between the art and life started to break down. Wagner stepped into the archetype of the heroic Artist which was quite specific to 19th-century Germany and included great men such as Goethe, Mozart, and Beethoven. There was a quasi-religious tone to this in that the Artist was expected to fulfil a role that had been left vacant by receding Christianity. Thus, Wagner's life can be thought of as an experiment in the idea that life and art could merge together. More poetically, he wanted to live life as if it were a work of art.

Wagner achieved his goal to a very large extent, and a big part of the reason why Nietzsche became so enamoured of the composer was because he found himself sucked up into the same vortex where the boundary between reality and art seemed to break down. From the very first time he met Wagner, Nietzsche remarked how it felt as if he was "living in a novel" and that the coincidences that kept occurring were like something out of a fairy tale.

Our analysis of the relationship between Wagner and Nietzsche will therefore also be a case study in the idea that life and art can merge and what that might look like. What we will show in this book is that the evolution of the bond between the two men must be thought of in terms of a story. This is not a metaphor or vague symbolic statement. We can be very precise about what it means by following the scholarship on stories done in the 20th century, including and especially that of Joseph Campbell. Thus, we can show in detail that Nietzsche and Wagner's relationship follows what we will call the Orphan Story pattern, a pattern it shares with two of the most important relationships in Western history. What we will argue is that Wagner was Socrates to Nietzsche's Plato, Jesus to Nietzsche's Peter.

It is fitting that our subjects will be two men from the 19th century since it was in that century that a question arose of whether life imitated art or vice versa. Our analysis will call into question whether there exists any meaningful difference to begin with. If reality is already structured in the form of art (i.e., a story), then life is already art and art is already life. Whether that is true by default or whether it was only true because Wagner and Nietzsche made it true is a question that is difficult to resolve. But, even if it is the latter, then that simply means that Wagner had successfully turned his life into a work of art such that the boundaries between the two broke down. Nietzsche would develop a similar idea in his mature philosophy, i.e., the notion of self-creation through art, philosophy, etc.

Thus, in answer to our original question of why we should study the relationship between Wagner and Nietzsche, we have several answers. Firstly, to tell the incredible story of how Wagner took a young philology student under his wing and turned him into one of the greatest philosophers in Western history. Secondly, to show that the relationship between the two men must be understood in the form of a story (a *journey into the sacred*). Thirdly, to marvel at the incredible "coincidence" that the story between the two men would play out almost identically to those in Wagner's operas. All of which will lead to a conclusion that Wagner and Nietzsche were right and that we can become the authors of our own story rather than just characters in someone else's.

Part 1: Preliminaries

Why Wagner and Nietzsche Were Never Friends

Let's begin this book with a thought experiment. We'll pretend that neither Richard Wagner nor Friedrich Nietzsche were famous men but that everything else about their relationship remained the same. In this alternative world, two ordinary, non-famous individuals meet for the first time. The elder one is fifty-five years old and the younger one is twenty-four. The older man has a family and a successful career, while the younger is just coming to the end of a university degree. What sort of relationship could we expect to form between them? That would obviously depend on the context. It may be that the younger man is trying to enter the same field as the older. In that case, the older man might become an employer or some kind of mentor to the younger. Another option is that the two men happen to live in the same area and make acquaintance while passing each other's houses or seeing each other around town. A third option would be some kind of family connection that brings them together, e.g. a relation via marriage.

However this relationship between our two hypothetical men begins, it is simply a fact that a generation gap exists between the two that will inevitably exert its influence. Barring any special circumstances, we can assume that the older man will have more resources, more connections, and an established place in society, while the younger man, who has not even graduated university, is likely to have none of those. The older man will almost certainly have more and varied life experiences than the younger man who is still going through his education. These factors form the background dynamic between the two and they dictate that the most probable relationship to emerge between the men will be a mentor-protégé one. This is true whether the relationship is formal or informal in nature. It follows from the fact that the older man has already done what the young man is only getting ready to do. He has established his career, gotten married, had children, and become involved in politics or religion or any of the activities undertaken by adults in his culture. A mentor-protégé relationship between the two men doesn't need to be formalised or even consciously understood by the participants. It would follow naturally from the differences between them.

For these same reasons, a genuine friendship between two such men would be highly unlikely because a friendship implies a relationship between equals, where equality can relate to social standing, financial status, emotional maturity, and perhaps most importantly, life experience. Especially for the young man, a friend is somebody with whom he can share the experiences of that phase of life as an equal. The kinds of experiences that the young university student is likely to undertake with his friends are almost certainly not going to be participated in by a fifty-five-year-old, not just because of the social awkwardness that would obtain but because the older man is unlikely to be interested. He's been there and done that, and, in any case, he now has a reputation to uphold and a family to think about. Unlike the younger man, he has something to lose.

If we accept these general truths about the kind of relationship that can exist between two men separated by a generation gap, then returning to the specific pairing between Nietzsche and Wagner, we can add more cultural context to enhance our perspective. Nietzsche and Wagner lived in Victorian-era Prussia, not exactly a society that was known for its free and easy-going cultural norms. In fact, it was a culture in which obedience to authority, including the authority of elders, was inculcated from a young age. Parents expected to be obeyed by their children, school teachers expected to be obeyed by their students, and an older man in a relationship with a younger would expect his authority to be recognised too, even in an informal setting. That would have been true in general, but it would have been even more true if the older man was a recognised master in his field, as Wagner was. We have to remember that the almost insolent attitude that post-war Western culture has towards age and experience did not exist in the 19th century and certainly not in Germany.

Of course, when any group in society has a default power advantage over another, it inevitably happens that the powerful group abuses that dynamic. It is a curious coincidence then that, in all of Wagner's mature operas, the use and misuse of the power dynamic between an older and a younger man sits at the core of the drama. King Marke's domination of Tristan destroys the love between him and Isolde and leads to both their deaths. Although the ages are not precisely specified, we can be very sure that Hagen is the older man who uses his experience to bring down the younger Siegfried in the final opera of the *Ring Cycle*. The plot of *Die Meistersinger* revolves around the middle-aged Beckmesser trying to elbow aside his younger rival, Walther, in a contest over who gets to marry the young Eva. In *Lohengrin*, we see an almost identical dynamic to *Meistersinger*, with the titular hero set against a more experienced and well-connected adversary in Telramund. In *The Flying Dutchman*, the titular hero is the more experienced campaigner who steals the love of the young woman Senta from her contemporary Erik. Finally, the plot of *Parsifal* begins with the experienced Grail knight, Gurnemanz, sending the young hero away in a rage at his inability to understand a complex religious ceremony that has been conducted before him. Parsifal is made to wander alone and face his adversaries without the training or guidance of a teacher.

Part of the enormous appeal that Wagner's operas had in his day surely came from the fact that the intergenerational conflict presented in his operas mirrored the broader social and political context. In the aftermath of Napoleon, the revolutionary spirit that still burned brightly in the hearts of the younger generations was severely repressed by the established powers of that era, primarily Prussia and Austria. This repression gave rise to a number of rebellions and uprisings, including the one in Dresden in 1849 that Wagner directly participated in and which would see him sent into a long period of exile. In his public and private writings, Wagner railed against what he saw as the dull, unimaginative, and moribund state not just of opera but of German culture altogether. From his perspective, the repression of the older generation was not just holding back political progress but cultural progress through the arts. Wagner saw himself and his contemporaries as the younger man being oppressed by the older, and it's clear that this belief flowed through into his operas.

Putting all this together, considering the default general asymmetry in a relationship between a twenty-four-year-old and a fifty-five-year-old and considering the social and cultural factors of 19th-century Germany that exacerbated this asymmetry, it should strike us as strange that the default analysis made by commentators on the relationship between Wagner and Nietzsche has been that they were "friends". Not only was Wagner the older man with all the general advantages that we have just discussed, he was also a famous man and a man whose fame was growing. As if all that wasn't enough, there are the personal factors involved. Wagner had one of the most dominating personalities of his age. He could be charming and witty but also abrasive and hurtful. He demanded loyalty and commanded attention. He did so not just among general company but even among some of the most distinguished and powerful people of his time, including the young king of Bavaria. Many of those people, who were highly accomplished in their own lives, fell under his spell and remained faithful to him even as he treated them appallingly. So, we must ask the question again and even more forcefully: why have seemingly all commentators on the Wagner-Nietzsche relationship taken the default position that the two men were "friends" when there are so many factors against such a reading and almost none in favour of it?

One of the primary reasons is certainly a bias that Nietzsche himself wrote about in his later philosophy. He said that we judge peoples, nations, and events based on their finished state. We judge ancient Greece based on the golden age of Athens. We judge Rome based on the achievements of the imperium. We judge individuals based on the peak achievements attained during the mature phase of their life. We use the properties of this end state to judge all prior states that led up to it. When we apply this bias to Wagner and Nietzsche, our starting point is a relationship between a great composer and a great philosopher. Since these epithets imply a level of equality, we assume a relationship of friendship must have existed between the two men, since friendship is based on equality. But this is the exact error Nietzsche was talking about. We take the end state as the basis for the whole analysis. When Nietzsche met Wagner for the first time, he was not a great philosopher. He was not a recognised philosopher at all. By contrast, Wagner was already considered a great composer, including by Nietzsche himself. From the very beginning, there was not equality but asymmetry.

This error of starting at the end also applies to the way in which commentators have allowed Nietzsche's own writing to cloud the issue of the relationship with Wagner. Nietzsche's later writings are considered his greatest. In fact, they are considered some of the great writings of Western philosophy. Every one of them was written after Nietzsche's break with Wagner, and most of them contain the scathing critique of the composer that Nietzsche made in his later years, labelling him a decadent. The forcefulness of this critique in Nietzsche's classic works has led readers to believe that this was Nietzsche's "true" opinion of Wagner. Starting from that proposition, many analysts have gone off in search of evidence for this same attitude in Nietzsche's earlier works, even finding sentences in the 1876 essay *Richard Wagner in Bayreuth* which they claim show that Nietzsche had already begun to dissociate from the composer. But even if such sentences exist (if they do, I couldn't find them), this would not negate the fact that *Richard Wagner in Bayreuth* is a gushing hagiography whose closest parallel can only be found in the gospels. Any marginal criticism that Nietzsche made of Wagner in that work is completely overshadowed by that fact. The real question of *Richard Wagner in Bayreuth* is why Nietzsche felt the need to lavish such effusive praise on Wagner and why he just happened to do so right before the famous falling out between the two men.

But even these questions commit the error of judging events based on the end state. Nietzsche's explicit criticisms of Wagner only show up in his later writings. Because those works are considered classics, their content is assumed to be "superior" or "more truthful" than what came before. Some take this attitude so far as to write off the earlier works as irrelevant. No less an authority than one of Nietzsche's foremost English translators, R.J. Hollingdale, labelled the early philosophy of Nietzsche a "false start". But, to say it one more time, this is the exact error of thinking that Nietzsche himself pointed out. It denies the process of becoming. Therefore, it denies the way in which all of us actually develop in our lives. It would be like saying that Michaelangelo's early sculptures were a *false start* or Wagner's early operas were a *false start*. That's not how human development works. Our early attempts are never as good as our mature ones, but without those earlier efforts, we would never get anywhere at all. Such things cannot be a *false start* because there is no other way to start, unless one is a *savant*.

Nietzsche was not a savant. His early philosophy constituted the foundation for his mature works, and Wagner was crucial in his development, not just as an inspiration but as a public defender of his early writing. And here we get a glimpse of the real relationship that existed between the two men at the beginning, not at the end. As a first approximation, we can say it was a mentor-protégé relationship, although, as we will see shortly, there was something much more fundamental and important going on. What we need to do if we want to understand this strange relationship between a famous composer and a young university student is to take a leaf out of Nietzsche's book and examine both men and their relationship as a process of becoming. That means we do not judge them solely from the great heights that they later achieved; we judge them as human beings who evolved from childhood through adolescence and into maturity. When we do this, we understand their relationship as taking place during a specific phase of their lives.

Nietzsche was a bookish twenty-four-year-old philology student coming to the end of a university degree. Wagner was a famous man with an imposing and dominating personality. At the time of their first meeting, Wagner's fame had been growing in Germany for some time, predominantly among the class of people of which Nietzsche was a newly minted member, i.e. the educated elites. For his part, Nietzsche's interest in Wagner had begun about eight years earlier, and the manner in which it was sparked tells us a lot about the young man. While at school in Naumburg, Nietzsche and two friends formed a musical and literary society called *Germania*. The friends were subscribers to a music magazine called the *Neue Zeitschrift für Musik,* which often featured positive reviews and news on Wagner. It was one of the other members of the group, Krug, who first introduced Nietzsche to Wagner's music. Wagner was a prominent exponent not just of "new music" but of a *new German culture.* Nietzsche and his school friends were interested in that new culture not just as passive spectators but with an eye to actively contributing. In the years leading up to their meeting, Nietzsche's enthusiasm for Wagner grew. Thus, when they did meet for the first time in late 1868, Nietzsche knew a great deal about Wagner, but Wagner knew nothing of him. Once again, we see that the asymmetries involved are all in Wagner's favour, and such an asymmetrical relationship can never be a "friendship".

Further evidence against the friendship idea comes from the fact that Nietzsche always addressed Wagner by the epithet *Meister* (master) in the correspondence between the two. This touches on another subject that Nietzsche wrote about often in his later philosophy, where he criticised the "democratisation" process that had already begun levelling out social distinctions in the 19th century. Nietzsche lamented the erasure of *gradations of rank* between men. He would have seen the reduction of all relationships to "friendship" as not just sloppy scholarship but as yet another hallmark of this democratisation process. All the evidence suggests that Nietzsche saw Wagner as a superior man and accorded him the status that came from that position. Moreover, Nietzsche thought of Wagner as a teacher. Once the relationship was established and Nietzsche was a regular guest at the Wagner home in Switzerland, he eagerly wrote to friends stating how much he was learning from the *Meister.*

What exactly was Nietzsche learning from Wagner during this time? We know that the young man was a talented and enthusiastic musician. In fact, he and Krug had sat down at the piano and attempted to play the score of *Tristan and Isolde* back in 1861. We know that Wagner was not shy about playing his works for guests of the house, and so Nietzsche had the rare honour of receiving personal performances from the famous composer. No doubt, he would have informally picked up much about music theory and the art of composition while in Wagner's presence. But Wagner was not giving musical instruction to Nietzsche, and he wasn't particularly impressed with the young man's musical abilities anyway. On the contrary, Nietzsche's musical talents, or lack thereof, were the subject of one of the scathing jibes that Wagner often dished out to those around him when his mood turned sour.

Nietzsche was clearly not receiving any kind of technical musical instruction from Wagner, at least not in a direct sense. What he was receiving were Wagner's broader ideas around the role of music and especially Wagner's innovations in opera for the new German culture that the older man had become concerned with earlier in his life. As we will see later, Germany, which was not even a unified nation at the time when Nietzsche and Wagner first met, had been going through a cultural identity crisis for decades. Both Wagner and Nietzsche had been born into that milieu, but it was the older man who had not only sketched out a plan to address the problem but had also made significant progress towards implementing it. Wagner may have been a narcissist, a bully, and a prima donna, but he also had the ability to charm and inspire those around him. The elation that we read in Nietzsche's letters from the first years of their relationship is testament to the fact that Wagner's inspiring vision had worked its magic on the younger man.

When we approach the relationship between Nietzsche and Wagner from the point of view of the stage of their lives that each was going through at the time, we get a very different perspective from that which has become common and which is heavily influenced by Nietzsche's later writings. Nietzsche was one of many young men who were hungry for a new culture that addressed the identity and political crisis in Germany. Wagner had already identified the problem decades earlier and had quite literally made it his life's mission to address it. What's more, he had begun to succeed at that mission. Thus, when the two men met for the first time, not only was there the inherent age difference between them which made Wagner old enough to be Nietzsche's father, not only was Wagner a famous man with all the drama that comes with that, but he was increasingly seen to be a heroic figure who was advancing a revolutionary new art form. That art form, the *Gesamtkunstwerk*, was a combination of music, drama, poetry, acting, stage design, and more. It involved detailed and intricate reworkings of famous mythical stories. Nietzsche was not just an enthusiastic musician; he was starting to win acclaim as perhaps the most promising philologist of his generation. Nietzsche would have known all of the Germanic myths that Wagner was using in his operas as well as his numerous references back to the Greek tragedies that both admired. Of all the young men in Germany who were inspired by Wagner's new art, very few were in a position to understand and appreciate that art more than the young philologist. The "education" which Nietzsche was receiving was to meet the kind of man who could create such art and see how he worked, how he lived, and how he thought. It was an initiation into greatness, with all the negative and positive qualities that come with it.

Thus, we can put to bed once and for all the idea that Wagner and Nietzsche were "friends". The twenty-four-year-old Nietzsche would never have described the relationship that way. He had dreamed of greatness as a teenager, and now he had direct access to it. He was a young man meeting his hero. As a famous, powerful, and accomplished man, Wagner already had an inner circle of supporters who were helping to bring his vision of the new art and the new German culture to fruition. It was into that circle that Nietzsche would eventually be invited. It was an invitation that was Wagner's to make and Wagner's to cancel any time he liked. He made it some months after their initial meeting in a letter to Nietzsche where he all but ordered the young scholar to visit him and included the words, "Now let me see what kind of man you are." Does this sound like the invitation of a friend? No. It is the invitation of a *Meister* to his new apprentice.

In the same letter, Wagner writes, "My experiences with my fellow Germans have been less than wholly delightful so far. Come and restore my not entirely unwavering faith in what I – together with Goethe and a few others – call German freedom." Nietzsche had been invited into a small and select circle of people who were pursuing this *German freedom, German culture*, and the *artwork of the future*. Wagner was the hero at the centre of it all, and the word *hero* really is appropriate here because Wagner's new art form required truly heroic dedication and passion not just in its performance but in its preparation and organisation. Nietzsche would later contribute directly to the fulfilment of that art. He would accept Wagner's call and join the fight for *German freedom*. This was not a *friendship*. In fact, it was not even a mentor-protégé relationship. Wagner's invitation to Nietzsche was to join him in the pursuit of grand, world-changing goals. When Nietzsche accepted, he became not a friend of the composer but a disciple. He became a *Wagnerian*.

A Model of Human Development

In order to understand how it was that Nietzsche became a disciple of Wagner we have to do what most commentators have not done which is to start at the beginning by describing Nietzsche's life prior to Wagner. But, more than that, we need to have a framework by which to understand what kind of life Nietzsche was living and why the connection with Wagner caused a radical shift which would place the young man onto the path that we know he would eventually take, that of becoming a philosopher.

The framework we will use for that purpose is the one I laid out in my book *Archetypology: The Archetypal Study of Human Nature*. As the name suggests, archetypology places the concept of the archetype at the centre of analysis. The theory is inspired by the work of the great Swiss psychologist, Carl Jung. Archetypology builds on the work of Jung by expanding the concept of the archetype beyond the psychological and into the biological and socio-cultural realm, thereby connecting it back to what Wagner called Life and Nature.

A detailed outline of archetypology is not required for our purposes here. This book has been written so that no prior knowledge of the model is needed. Nevertheless, we will need to introduce the basic concepts. Fortunately, these are very straightforward as they map to our common-sense understanding of human development.

Archetypology posits that there are four main stages of development we go through in life. We name these stages according to four archetypes: the Child, the Orphan, the Adult, and the Elder. Each of these maps to the biological concepts of childhood, adolescence, maturity, and senescence, but the core idea of archetypology is that the archetypes are not merely biological or psychological in nature. They are integral. We can think of each archetype as a complex symbol that points to biological, socio-cultural, and psychological truths. For example, the Child phase of life has distinctive biological properties, but it also has unique psychological and socio-cultural properties. These are all aligned with each other and therefore form a natural unit of analysis.

When applied to the task of writing a biography, such as the one we are compiling of Nietzsche in this book, archetypology prompts us to divide the life of the individual into the four archetypes of the Child, Orphan, Adult, and Elder. This may sound like a fairly obvious thing to do, and yet, when we look at the biographies of famous people, we find that they almost exclusively concentrate on the Adult phase of life. It is not a surprise that this should be so because that is the time of life when every individual is at the peak of their powers in terms of real-world achievement. What is true of all of us is even more true of the exceptional individuals who are worthy of having biographies written about them. For people of world-historical importance, it's almost certain that the most dramatic, interesting, and important events occurred during the Adult phase of their lives, and therefore biographers focus on those to the exclusion of the less dramatic events of childhood or adolescence. Note that this is true even of the sub-genre of biography concerned with the lives of religious figures, i.e. hagiographies, myths, and legends. The gospel story of Jesus, for example, has almost nothing on his childhood or adolescence (Child and Orphan archetypes). Even the early years of the Adult phase of his life are not covered. Understandably, the gospel story focuses only the dramatic few years that ended up changing the world.

By using the archetypal approach, we at least remind ourselves that human development includes more than just the Adult years of life. In fact, the Adult years can be seen as the culmination of the evolution that has occurred during the Child and Orphan phases. To what extent our mature identities are defined by these earlier phases is a question that still has no definitive answer, although it was in the 20th century where such questions began to be studied in earnest and where the developmental phases of the Child and

Orphan years of life were sketched out in detail. In any case, our analysis in this book will hopefully contribute to a correction in our understanding on this score because we will posit that Nietzsche was in the Orphan phase of his life when he met Wagner, and it was the relationship with Wagner that led directly to his mature (Adult) identity as one of the great philosophers in the Western canon. In other words, we will be studying the process by which he became a philosopher. This is in stark contrast to almost every other Nietzsche biography, which begins with his mature writing and works backwards.

This leads us to the final concept we need before we begin our analysis proper. Each archetypal phase of life has a dominant relationship with one other archetype. During the Child years, it is the connection with our parents which dominates. This sounds incredibly obvious, yet it took until Freud for somebody to take the Child-Parent relationship seriously enough to study it in detail. In any case, this pairing is so fundamental and universal that it requires no further explanation. It is the second pairing which is far less well-understood and that is the one between the Orphan and the Elder archetypes. This relationship is crucial in human development because it is the Elder's role to initiate the Orphan into the institutions of society. Therefore, the Orphan-Elder relationship is not just vital to the individual, it is also about the propagation of a culture.

The Orphan-Elder relationship sits at the heart of some of the most important events in Western history. Jesus was the Elder to the disciples. Socrates was the Elder to Plato. Julius Caesar was an Elder to Brutus. Freud was the Elder to Jung. It is because Nietzsche met Wagner during the Orphan phase of his life that Wagner would become his Elder. Therefore, we can draw a direct parallel between their relationship and the great names just mentioned. In fact, as we will see later, not only is the basic relationship the same, but the evolution of it follows an identical pattern. In short, we are going to say that the relationship between Wagner and Nietzsche was (almost) identical in form to that between Jesus and the disciples and Socrates and Plato. It will take the rest of this book to see just how deep these parallels go.

PART 1: PRELIMINARIES

Nietzsche's Childhood and Adolescence

In order to see how extraordinary the relationship with Wagner was, including the speed of its development, we need to sketch out the details of Nietzsche's life prior to meeting the composer. Let's begin with the first archetype in our sequence: the Child.

We have little information about the Child phase of Nietzsche's life. However, there was a dramatic event that occurred when Nietzsche was still a young boy. His father died when he was five, and his brother passed almost immediately afterwards. It's very difficult to know how much of an impact this had on Nietzsche. Some commentators have used his father's death to speculate that Nietzsche's relationship with Wagner had an Oedipal dimension to it, since Wagner was about the same age as Nietzsche's father. One piece of evidence against this reading is that Nietzsche very rarely mentioned his father in both his philosophy and his personal writings. For a writer who was so open about his inner thoughts in most other areas of his life, this absence signals that his father's death was not an ongoing problem for the older Nietzsche. By contrast, Nietzsche never stopped writing about Wagner. In fact, two of his last five books had the composer as the main theme of the work.

One important outcome of the untimely death of his father and brother was that Nietzsche spent most of his childhood raised as the sole male in female-dominated homes. Despite achieving independence later on, his mother and sister remained pervasive influences throughout his life. Indeed, they became his primary caregivers when he later lost his mind. This was certainly an important influence on Nietzsche and may explain, among other things, his inability to form romantic relationships with women. In the case of Nietzsche's failed attempt at courting Lou Salomé, both his mother and sister were actively involved in subverting that relationship. Nevertheless, all these seem to be minor points. The overall impression we get is that Nietzsche's Child phase of life had no extraordinary influence on his later development. By contrast, the events that occurred at the beginning of Nietzsche's Orphan phase became crucial to his later identity.

Since the properties of the Orphan are central to our analysis in this book, let's now spend some time introducing the archetype. The name of the Orphan derives from the fact that the primary mission of this time of life is to separate from our parents and begin to forge an independent identity that will reach maturity during the Adult phase. Nietzsche's life shows us a prime example of this since he was able to escape the female-dominated household of his childhood by receiving a scholarship to study at the prestigious Schulpforta. Because the school was too far away from home for daily travel, Nietzsche became a boarder, and this gave him a physical separation from his mother and sister. Schulpforta was also renowned for the subject that Nietzsche would later become a professor of: philology.

The Orphan phase of life is the beginning of the development of the full range of identities that we carry into adulthood. For analytical purposes, we can divide that identity formation into several categories. One of these follows from the onset of biological maturity, and that is our sexual identity. Most societies have strict regulations around the expression of sexuality in young teens with the intention of channelling the sexual instinct into marriage. In the post-war West, we have largely thrown away the rule book in this respect, but that was definitely not the case when Nietzsche came of age. The Victorian era was notorious for its repressive attitudes towards sexuality, and even though these were less restrictive for young men than their female counterparts, the result was much the same. Especially in the case of the educated and upper classes of society, sexuality began with marriage, and marriage did not take place until the individual had established themselves in society. In short, sexual identity did not begin to develop until the Adult phase of life. Nietzsche made two famously clumsy attempts to get married later, but during the Orphan years, he had next to no contact with females. Schulpforta was an all-boys school, and women were not allowed to study at university during this time. As a result, Nietzsche would never properly develop a sexual identity.

The other domains of identity outside the family are the economic, political, and military ones. For each of these, the Orphan phase of life represents an apprenticeship period. No society expects its Orphans to instantly transition from childhood to adulthood. There must be a time when we learn and build up our skills. Thus, the Orphan phase of life manifests in the socio-cultural domain as a time of education and training, and seemingly all cultures have a set of predefined roles, both formal and informal, to demarcate this fact. Common terms for the Orphan in the socio-cultural realm include 'student', 'apprentice', 'novice', 'trainee', 'recruit', 'learner', 'beginner', 'debutant', 'fledgling', or 'probationer'. Note that almost all of these terms imply a relationship with another person. A student implies a teacher. An army recruit implies a drill sergeant. A trainee implies a trainer, and so on. If all of the former roles pertain to what we have called the archetypal Orphan, all of the latter pertain to the archetype of the Elder. Thus, the Orphan-Elder relationship in all its variations is a crucial component of the Orphan phase of life. Our separation from our parents coincides with the beginning of these Orphan-Elder relationships.

There is one other domain of identity we have not yet mentioned, and that is the religious. The anthropological literature tells us that most cultures have religious ceremonies and practices that mark the onset of the Orphan phase of life. These can take a wide variety of forms, but we can say that the main purpose of any religious initiation is the communication of the core meanings of the culture. These are inculcated via rites of passage and also by stories and myths. In the modern West, we also communicate our core values through the scholarly-style instruction provided in the education system. Thus, Nietzsche's education at the Schulpforta was primarily religious in the broadest meaning of that term. It occurred at a time when mass education was not yet fully developed. We would say that Nietzsche was being trained for the mature archetype of the Scholar-Monk that had existed since the medieval period in Europe. (In this respect, an unspoken vow of chastity makes sense).

If we now apply these considerations directly to the life of Nietzsche, we find that the beginning of the Orphan phase of his life was marked by two primary forms of initiation. The first was his induction into high school, which was an intense and difficult transition involving the military-style practices of the 19th-century Prussian education system. The second form of initiation would have been his Confirmation ceremony at the Lutheran church of which he was a member. Confirmation is the coming-of-age ceremony given to Christians. The purpose of the rite is to instil the Holy Spirit in the initiate. It also marks a change of status within the congregation as the individual begins working towards full membership, i.e. adult status. In both of Nietzsche's initiations, we can identify the Elder whose role was to induct him. In the case of high school, that would have been his teachers. In the case of the church, the priest or bishop is the Elder who initiates the Orphans during the rite of Confirmation.

Since it will become crucial later in our analysis, let us now give a formal definition of the role of the Elder. The Elder is responsible for the initiation of an Orphan into an institution of society with an associated duty of care to the younger person to train, educate, and guide them to full membership in that institution. Institutions can be both highly formal or highly informal in nature. The army is a classic example of a formal institution, while voluntary and ad hoc associations are examples of informal ones. In both cases, however, the Elder archetype is fulfilled by the individual who has the authority to grant admission and who subsequently initiates the Orphan. Since many formal institutions have an internal hierarchy of command, we can also distinguish between the Elders in leadership roles who have ultimate responsibility versus the lower-level Elders who are responsible for day-to-day activities. For example, a general is an Elder with ultimate authority to grant admission to new recruits to the army, while the drill sergeant is the lower-level Elder who is responsible for the actual training of those recruits.

Every Orphan initiation into an institution implies a change of identity for the individual. In more extreme cases, the change of identity can be very dramatic. Let's take the example of the initiation of an army recruit.

The recruit must leave their civilian identity at the front gate. Normal, everyday clothing is exchanged for combat fatigues. For those with inappropriate hairstyles, a new haircut is in order, probably involving a short razor. New forms of address are learned. New forms of behaviour are inculcated. In highly formal environments like the army, the exoteric, outward-facing identity of the recruit is strictly determined, and all recruits are expected to live up to the mark. In some sense, we might say that the army denies or suppresses the esoteric or inner identity of the trainee. But another way to look at it is that the esoteric identity must conform to the exoteric. Whatever the recruit happens to feel about the training being given to them is irrelevant. What *is* relevant is that they do as they are told, i.e., that their exoteric behaviour matches expectations. We might more accurately say that the recruit must reconfigure their esoteric identity to develop the discipline and determination required to maintain the exoteric behaviour required of them. The recruit is required to learn a completely new set of exoteric behaviours as well as the esoteric states that facilitate them. Thus, there is both an exoteric and an esoteric reconfiguration. Because this new form of identity does not come naturally, it must be learned by the recruit (the Orphan archetype), and it must be strictly taught by the drill sergeant (the Elder archetype).

Nietzsche would go through army training in his early twenties in accordance with the requirements of Prussian society at that time. However, as we have already alluded to, his high school initiation was already of military-grade intensity. We must remember that this was the 19th century, and the Prussian discipline that had earned its military a fearsome reputation also manifested itself in the way in which education was conducted. Nietzsche's school regime required him to rise at 4am to be ready for the start of class an hour later. Classes continued through the day and into the early evening before an early bedtime of 9pm. Saturdays were also school days, with only Sunday reserved for rest. The teenage Nietzsche initially struggled to get used to this military-style education, but once the difficult period of adjustment was over, he excelled, and it was this environment which prepared him for his meteoric rise through the ranks of academic philology later.

In short, Nietzsche received the kind of initiation that matches what the anthropological literature tells us is common for young men across cultures. He was physically separated from family life and thrust into a new way of living. He was initiated into an institution of society that had a strong scholarly ethic. The Elders of that institution held its students to a very high standard; obedience and discipline were paramount. Nietzsche excelled in this environment, which prepared him directly for university, where he would become one of the most promising young philologists of his era.

This gives us a solid overview of the personal journey that Nietzsche had gone through in the Child and early Orphan phases of his life. We will return to the later Orphan phase later, which is the time when he met Wagner. However, it's important to realise that the Orphan years in particular are crucial because they are about the individual's initiation into the broader culture to which they belong. This broader culture forms the background against which any biographical sketch must take place. Therefore, we need to spend some time understanding in greater detail what sort of society Nietzsche was born into, especially because Wagner had been born into much the same milieu and their relationship took on forms quite specific to that era. Let's now turn our attention to the socio-cultural backdrop of central Europe in the 19th-century.

The Upheaval in 19th Century Germany

To the list of difficulties in understanding the Nietzsche-Wagner relationship that we have already mentioned, there is one more to add, and this is the fact that the image that has been handed down by history is of two supreme individuals. This is certainly warranted in the case of Nietzsche, who became a philosopher-hermit whose writings are radically subjective in nature, a feature that he did not shy away from but rather placed at the centre of his thought. In addition, Nietzsche was the supreme believer in genius and claimed that the purpose of society should be to facilitate the development of great individuals. Wagner was exactly the kind of individual man of greatness that Nietzsche was talking about. Wagner's individualism comes from the bombastic nature of his personality, his writings, and his operas. He was not in the slightest bit shy of criticising those he perceived as his enemies, and he did so without providing any argumentation, logic, or empirical evidence for his claims but simply asserted them through the force of his character.

The individualistic tenor of Nietzsche's life led one of his main commentators, Stefan Zweig, to proclaim in the opening line of his book on the philosopher, "The tragedy of Friedrich Nietzsche is a monodrama: no other figure is present on the brief-lived stage of his experience". Needless to say, we completely disagree with Zweig on this point. To the extent that Nietzsche's life was a tragedy (is that really true?), it was a tragedy that would never have happened without Wagner. If anything, it was a tragedy born out of the broken relationship with Wagner. But, more generally, this whole idea of a monodrama is highly problematic. It is worth quoting the extended text of John Donne's famous sermon in response:-

> *"No man is an island entire of itself; every man is a piece of the continent, a part of the main; if a clod be washed away by the sea, Europe is the less, as well as if a promontory were, as well as any manner of thy friends or of thine own were; any man's death diminishes me, because I am involved in mankind. And therefore never send to know for whom the bell tolls; it tolls for thee."*

Zweig's error is the one we have already noted: he began at the end. When Nietzsche became a philosopher-hermit, we can argue that he was an island unto himself. But it had not always been so. We have already seen that Nietzsche had an excellent schooling where he had numerous friends and colleagues, and we will spend most of this book sketching out the relationship with Wagner, which was instrumental in his development.

There is a subtle irony here because Wagner was a major exponent of the Romantic tradition in art and philosophy and one of the main tropes of that movement was the idea that civilisation was an inherently corrupting influence. The antidote was the so-called *child of nature*, whose strength came precisely from not having been initiated into a culture. Almost all of Wagner's mature operas contain this trope to some extent, but its purest expression is the character of Siegfried from the Ring Cycle, who is raised in a forest. The contradiction in the Romantic ideal of the child of nature is that it was a story written by men who had been raised not in forests but in cities.

In any case, stories are one of the two universal mechanisms that all cultures use to initiate new members. The other mechanism is what the anthropologist Arnold van Gennep called the *rites of passage*. In most cases, the rites and stories of a culture are closely correlated, if not used simultaneously. The 4th-century scholar Sallustius referred to stories used in rites of passage as *mixed myth*. We have a prime example of this in the extensive rites of the Catholic Church. A Catholic mass consists of the Liturgy of the Word (stories) and the Liturgy of the Eucharist (rite of passage). Both of these practices are tightly coupled since they revolve around the story of Jesus. The stories and the rites reinforce each other.

Therefore, for any given culture, to understand how initiation into the core ideas of the culture occurs, we need to look for the institutions that manage its rites of passage and its stories. It should not surprise us to find that 19th-century Germany, and the West more broadly, was a time of major upheaval in this respect. Christianity had been the core religion and therefore the core initiatory system in northern Europe for the best part of a millennium. By the 19th century, however, the influence of the religion had very much begun to wane, especially among the educated elites of European society. This loss of faith was directly related to the rise of historical consciousness that occurred at around the same time, not to mention the fact that the global nature of European civilisation had allowed a deeper appreciation of non-Christian cultures such as Japan, China, and India. Alongside the increasing dominance of scientific materialism, the mythological ground on which Christianity had stood was slowly giving way.

In addition, there was another set of problems that had been opened up by the Reformation. One of the ways to understand these is in the appearance of a debate over the difference between being a "Christian" and being a "disciple of Jesus". This issue ties back to our earlier question of how initiation into a culture works. Ritual and myth are about the imitation of the heroes of the past. It is clear from the gospel story that Jesus expected his disciples to emulate him directly. He wasn't just teaching them in an academic or abstract fashion; he was having them walk the same path that he did, and he expected them to follow his example after his death. It is for this reason that the word *disciple* means something more than *student*. A student learns a theory or an abstract principle. A disciple commits to a lifestyle based on imitation of the master.

Because of the increasingly abstract nature of modern education, we don't automatically associate the process of learning with imitation and mimicry, yet these are still widely practised. Plumbers, carpenters, and other trades learn their craft through imitation during their apprenticeship. The same is true of musicians and other artists. Our modern focus on the written word as a pedagogical device is a practice which was born out of the scholarly tradition of university education in the Middle Ages. While it made sense for scholars, for whom the written word was their speciality, it made far less sense for other domains of life. A prime example of this difference can be found in the early life of Wagner, who received a theoretical musical education as a young man, but who eschewed that in favour of learning and transcribing works by ear, including and especially those of Beethoven. By playing along to Beethoven on the piano, Wagner was directly imitating one of his culture heroes. His early learning was done through mimicry.

Coming back to Jesus and his disciples, it is clear that the education Jesus was giving was not just about understanding his teachings in a theoretical or intellectual sense; it was a complete change of life for those who were willing to join him. The disciples were expected to leave their jobs and even, in some cases, their families. Such sacrifices are very often a core component of initiation in the religious sphere. We saw earlier that Nietzsche had needed to make a similar, although less dramatic, sacrifice in order to attend Schulpforta. That is why we can say that Nietzsche's scholarship there was a proper initiation since it was very much a lifestyle change, one that the young teenager took quite a long time to adjust to.

But there is an important difference between the initiation offered by Jesus and the one Nietzsche received. Schulpforta was a distinguished school which was recognised and celebrated by the wider society of Nietzsche's time. By contrast, to become a follower of Jesus required the individual to place themselves in direct opposition to the Jewish religious authorities and then later the Roman imperial state. Jesus asked his disciples to follow his example of challenging these authorities even though it put their lives on the line, just as he put his own life on the line. After the death of Jesus, the disciples faithfully carried out the task and, especially in the case of Peter and

Paul, met the same fate as their master before them. The difference here is between initiation into a recognised and accepted institution of society versus initiation into an institution that is in opposition to powerful segments of society.

In the case of Jesus, rebellion was part of the initiation he was offering. This rebellious attitude continued on for centuries after the death of the prophet. The Roman state set out to persecute the Christians on a number of occasions, thereby affording those who wanted to imitate the master the opportunity to die for the cause. The Romans had no compunction about killing both external and internal enemies as a method of pursuing the goals of the state, and this worked to crush opposition in most cases. But the example of Jesus had the highly unusual effect of creating a group who not only did not fear death but exalted it as a way to imitate the prophet. Thus, it was in the 2nd century AD that the concept of the Christian martyr was generalised as a response to Roman persecution and became part of the tradition.

What happened next is something that has perplexed thinkers down through the ages and which set up the paradox that would later lead to the issue of what was the difference between a "Christian" and a "disciple". During the latter phase of the Roman Empire, the Christian religion was incorporated into the Roman state. That institutional structure subsequently gave rise to the Catholic Church, which survived the Dark Ages and went on to unify Europe into what was essentially a Christian caliphate around 1000 AD. Whatever else can be said about that, it rendered the original concept of being a *disciple* problematic at best. Jesus had expected his disciples to follow his example and live as he did. That entailed rebelling against the corrupt authorities of his time. But what could it mean for a medieval peasant of Europe to imitate Jesus in this respect? At the very least, the part of the imitation involving a rebellion against the authorities had to be airbrushed out of the story since it was those exact authorities, i.e., the Catholic Church, which were promulgating the religion in the first place. Ironically, in the meantime, the Church had reverted to the old Roman tradition of putting to death anybody who threatened its authority, as can be seen from the numerous killings of heretics and the Inquisition.

This strange state of affairs continued on for about five hundred years until a rebellious (there's that word again) group of scholar-monks began to realise that there was a problem. It is no coincidence that these scholars had direct access to the original Greek texts of the Bible and therefore to the foundational myth of the religion. They were able to see which parts of the story had been airbrushed out by the Catholic Church. More generally, the Protestants correctly saw that the rites that had been built up by the Church were problematic, especially given that the gospel story makes clear that Jesus considered the rituals of his time to be outdated, if not entirely corrupt. That message could only have resonated strongly among those who watched the increasing decadence of the Catholic leadership. Thus, the corruption of the Church placed it in an identical position to the religious authorities in Jesus' time, and what could be more fitting than to emulate the master in rebelling against it? In this way, we can very much say that the Reformation was based on *imitation*.

The reason to go into some detail about this history is because these developments form the context not just to Nietzsche's own life but to the broader cultural trends of his age. Nietzsche's father was a Lutheran pastor, and Luther was still viewed as a heroic figure in 19th-century Germany. In Luther, we have the strange combination of a specifically German culture hero who was advocating on behalf of the ultimate culture hero that had been the foundation of modern Western civilisation, Jesus. Of course, the story of Luther is very similar to that of Jesus. Like Jesus, Luther held the strong conviction that the religious authorities of his time were corrupt. Also like Jesus, he had the ability to communicate his position with clarity and passion, winning him a great deal of support among his contemporaries. That support made him a danger to the authorities and he required great courage to stand up to them. All of this places Luther very much in the context of a disciple imitating the master's example as mediated through a myth that had been handed down over millennia. That is the incredible power of stories as initiatory devices.

But there are a number of important differences between Luther and Jesus. Just like the other Protestants, Luther was a university man. The Reformation was driven by men whose rejection of the Catholic Church was justified by the fact that they believed they had access to the direct source of truth in the Bible. There is a subtle irony here in that the Catholic Church had founded the universities and educated the very scholars who would later turn against it. The Protestant reformers had come to see that the official translation of the Bible, the Vulgate, was riddled with errors. Moreover, those scholars also accused the church of misleading the congregation by omitting large sections of the text. All of this is relevant to the young Nietzsche since his high school and university education placed him on the same track as scholarly heroes like Luther, for whom the question of the truth of the interpretation of texts was quite literally a matter of life and death. There really was a heroism tied to the archetype of the scholar in this cultural milieu, and Nietzsche was being inducted into that mythology.

With the Reformation, the Catholic Church lost control of both primary methods of initiation mentioned earlier: rites and stories. It's no coincidence that a big part of the fight that had been going on for centuries was to ensure that both the Bible and the rites of the church were not translated into vernacular languages. All this changed with the victory of the Protestants. One of Luther's greatest achievements was his translation of the Bible into German. Nietzsche was born into a culture that arose out of these developments. We can now see why that culture had, from the very first, been preoccupied, even obsessed, with the written word. The reason why literacy rates in Protestant communities rose sharply in the aftermath of the Reformation was because being able to read the Bible for yourself became an article of faith. It was the heroic scholar, Luther, who had ushered in this change.

All of this was true for the general culture that the Reformation brought into being, but we can't fail to see that it was even more true of Nietzsche as an individual. Not only was he the son of a Lutheran pastor and a devout mother, but he was also sent to a school whose military-style discipline was dedicated to exactly the kind of scholarship that Luther and the other Protestants were masters of. The interpretation and translation of the holy books was the life's work of such men, and Nietzsche was receiving a first-class education in the same methods. But, alongside the Christian tradition, there was the other tradition that had heavily informed European culture: the Greeks and Romans. The Renaissance had most conspicuously revived interest in this kind of classical scholarship, and it had also seen a surge of interest in the 18th and 19th centuries. Thus, Nietzsche's original enrolment at the University of Bonn saw him studying both theology and classical philology, essentially the two foremost influences on modern Western culture.

In short, Nietzsche received a first-class initiation into the kind of scholarly life that had existed in Europe since medieval times. The university was a genuinely new kind of institution that medieval Europe created for itself through the influence of the Catholic Church. As a result, university scholars were always Christians, often devoutly so. But there are two things about this tradition that are highly unusual when viewed from a broader historical and cross-cultural perspective. The first was the diverse array of culture heroes and stories that had been handed down from antiquity. Through the Christian tradition, there was the figure of Jesus as well as all the other major figures of the Bible. Then there were the Roman and Greek traditions with culture heroes such as Socrates, Plato, Alexander and so on. This meant that modern Western culture from medieval times onwards had at least two different sets of culture heroes to draw on in addition to the indigenous mythology of the various regions of Europe.

The second thing that is highly unusual about this is the abstractness of it all, and this brings us back to the issue of imitation. The stories of Jesus or Socrates took place in societies which no longer existed. If initiation is supposed to entail imitation, how could one imitate a man like Socrates if one didn't live in a Greek city-state? And how could one imitate Jesus in rebelling against the religious authorities when it was those religious authorities who claimed to speak on behalf of Jesus? The way to resolve this was to take a more abstract approach to the lessons handed down from antiquity, but that de-emphasised imitation in favour of abstraction. That is why the issue of the difference between a "Christian" and a "disciple" arose. The Christian knows the doctrines of the faith but does not necessarily practice what he preaches. Without the requirement for imitation, Christianity eventually devolved into hypocrisy. This was especially problematic among the Protestants since it was Protestantism that reinvigorated the idea that imitation was required of the faithful, and yet how could one translate the example of Jesus into the modern world? The growing problem of hypocrisy meant that the abstractions of the faith had become even more stretched and hollowed out by the 19th century. This was a big part of the reason why Christianity lost relevance among the educated classes. In many respects, Nietzsche represented a paradigm example of that class since he renounced his belief in Christianity at exactly the time he began his university studies.

At the same time as this loss of faith in Christianity was happening, scholars had begun to approach religion from a secular point of view. In the years before his renunciation, Nietzsche had been reading Ludwig Feuerbach, David Strauss, Ernest Renan, and others who interpreted the Bible not as the sacred word of God or as holy revelation but as the projection of human psychology. Jesus was no longer the son of God but just a man who thought he was the son of God. The miracles he performed were no longer real but either figments of imagination or standard literary tropes that had been inserted into the story. Whether we agree or disagree with any of that, the point is that these new interpretations also functioned as initiatory devices. When we say that Nietzsche "read them", it's clear that he did more than that. He believed them, and he believed in the broader movement of which they were a part. Nietzsche's renunciation of faith was not just nihilistic rebellion for its own sake; it was a decision to renounce theology in favour of a different way of life, philology. It was a decision to follow a different group of Elders (Feuerbach, Strauss, Renan) on a different initiatory pathway.

The point of going over these historical and cultural details is to show that Nietzsche was not an island unto himself but was a member of a culture and had received a strong initiation into a specific role within that culture. His enrolment at Schulpforta and his subsequent university studies place him in the category of the scholar-monk that had been a staple archetype in Europe since medieval times. The scholar-monks had inherited a synthesised tradition with heroic figures such as Luther and Calvin concerned with the Christian lineage, while other great scholars such as Montaigne or Goethe drew inspiration more from Greece and Rome. One way to view Western history since medieval times was as a back-and-forth battle between these two traditions, the Renaissance tilting the balance in favour of Athens and the Reformation in favour of Jerusalem. If that's true, then the 19th century saw the waning of Jerusalem and the return of Athens. Nietzsche made the choice to become part of that movement. In a letter to his sister, he put it this way, "Hence the ways of men part: if you wish to strive for peace of soul and pleasure, then believe; if you wish to be a devotee of truth, then inquire…"

This focus on "truth" may seem to set up a direct connection between the initiation that Nietzsche received during his high school and university education and the life path that we know he would eventually end up on as a philosopher. Yet, that is not strictly true. The discipline of philology as it was practised in Nietzsche's time had more in common with linguistics and literary criticism than with philosophy. While it was not uncommon to study the written works of the ancient Greek philosophers, this was normally in service of answering technical questions about textual interpretation. It certainly had nothing in common with the aphoristic style of Nietzsche's mature philosophy and especially not its belligerent and bombastic tone and its radically subjective approach to the subject. In fact, as we will see later, Nietzsche's philological mentor, Ritschl, would condemn his first published work of philosophy, *The Birth of Tragedy*. The rest of the philological establishment would also reject the work. Therefore, it was certainly not his philological colleagues and teachers who would encourage Nietzsche towards his eventual life path as a philosopher. On the contrary, they impeded it.

The question then arises: how did Nietzsche go from being an upstanding philological scholar with impeccable credentials to being a philosopher-hermit whose works, in his own lifetime, were read by almost nobody? To the extent that commentators attempt to answer this question at all, they almost always either implicitly or explicitly find the answer in Nietzsche's psychology or some other qualities of his character. This fits with the romantic notion we have in our culture that people are somehow destined to become what they actually do become. This is especially true for the major figures in any field of endeavour. We like to believe that they are all savants who were born to become great. Since Nietzsche eventually became a great philosopher, we are predisposed to think that he must have been born that way and that all the events that happened along the path to get there were the natural working out of this inner genius. While not denying the role of character in the evolution of identity, it is clear that there were larger social forces at play in the case of Nietzsche that facilitated the radical change of track that led to him becoming a philosopher-hermit. Therefore, we cannot fully understand Nietzsche without understanding this milieu and what it was unusual.

The normal state of affairs in any culture is that there is a well-defined and understood tradition in place and an equally well-defined set of Elders whose job is to safeguard it and propagate it to the next generation. History shows, however, that there are times of upheaval when a paradigm shift is taking place in a culture, usually due to some combination of external pressure and internal fissures. We have already seen that 19th-century Europe was an example of this latter type, and Germany was at the centre of the tension. A number of different schisms had opened up. There was the Catholic-Protestant division, with the latter splitting up into hundreds, if not thousands, of alternative interpretations of the faith. Then there were the secular approaches to the same set of stories taken by thinkers such as Feuerbach, Strauss, and Renan. Shakespeare enjoyed a massive spike in popularity, as did the medieval myths that were being rediscovered. As if that wasn't enough, breakthroughs in archaeology and historical research led to renewed interest in the ancient world. The Orphans of the 19th century were offered all of these varying traditions as a kind of smorgasbord to choose from. The result was an identity crisis felt at both the collective and individual levels.

What this meant for Nietzsche and other members of the upcoming generation was that there were a number of options available and, by cross-cultural and historical standards, a perhaps unprecedented freedom about which one to choose. We have seen that Nietzsche exercised his freedom of choice to decide in favour of the new secular wave of thinking. He received a very successful initiation into that thinking. He thrived in the military-like conditions of Schulpforta, and his subsequent university enrolment placed him under the tutelage of one of the best philologists of his time, Ritschl. Nietzsche was initiated during this time by a strong set of Elders culminating in his relationship with Ritschl, who ensured his ascent through the ranks of academic philology. But his success in this domain did not rule out the other possibilities that were available to him. Because of the cultural upheaval of the age, a large number of potential life paths had opened up, at least for the educated and upper classes of society (things were very different for the working poor). Although Nietzsche had landed on the pathway of the scholar, this was by no means the only area that was of interest to him. In fact, Nietzsche was known among the philological faculty in Leipzig for being a very keen and accomplished musician. Meanwhile, he also toyed with the idea of swapping the literary sciences for one of the other sciences where great breakthroughs were being made at the time, chemistry. He even dreamed of starting an artistic or intellectual commune with a few friends, apparently not dissimilar from the hippie communes of the 1960s (the juxtaposition of Nietzsche with a 20th-century hippie is a strange one and yet there are a number of parallels, including Nietzsche's principled attempt at vegetarianism).

In many respects, the 19th-century was the precursor to the cultural model that we now take for granted, where the fact that even university students do not have a fixed destination in life is not seen as a problem. Nietzsche belonged to perhaps one of the first generations where this level of indecision was a normal part of the coming-of-age process. It is fair to say that, in his relationship with academic philology, philology wanted Nietzsche more than he wanted it. But, it's also easy to imagine why Nietzsche would have stuck with a discipline that he clearly had great talent for and which was showering accolades on him.

The brilliant young philologist had numerous options in front of him and indecision was a luxury he could afford. Nevertheless, what we still have not identified is where Nietzsche got the idea to pursue the path of philosophy. The first major event that pointed in this direction came in 1865. Nietzsche had been studying at Bonn under Ritschl when a major academic battle erupted between his teacher and another leading philologist called Jahn. These days we think of scholarly disagreements as being relatively tame affairs involving politely worded criticisms in journals or newspapers. The Ritschl-Jahn dispute was far more intense. There were physical altercations on campus between supporters of the two men, and even the Prussian government got involved at one stage. Ritschl came out the loser in the battle and was forced out of Bonn University only to immediately find another position at the University of Leipzig. Nietzsche and a number of other loyal students moved to Leipzig to continue to study under him. From this we can see that Nietzsche's relationship with Ritschl was a very close one and that his attitude to philology was not flippant or cynical, since he was prepared to move cities to continue his studies.

It was just months after the move to Leipzig that Nietzsche was browsing in a bookshop and stumbled across the work of Arthur Schopenhauer. Schopenhauer's philosophy captivated the young man. It is curious that this happened almost a year after Nietzsche had renounced Christianity and gave up the idea of becoming a pastor. At just the moment in his life when he had exercised his *will* on a truly life-altering decision, he stumbled upon a philosopher who had made the subject of the will central to his work. It is clear that Schopenhauer had a major influence on Nietzsche, and we might surmise that he planted the seed of philosophy in his mind. However, there is no indication on Nietzsche's part that this was some kind of epiphany that led him to drop everything and become a philosopher. Even if he had wanted to pursue such a radical course of action, there was no obvious way to do it. Schopenhauer had been an outcast from the academic philosophical establishment of his day. After a brief attempt to promulgate his work at the University of Berlin, in direct competition with the superstar philosopher of the time Hegel, Schopenhauer retired from formal institutions and wrote his work in seclusion. As a result, there were no formal institutions where Nietzsche could go to practise Schopenhauerian philosophy, no Schopenhauerian Elders under which he could begin a pathway to the life of a philosopher.

There was, however, a famous opera composer who had also become a devotee of Schopenhauer. Wagner had always had an interest in philosophy. The work of Feuerbach had been particularly influential in his younger days, but Schopenhauer became his guiding light later on. The strange thing is that Wagner's life had little in common with the work of either philosopher. Wagner had chosen to take a different route from the scholarly one. Like many of his generation, he was not satisfied with a life of contemplation but wanted to put ideas into action. Another famous person in the same category was none other than Karl Marx. Many people would have heard the quote from Marx that the philosophers had merely described the world while the point was to change it. Fewer would remember that Marx wrote that in a critique on Feuerbach. Wagner would draw a similar kind of conclusion, and, like Marx, would briefly take an interest in politics. However, Wagner was always primarily concerned with channelling his world-changing energies into the domain of art and culture. He was not interested in the static or passive arts. He wanted to create a lively, energetic, living art that was in tune with an equally buoyant broader culture. That was how he envisaged changing the world.

We know that Nietzsche had been an enthusiastic proponent of much the same set of ideas. In fact, there was a strong general movement at that time towards the creation of a distinctly German culture, not for political reasons but as an end in itself (nationalism as a political force would come later and would utilise *cultural nationalism* for its own ends). Thus, Nietzsche and Wagner shared a strong interest in a lively and vigorous culture and in Schopenhauerian philosophy. Although it may seem like a contradiction given Schopenhauer's pessimism, his concept of the will also aligned broadly with the desire for Life and Nature, to use Wagner's terms. Nietzsche was on his way to becoming a bookworm by profession, but deep down he dreamed of something more. As for Wagner, although he almost certainly was not consciously aware of it, he had filled a gap that had been left by the decline of the Christian church in that he took on the role of one of the primary storytellers of 19th-century Germany. Since stories are one of the two primary initiation mechanisms in any culture, Wagner had become an Elder of general cultural importance for 19th-century Germany, and Western culture more generally. The young scholar who had spent almost a decade studying stories in an academic fashion was about to come into contact with an Elder who had made it his life purpose to create stories that were alive and vital.

Schopenhauer had not created any formal institutions, but his influence on the two men would help to forge what would become an incredible informal bond. We can now see why this informality fits against the broader cultural background of 19th-century Germany because what was going on was a breaking down of the formal boundaries and categories that demarcate the roles in a culture. The fact that Nietzsche and Wagner would unify around a philosopher who had been spurned by the official institutions of the time is therefore not a coincidence. Neither did Wagner see any contradiction in incorporating and exploring the ideas of Schopenhauer and Feuerbach into his art, just as he borrowed from medieval myth, Christianity, and even Eastern religions. Part of the reason why Wagner became a controversial figure was because he reserved the right to speak about such matters with an authority that the official institutions (e.g., academia) reserved for themselves. More than that, however, Wagner's explicit goal was to take these ideas out of the realm of intellect alone and incorporate them into a living, breathing art form and thereby into a vibrant culture.

As one of the most influential storytellers of his era, Wagner manifested the archetype of the heroic Artist who could take over the roles of priest, bishop, and pope (and philosopher!) as the custodian of the deeper truths that governed human affairs. That was a peculiarly German idea, but what we will show in this book is that he made it work. It was in precisely that role that Wagner became the prophet and Nietzsche his disciple.

PART 1: PRELIMINARIES

Why Appearances Deceive: The Dionysian and Apollonian

Now that we have the broad personal and cultural background sketched out, we can start to get more specific about the events that would lead to Nietzsche becoming a philosopher. For that purpose, it seems fitting that we should make use of the two concepts that were central to his very first published work of philosophy. Readers of Nietzsche would be familiar with the *Dionysian* and *Apollonian*, first introduced in *The Birth of Tragedy* in 1872. Since our purpose in this book is to create a form of biography that explicitly recognises the development and evolution of identity, we will adapt Nietzsche's concepts as follows. By the Apollonian, we refer to the structured, ordered, exoteric aspects of identity. By the Dionysian, we refer to the unstructured, irrational, esoteric aspects.

Our earlier analysis of Nietzsche's Orphan phase of life already fits neatly into these categories. In the period 1865-68, Nietzsche was safely ensconced at the University of Leipzig as a student of Ritschl. He was respected among his fellow students, and he was already beginning to make great progress in a prospective career as a scholar, as evidenced by the fact that he had published several articles in professional philology journals, a significant achievement for somebody who had not even completed their degree yet. All of this belongs to the Apollonian world. It was structured, orderly, disciplined, and professional. But we have had a glimpse that Nietzsche was not one hundred percent satisfied with this life, as seen in his discovery of Schopenhauer. His sentiment towards the academic lifestyle can be gleaned from a letter sent to his friend Gersdorff in 1867 in which he writes, "...the whole of our method of working is horrible. The hundred and one books lying on the table before me are only so many pincers consuming all the vitality out of the nerve of independent thought." Nietzsche goes on in the letter to contrast the life of the modern scholar against that of the ancient Greeks, who, even among those that history regards as intellectual giants, were never just scholars but also involved in sports, politics, and military activities.

It's noteworthy that Nietzsche wrote the letter to Gersdorff in April of 1867 at just the same time that he had achieved success by having a paper published in a professional journal. Given how well he was doing in his studies, we might have expected him to have a positive attitude towards the situation, and yet we can see that his inner thoughts were not of excitement but, at best, trepidation. The tone of these letters can be compared to those he would later write during the height of his relationship with Wagner, a tone which can only be described as ecstatic. Whereas the letters written during his university studies make Nietzsche sound more like a grizzled old professor coming to the end of his career rather than a promising young student who was just beginning it, his later letters to Wagner reveal that the composer had unleashed something very important in the young man. We can call that something *the Dionysian*.

The Apollonian can be thought of as our outward-facing identity, including our membership in the institutions to which we belong and the relationships we have within those institutions. We mentioned earlier that institutions can be both formal and informal in nature. We can now enhance that distinction by noting that institutions have both an Apollonian and Dionysian aspect. The Apollonian refers to the formal, exoteric nature of the institution, while the Dionysian is its informal, esoteric nature. It follows that some institutions are more Apollonian and some are more Dionysian, although, just as Nietzsche analysed Greek tragedy as a balance between these forces, we can also say that healthy institutions have a balance of the two. We can then say that the world of 19th-century German academia was strongly Apollonian in nature. This makes sense because scholarly work is itself formal, disciplined, and structured. It is about putting things in order. Thus, Nietzsche's identity as a scholar was Apollonian not just in the sense of being his exoteric profession but also in the fact that the institution and the work he carried out within it were rational and orderly.

It shouldn't be surprising, then, to find that the Dionysian aspect of Nietzsche's character was suppressed during this time. The key phrase from the Gersdorff letter is "independent thought". Nietzsche felt himself constrained by the excessively Apollonian rigour of the scholarly world, and he yearned to break free from it. His academic Elder, Ritschl, could not assist with this task since he belonged to the Apollonian side of life. What Nietzsche needed was a Dionysian Elder, one who could unleash the side of his character that had been penned in. Schopenhauer had provided inspiration in this respect. But it was Wagner who would unexpectedly step into the role in late 1868 when the two met for the first time. Here we get our first glimpse of an answer to our earlier question, What would Nietzsche learn from Wagner? The provisional answer is: the Dionysian.

But we can be even more specific than that. Nietzsche was a budding philologist. Philology is the academic study of language, text, myths, and stories. It is a scientific discipline that aims for objectivity. Therefore, it is an Apollonian approach to the subject matter. What would a Dionysian approach to the same subject matter look like? One answer to that question is that it would be the creative use of language, text, myths, and stories. In short, it would be *art*. Art is exactly what Wagner had dedicated his life to. Not only that, Wagner had railed against the art of his day as itself being excessively Apollonian. Although he didn't have the concept at the time, we can see in hindsight that what Wagner dreamed of earlier in his life was a Dionysian kind of art. In his 1849 essay *The Artwork of the Future,* Wagner laid out an approach to opera that took the elements that philology studied (language, text, and stories) and turned them into a living and expressive work. Wagner had not only set out a basic theoretical framework of how to understand what this meant; he had achieved substantial results towards its fulfilment in his operas. His immersive art form was already known for its ability to lift the audience into realms of almost religious ecstasy. Nietzsche must have felt that himself when he saw Wagner's operas performed on stage. Wagner's Dionysian artwork resonated with the parts of Nietzsche that were yearning for expression, just as it did for those in Germany who also felt something in the composer's work that they weren't fully conscious of.

For this reason, we say that Wagner and Schopenhauer belonged to the Dionysian side of Nietzsche, his inner character, which sought but could not find full expression in his Apollonian identity. Another way to say the same thing is that Wagner and Schopenhauer had become Dionysian Elders in opposition to Ritschl, who was Nietzsche's Apollonian Elder. The young philologist was well aware that the Dionysian side of art was completely absent from the scholarship of his time, which denied this living, breathing aspect of creative work and therefore of life in general.

What was true of Nietzsche's personal circumstances was also true of Germany more broadly. In the aftermath of Napoleon's destruction of the Holy Roman Empire, a reactionary political movement had overtaken the region, led by the imperial ambitions of Prussia and Austria. The old cultural traditions and institutions had become Apollonian structures that set about suppressing the Dionysian revolutionary impulses and ideas that had sought expression in the French Revolution. The repression enforced on the young guard had led to a build-up of pressure that overflowed in various uprisings, such as the one Wagner was involved with in 1849. Wagner had been on the side of these Dionysian forces struggling for expression and being held back by the antiquated structures of the old world. We are now ready to understand how Wagner became what we are calling a Dionysian Elder, not just in his relationship with Nietzsche but with Germany more broadly.

Why Wagner was Primarily a Storyteller

In clarifying our understanding of Wagner, we run into a very similar problem that we have already addressed in relation to Nietzsche, i.e., of judging based on the image that has been handed down through history. Wagner is remembered primarily as a composer. It's not hard to see why. A number of his compositions, or sections of them, are still known to this day even among people who have no interest in opera or classical music. Everybody knows the *Bridal Chorus* from *Lohengrin* and the main theme from *Ride of the Valkyries*. Among those with a passing knowledge of the classical music tradition, the *Tristan chord*, *Liebestod* and most of the overtures to Wagner's operas would be known, along with his extensive use of chromaticism, which broke with the conventions of his day. Furthermore, there is Wagner's innovative use of the *leitmotif*, something which would be copied extensively in modern film and TV.

In contrast to these well-known musical innovations, the stories (librettos) of Wagner's operas have received relatively little attention. This is perhaps because Wagner relied heavily on adaptations of medieval myths, and therefore most of his librettos are not completely original creations. Only readers familiar with the originals would know to what extent Wagner modified the myths to convey a new set of meanings in his own work. In some cases (such as *Parsifal*), the changes are significant enough to be considered a completely new story. All this places a barrier in the way of understanding. A further barrier for the uninitiated is the length and density of Wagner's work. It is not possible to unpack the symbolism and meaning of a Wagner opera in a single sitting, even when a single sitting takes five hours and potentially several days to get through. For these reasons and more, the librettos of Wagner's operas are often written off as unimportant or "symbolic", thereby reinforcing the notion that he was first and foremost a composer of music.

This way of viewing Wagner is not just incorrect in itself but, more importantly, it is completely at odds with the way he thought about his art. From very early on in his career, Wagner set out to overturn a number of operatic conventions, not just because he was an iconoclast, but for the express purpose of foregrounding the story. Nominally musical innovations such as the *leitmotif* or the *endless melody* were the technical means by which Wagner aimed to achieve his larger vision. He wanted to create a *unity*. That unity was arrived at by making the story the central core of the artwork. Everything else, including the sets, the costumes, the stage, the acting, and even the music, would be made to serve the story. As Wagner put it in his 1849 essay *Artwork of the Future*, "This purpose of the Drama, is withal the only true artistic purpose that ever can be fully realised; whatsoever lies aloof from that, must necessarily lose itself in the sea of things indefinite, obscure, unfree."

It was his belief in the centrality of the story that explains the otherwise arbitrary fact that Wagner wrote his own librettos, an almost unprecedented practice at the time since almost every other composer of operas preferred to stick to their speciality of music composition and allow someone else to write the story. But there was nothing accidental about it. Wagner wrote the librettos himself because everything else in his *Gesamtkunstwerk* was supposed to follow from them. The music in Wagner is an extension of the story, not an end in itself. This demarcated Wagner's operas from the conventions of his day, a fact which he embraced by asserting that his new art form should not even be called *opera*. Rather, he proposed to call it *Drama* (this was an adaptation of another idea that was floating around in Germany at the time – the *Musikdrama*).

The central place of the story in Wagner's art ties in with several other core concepts he used to explain its meaning. He saw stories as being fundamental expressions of what he called *Life* and *Nature*, two terms that were popular in the German Romantic thought that Wagner was steeped in. This further related to the concept of a Folk which the philosopher Herder had introduced several decades earlier. According to this idea, it is only ever a Folk which can give rise to a Culture. Anything else is *indefinite, obscure, unfree*. Finally, Wagner anticipated some of Freud and Jung's concepts of the instinctive or unconscious aspects of being. He saw the purpose of art as what Jung would later call the process of individuation, of making conscious what had previously been unconscious. As he put it in *Artwork of the Future*, "In like manner will Art not be the thing she can and should be, until she is or can be the true, conscious image and exponent of the real Man, and of man's genuine, nature-bidden life."

With this brief introduction, we can start to see more specifically how Wagner's ideas around art were complementary to the idea of studying stories in an objective and scientific fashion, as in the case of philology. Not that Wagner was the slightest bit interested in compromise or balance. He more or less declared war on what he saw as the sterile and overly intellectual academia. We have already referred to Marx's famous quote on Feuerbach that philosophers have merely described the world while the point was to change it. We can imagine Wagner writing something almost identical in relation to stories: the philologists have merely described stories; the point is to live them and through them to become conscious of our true selves (and our true culture).

Put into the terminology that Nietzsche would later introduce, Wagner believed that the operas and the stories of his own era had become excessively

Apollonian in that they were formulaic and detached from everyday life. The elitist nature of art had created an insular world that was more about status signalling than about the true expression of a culture. For these reasons, Wagner made the Dionysian side of art his primary concern. Thus, when Wagner talks about *Drama,* he takes the Apollonian structure of a story as given and focuses all his attention on the performance of that story on the stage. In fact, Wagner explicitly contrasts this performed Drama against stories conveyed in written language i.e. literature. Of the latter, he writes in *Artwork of the Future,* "The Literary Drama can only redeem itself from this state of misery by becoming the actual living Drama."

The *Literary Drama* belongs to the Apollonian realm, while the *living Drama* concentrates on the Dionysian in the sense that it is communal while also, under Wagner's express instruction, being explicitly emotive. Wagner was deliberately trying to free opera from what he perceived were its contrived intellectual modalities. His reconnection with Nature and Life was first and foremost a reconnection with Feeling in contrast to the dry and bloodless approach to art that he believed prevailed in his time. In order to achieve this, he had to retrain both his singers and his orchestra to get them into this Dionysian mindset and express the actual living Drama as he wanted it performed. This was one of the core ideas that Wagner would impart to Nietzsche, who would later infuse his philosophy with the same form of expression, incorporating feeling and emotion into a discipline that had concerned itself only with dry intellectual rigour.

In his letter to Gersdorff, Nietzsche had complained that the academic life strangled *independent thought.* This was an almost identical grievance to the one Wagner had made as a younger man against the artistic establishment. Wagner wanted to make independent art, where *independence* meant freedom from the aristocratic patronage system and its repressive expectations. He would eventually get the independence he desired, but he would pay a significant price for it. As Nietzsche well knew from Schopenhauer's example, independence is often just another word for incomprehension and even ostracism. But the willingness to suffer for one's independence was heroic, and it was this kind of heroism that Nietzsche found in the example of Schopenhauer and, later, Wagner.

That was one way in which Wagner was an inspiration to the frustrated young scholar seeking something more. But Wagner was also the exemplar of the Dionysian, of the living, breathing expression of life and Nature. For these reasons and more that we shall see shortly, Wagner and Nietzsche would enter into an Orphan-Elder relationship that was as Dionysian as the existing bond between Nietzsche and Ritschl was Apollonian. The Wagner-Nietzsche relationship was entirely informal in nature. It was so informal that neither man knew how to understand it, and commentators ever since have had to fall back on the "friendship" analysis. It's for that reason that our main focus in this book will be to elucidate an Apollonian framework for understanding the Wagner-Nietzsche relationship. We now have almost all of the concepts we need to carry out our analysis. The final ingredient is the most important, but the implications of it are also going to be the hardest to swallow for modern readers used to thinking about the world in terms of scientific cause and effect.

In one respect, what we have described so far about both Wagner and Nietzsche's lives before they met was nothing out of the ordinary. Nietzsche was a bright student who was on track to become a professional scholar. To be sure, it was an elite track, but one that was well-defined. Wagner's life path had been much more varied and dramatic, but that was not out of the ordinary for somebody in his line of work. Even today, we expect a level of eccentricity from artists, including "delusions of grandeur". That was even more true in the 19th-century. People expected great artists to be larger-than-life characters. Thus, we can say that both men were fulfilling roles that were understood in the culture of their time.

What we now want to say is that what happened when the two of them came together was that a story began, and their relationship developed along lines set out by the nature of that story. To those who interpret the idea metaphorically, this will sound trite. To those who interpret it in terms of cause and effect, it will sound absurd. We need another way to think about stories. As a first approximation, we can put it this way: stories are a pattern with slots that need to be filled. When those slots get filled, the pattern comes to fruition. Stories draw events into their pattern like metal shavings are drawn to a magnet's field.

This excessively Apollonian way of thinking about it is incorrect when applied exclusively because, as Wagner, Nietzsche, and Schopenhauer knew, the human will plays a major role in such matters. Nevertheless, it is only by focusing on the Apollonian, structural aspects of the story that we allow the Dionysian qualities, such as the will, to come into proper focus. What we are aiming for is a balance between the Apollonian and Dionysian, and we can only do that by addressing the shortfall in the Apollonian appreciation of the relationship.

With that in mind, we first need to identify the pattern of a story and what prerequisites are required for a story to take place. We will then find that the relationship between Nietzsche and Wagner provides ample evidence for our hypothesis that stories draw events into them like a magnet, because what happened when the two men met was that they entered into a specific kind of story, one that we will call the Orphan Story.

The Orphan Story Template

Nietzsche dedicated his first published work of philosophy, *The Birth of Tragedy*, to Wagner. These are the final sentences of the dedication text that begins the book:-

> *"But perhaps those same people will find it distasteful to see an aesthetic problem taken so seriously, if they can see art as nothing more than an entertaining irrelevance, an easily dispensable tinkle of bells next to the 'seriousness of life': as if no one was aware what this contrast with the 'seriousness of life? amounted to. Let these serious people know that I am convinced that art is the supreme task and the truly metaphysical activity of this life in the sense of that man, my noble champion on that path, to whom I dedicate this book."*

Nietzsche wrote this in 1871, and he refers to a development that had already occurred in Western culture whereby art was seen as an "entertaining irrelevance". This trend has only become more pronounced in the post-war years with the explosion of the entertainment industry creating mass markets for all forms of art, including literature and film. Alongside the increasing dominance of the scientific materialist paradigm in the intellectual domain, the status of art in broad terms has been significantly reduced from what it was in the 19th century when Nietzsche was already complaining about the problem. Stories and art are no longer seen as devices for the interrogation of truth and meaning but as light-hearted diversions from the *serious* work of science, scholarship, and business.

Nietzsche couldn't have been more clear about his disagreement with these developments, stating that art is *the supreme task and metaphysical activity* of life, a position he attributes to Wagner directly. He would (somewhat) renounce this position in his later philosophy after his break with Wagner. We will see why later in the book. For now, we can simply assert that our analysis agrees with Nietzsche's earlier sentiment that stories are far more than *entertaining irrelevances*. If they were, then the relationship between Wagner and Nietzsche would also be just an entertaining irrelevance since we are going to assert that that relationship must be understood as a story. Instead, we say with the Nietzsche of 1871 that stories are metaphysical in nature and provide the key to understanding some of the most important developments in Western history.

Wagner wanted his stories to be infused with Life and Nature as opposed to the overly contrived and intellectual art of this time. The composer focused his attention on the Dionysian aspects of stories in order to achieve his goal. We will return to the Dionysian, or esoteric, aspect of stories shortly. To begin with, however, we need to outline their Apollonian nature, i.e., the underlying structure which determines a story's form. Fortunately, we do not need to reinvent the wheel here because the 20th century saw some major advancements in our understanding. The most important of these was the concept of the *hero's journey* as outlined by Joseph Campbell in his book *The Hero with a Thousand Faces*. Campbell's work was based on an exhaustive analysis of stories from across cultures, leading to the conclusion that the underlying pattern is a universal. Whether that is true or not, it is certainly the case that the best-known stories in Western culture follow the *hero's journey* pattern, including every one of Wagner's operas.

Our approach to story analysis in this book combines the *hero's journey* concept with the Jungian archetypes. By categorising stories based on the archetype of the hero, we hone in on the qualities specific to that archetype. For example, there are numerous stories featuring a Warrior hero. These include such famous works as Sophocles' *Ajax* and Shakespeare's *Macbeth* and *Othello*. A large part of what makes these stories great is that they explore the key challenges faced by the archetype. A Warrior must be skillful in the use of violence. But this raises a temptation to use those skills for selfish or unethical ends. Thus, stories featuring a Warrior hero almost always revolve around the moral and psychological issues that come from the use and misuse of violence.

It follows from this that we can identify a generic story structure for archetypes such as the Child (children's literature), the Ruler, the Sage, and the Elder, where the hero of each story fits the archetype. The hero we are concerned with in this book is Nietzsche, and since the young scholar was still technically an Orphan when he met Wagner, the story type we need is the Orphan Story. At an abstract level, the Orphan Story has a fixed structure that we can identify. The easiest way to present it is to first lay it out in the usual order in which it appears and then show how it applies to some famous examples. The structure is as follows:-

1. The hero is separated from his parents (becoming an archetypal Orphan)
2. The hero hears news of the Elder or the institution to which the Elder is associated
3. The hero meets the Elder, who offers them initiation
4. The hero accepts and initiation commences, including induction into the institution led by the Elder
5. A Shadow Elder tries to subvert the initiation
6. There is a struggle between the hero, the Elder and the Shadow Elder
7. The Elder dies or goes missing (usually sacrificing themselves for the

hero)
8. The hero faces the Shadow Elder alone

Perhaps the best-known example of an Orphan Story from modern times is the original *Star Wars* trilogy, which presents us with an interesting pattern in that the first movie was an Orphan Story by itself, which was then extended to become part of a larger Orphan Story that plays out over the trilogy. The hero of the story is Luke Skywalker, and we can see that Step 1 of our template has been met by the fact that his parents are dead and he is living with his aunt and uncle on the planet of Tatooine. Step 2 requires Luke to hear news of the Elder or the institution of the Elder. That comes via the message from Princess Leia carried by RD-D2, a droid that Luke's uncle has just purchased. Luke goes to meet the Elder (Obi-Wan Kenobi), who, after the death of Luke's aunt and uncle, offers him initiation by taking him on the journey to help the princess. Luke accepts and initiation begins. That gives us Steps 3 and 4 of the template, with Luke being both inducted into the rebel political cause and also into the quasi-religious institution of the Jedi. Note here that the quest to save a princess has direct parallels to medieval knight stories, exactly the kind of stories that Wagner adapted in the 19th-century. Therefore, we can already see the connection between Wagner's operas and modern "space operas".

Step 5 is about the Shadow Elder, who will try to subvert the initiation of the hero. *Star Wars* gives us one of the most memorable Shadow Elders not just in the history of film but of stories in general: Darth Vader. The Shadow Elder is almost always fighting against the institution that the Orphan has been initiated into. Thus, Darth Vader is a member of the empire which is at war with the rebels. In the second and third films, he becomes directly involved in trying to subvert Luke's personal mission to become a Jedi Knight by trying to convert him to the *dark side*. All this constitutes Step 5 of our template.

Step 6 is the main body of the story as the Orphan hero, the Elder, and the Shadow Elder battle it out in whatever format is appropriate to the genre. People familiar with the *Star Wars* movies know what those scenes are, and they require little elaboration here except to say that this constitutes a fundamental part of the initiation of the hero who is learning the ropes during this time. For Luke Skywalker, that means learning to become a Jedi and a rebel fighter.

Step 7 represents a dramatic turning point in the battle with the Elder either dying or being incapacitated. Almost always, this is done as a sacrifice to save the hero. We see a picture-perfect example of this in the first *Star Wars* film when Obi-Wan sacrifices himself in a fight with Vader, which allows Luke and the others to escape. The death of Yoda fills the same role in *Return of the Jedi*. The death of the Elder is what forces the Orphan hero to take the final step of their mission and gather up the courage to face the Shadow Elder directly. That is Step 8 of the story. Thus, Luke battles Vader at the end of the first two movies and then faces a dual Shadow Elder showdown against Vader and Palpatine in *Return of the Jedi*.

We can summarise all this using our template. Note that the version below relates to the first *Star Wars* movie, not the whole trilogy:-

Orphan Story Template	Star Wars
1. The hero is separated from his parents (becomes an Orphan)	Luke Skywalker's parents are dead. He lives with his aunt and uncle
2. The hero hears news of the Elder or the institution to which the Elder is associated	Luke sees the message R2-D2 is carrying for Obi-Wan from Princess Leia
3. The hero meets the Elder, who offers them initiation	Luke takes R2-D2 to Obi-Wan who rescues them both. When the stormtroopers kill his aunt and uncle, he agrees to accompany Obi-Wan to save the princess
4. The hero accepts and initiation commences, including induction into the institution led by the Elder	They connect with Hans Solo and Wookie who will transport them. They are now fighting on behalf of the rebel cause
5. A Shadow Elder tries to subvert the initiation	Darth Vader captures the Millennium Falcon and brings it aboard the Death Star
6. There is a struggle between the hero, the Elder and the Shadow Elder	They sneak away and are now inside the Death Star
7. The Elder dies or otherwise goes missing (usually sacrificing themselves for the hero)	Obi-Wan faces off against Vader and is killed
8. The hero faces the Shadow Elder alone	Final battle between Skywalker and Vader

To reiterate the main point we are trying to establish here, the template we have presented is made up of the archetypal components of the story. Because they are archetypes, they are abstract enough that they can cover almost any story type, from a science fiction story like *Star Wars* to medieval knight stories through to classic tragedy. In a comedy such as *Star Wars*, the hero wins. This means they defeat the Shadow Elder and graduate from the Orphan to the Adult archetype. Thus, Luke Skywalker begins the story as a naïve young farm boy and ends as a Jedi Knight. In a tragedy, the hero fails. Let's now analyse a tragic Orphan Story via one of Shakespeare's greatest works, *Hamlet*.

Hamlet presents an interesting variation on Step 1 of the template (the separation of the hero from his parents) since the story is predicated on Hamlet's father being killed by his uncle, who usurps the throne and marries his mother. Thus, at the beginning of the play, Hamlet's father is dead, and his mother has betrayed him. These events prevent the initiation that Hamlet is supposed to have undergone, i.e., becoming king. The young prince is called to fight for his rightful initiation, which represents his ascension to the Adult phase of life. A second crucial variation that Shakespeare uses in the story is that the Elder role is going to be played by the ghost of Hamlet's father. It is this ghost which will tell Hamlet that he needs to kill his uncle and take the throne. Of course, a ghost cannot provide any real initiation or guidance, and so Hamlet is left to work through the issue alone. That is Hamlet's main problem throughout the story: he has no wise Elder to guide him. Instead, the very men who should play the Elder role, Claudius and Polonius, are actively trying to deceive him. It is these inversions which lead to the tragic outcome of the story. Thus, Shakespeare is still following the structure of the Orphan Story, but inverting certain elements to create a tragedy instead of a comedy.

We can map *Hamlet* onto our template as follows:-

Orphan Story Template	*Hamlet*
1. The hero is separated from his parents (becomes an Orphan)	Hamlet's father has been killed by his uncle who subsequently married his mother
2. The hero hears news of the Elder or the institution to which the Elder is associated	Horatio tells Hamlet about the ghost that the sentries have seen during the night
3. The hero meets the Elder, who offers them initiation	Hamlet goes to see the ghost for himself. It tells him to avenge his father's death
4. The hero accepts and initiation commences, including induction into the institution led by the Elder	Inversion: Hamlet is alone and cannot confide even with his friends. He has no Elder or institution to help him in his mission. His famous soliloquy represents this
5. A Shadow Elder tries to subvert the initiation	Claudius prevents Hamlet from returning to university. Polonius subverts Hamlet's relationship with Ophelia
6. There is a struggle between the hero, the Elder and the Shadow Elder	Hamlet has an opportunity to kill Claudius but fails to act. Claudius sends Hamlet away with the intention of having him murdered on the journey
7. The Elder dies or otherwise goes missing (usually sacrificing themselves for the hero)	Inversion: Hamlet accidentally kills Polonius, the man who should be his Elder
8. The hero faces the Shadow Elder alone	Hamlet returns for a showdown with Claudius. They both die

The failure of Hamlet to initiate into the kingship results in the end of the royal line. Thus, at the end of the play, Fortinbras enters and takes the crown of Denmark on behalf of Norway.

We have now presented examples of both a comedic and a tragic Orphan Story in two completely different genres. We could continue to walk through analyses of numerous other stories to show that they also fit our template. However, this would take us too far off course for our present purposes. The interested reader is invited to apply the Orphan Story template to other famous stories to verify its validity. Some examples from modern stories include the films *The Matrix, Avatar* and The *Lion King*. In the science fiction/fantasy genre, there is *Dune, A Wizard of Earthsea,* and *Lord of the Rings*. The first Harry Potter novel is not technically an Orphan Story but shares most of its traits. Any medieval knight's tale will almost certainly be an Orphan Story, as are many popular fairy tales such as *Cinderella* and *Snow White*.

There is one final set of fictional Orphan Stories that we need to mention because they are directly relevant to the subject of this book. All of Wagner's mature operas are Orphan Stories. In the case of *Lohengrin, Tannhäuser,* and *Tristan and Isolde,* the story that Wagner presents is almost identical to the medieval versions that had enjoyed a surge in popularity beginning in the early 19th-century. They are all familiar to us as the medieval knight quest, although Wagner focuses on the love story angle. Since the stories are all tragedies, they have a lot in common with Shakespeare's *Romeo and Juliet*, which had also become extremely popular at that time.

Wagner's final opera, *Parsifal*, was also an adaptation of an old medieval knight story, but Wagner made radical changes to it. As this story is crucial to the Nietzsche relationship, we will analyse it in great detail later in the book. We will also look at the *Ring Cycle,* which is a concatenation of a number of myths, including an Orphan Story for the character, Siegfried.

There is one of Wagner's operas that is worth showing at this point, and this is the comedy *Die Meistersinger*, which was an original work that had no basis in medieval mythology. It is also a perfect example of an Orphan Story. Rather than walk through the details of the plot, let's simply map it onto our template as follows:-

Orphan Story Template	*Die Meistersinger*
1. The hero is separated from his parents (becomes an Orphan)	Walther is a young knight already on a quest and therefore has left his home
2. The hero hears news of the Elder or the institution to which the Elder is associated	Walther and Eva are in love but Eva's father has promised her hand to whoever wins the Meistersinger song contest. If Walther wants to marry Eva, he must try to win the contest
3. The hero meets the Elder, who offers them initiation	Walther attends a meeting of the Meistersingers and tries to qualify for the contest. All Meistersingers reject him except Hans Sachs
4. The hero accepts and initiation commences, including induction into the institution led by the Elder	Sachs rescues Walther from a street riot. The next day, he gives Walther instruction on how to become a Meistersinger
5. A Shadow Elder tries to subvert the initiation	One of the older Meistersingers, Beckmesser, wants to marry Eva. He tries to disqualify Walther from the contest
6. There is a struggle between the hero, the Elder and the Shadow Elder	Beckmesser attempts to woo Eva with a serenade. Sachs repeatedly interrupts him, while Walther and Eva watch on from a hiding place
7. The Elder dies or otherwise goes missing (usually sacrificing themselves for the hero)	Sachs, who is a widower, also has feelings for Eva but deliberately withdraws from the contest so that Walther has a chance to win
8. The hero faces the Shadow Elder alone	Walther defeats Beckmesser in the song contest, becomes a Meistersinger, and marries Eva

For those with little interest in the underlying structure of stories, this kind of analysis may be a little on the dry side. However, apart from its importance as an aid to understanding, it also provides us with a useful insight into the life that Nietzsche led during his academic career. This is the kind of work that Nietzsche had been trained in for many years and which he sometimes felt was a dreary grind. However, he also saw that the Apollonian and Dionysian aspects of stories needed to be in balance, and even in his mature philosophy, he acknowledged the virtues of discipline and rigour that the scholar requires. In short, he still believed that the Apollonian approach was of value.

In any case, the reason why the Apollonian approach is indispensable for our purposes is because our hypothesis in this book is that the pattern of stories shapes reality. We can now be more specific about that because we have identified what that pattern is. Given an Orphan, an Elder, and a Shadow Elder in the right circumstances, we can expect a story to play out in something like the sequence described above. It will be objected that all the examples given so far are fictional and therefore not real. We will correct that in this book because the story we are going to tell about Nietzsche and Wagner is very real. But before we get to that, let's prove the veracity of the structure by showing how it fits two of the most important events in Western history.

Why Stories are Real

Recall the earlier Nietzsche quote from *The Birth of Tragedy*: "*art is the supreme task and the truly metaphysical activity of this life...*". Nietzsche explicitly contrasted this with the idea that art was just "an entertaining irrelevance." The latter view is still the default within our culture. We don't think of the movie *Star Wars* as an exploration of metaphysical truths. We think of it as a "pop culture phenomenon" or a "blockbuster" that's a hit with the kids. In one sense, that is true. Works of fiction are, by definition, not real. However, the underlying structure is real. Once we understand that, then we can understand what Wagner was talking about with the relationship between art, Life and Nature. When art strays too far from Life and Nature, it becomes contrived and decadent. In its supreme form, however, art seems to directly touch something fundamental, and that is what Nietzsche was referring to by his reference to metaphysics. What we now need to understand is that life itself is a story (at least potentially). The reason to believe that is because two of the most important events in Western history follow the exact structure of the Orphan Story we have just outlined.

The stories in question are those which played out between Jesus and his disciples and Socrates and Plato. In order to understand them as Orphan Stories, we are going to need to perform the exact same re-evaluation we have already begun to carry out for Nietzsche and Wagner. That is, we need to cast off the image that has been handed down through history and to walk back through the series of events that actually happened in the order in which they happened.

The first thing to note here is that neither Jesus nor Socrates wrote anything that has survived for posterity. Especially in the case of Jesus, the story that has been handed down to us was told by the disciples. In the case of Socrates, it was Plato who immortalised his teacher in writing. In both cases, it was the disciple of the master who wrote the story after the fact. But therein lies the first evidence that these were real-life Orphan Stories because, at the very least, the relationship was real. Plato really was the Orphan and Socrates was the Elder. The same relationship held between Jesus and the disciples. These are historical facts. These real-life relationships existed prior to the story that was subsequently told about them. Even if the story had never been put down into words, the relationships in question would still have the structure that we have outlined above.

If a story occurs, but nobody ever tells it, was it really a story? Our answer to that question is: yes. The structure of events can follow the story template without anybody necessarily telling that story. Again, we will prove that in this book because nobody has ever told the true story of Nietzsche and Wagner, yet, as we will see, their relationship followed the Orphan Story pattern.

A second decisive re-evaluation that we must make is to focus on the events in question not from the point of view of the Elder but of the Orphan. That means we need to analyse the New Testament not from the point of view of Jesus but from the point of view of the disciples, and we need to analyse the relationship between Socrates and Plato from the point of view of the younger man. When we do that, the disciple becomes the hero of the story. This method of analysis is going to be particularly jarring in relation to the New Testament because it means we need to set aside the idea that Jesus is the hero of the story and entertain the prospect that the story is really about the disciples. Incredibly, when we do that, we find that the New Testament matches exactly to the Orphan Story template.

The key to understanding this is simply to note that, while the gospel story features Jesus, all subsequent books of the New Testament are about the disciples. Because the gospel story has dominated, and because Jesus dominates that story, the idea that he is not the hero of the story seems absurd, especially because there is almost no mention of the disciples in the gospels. The two exceptions are Peter and Judas, who are respectively the foremost disciple and the one who will betray the cause. However, let's put aside our biases and walk through the order of events as told in the New Testament.

The New Testament begins with the gospel and the begins with initiation. Almost the first thing that happens is that Jesus offers initiation to the first disciples (Step 3 of the template). They accept the offer and join him (Step 4). The story continues with their travels around the region. Along the way, Jesus imparts his wisdom via the famous parables. He also gives the disciples tasks, such as sending them off with instructions to spread the word. Clearly, Jesus is the Elder in this relationship, and he is providing initiation to the disciples who are in the role of archetypal Orphans.

We must remember at this point that the institution that the Elder inducts the Orphan into can be both formal and informal in nature. The institution that Jesus created was highly informal. It was just a man walking around teaching whoever wanted to be taught. For many years after Jesus died, the word *Christian* simply meant '*follower of Christ*'. It didn't denote membership of a church because there was no church. In fact, Jesus promulgated his teaching in direct opposition to the formal religious institutions of the time, led by the Sadducees and Pharisees. That makes them the Shadow Elders in the story, and, sure enough, they try to subvert the initiation in various ways, including arresting Jesus. There is even mention of a specific individual who takes the Shadow Elder role, a certain Caiaphas:-

> "*Those who had arrested Jesus took him to Caiaphas, the high priest, where the teachers of the law and the elders had assembled.*" (Matthew 26:57)

This gives us Step 5 of the Orphan Story template: *a Shadow Elder tries to subvert the initiation*. Step 6 is fulfilled by the various challenges lodged by the Sadducees and Pharisees as they send individuals to Jesus armed with trick questions designed to trip him up. Meanwhile, we even find mention of violent confrontations in the story, such as the flipping of tables in the temple. All this belongs to Step 6 of our template: *there is a struggle between the hero, the Elder and the Shadow Elder*.

Finally, we have probably the most important *death of the Elder* in history. Step 7 of the template tells us that the Elder will sacrifice themselves for the hero. Jesus did not just sacrifice himself for the disciples but for all of mankind who, it is implied, can become his disciples in a spiritual sense. We won't dwell on the theological questions raised by this except to say that it perfectly fits with our template.

The final stage of the story is when the hero confronts the Shadow Elder alone. The New Testament gives us that part of the story in the Book of Acts and the subsequent books written by various disciples which document their activity after Jesus had died. The Book of Acts makes crystal clear that the disciples will be following in the footsteps of Jesus because we see his explicit instruction:-

> *"Therefore go and make disciples of all the nations, baptising them in the name of the Father and of the Son and of the Holy Spirit, and teaching them to obey everything I have commanded you." (Matthew 28:19-20)*

The disciples then confront the Shadow Elder alone, which no longer includes just the Jewish religious authorities but also the Roman imperial ones. Therefore, the rest of the New Testament can be seen as fulfilling Step 8 of our template: *the hero faces the Shadow Elder directly*. The New Testament therefore constitutes a perfect Orphan Story. We can summarise it using our template as follows:-

Orphan Story Template	New Testament
1. The hero is separated from his parents (becomes an Orphan)	Jesus' disciples are fishermen and tax collectors. This implies separation from their parents and also, due to the difficulty of the work, that they were young men
2. The hero hears news of the Elder or the institution to which the Elder is associated	The Gospel tells us that word of Jesus had spread quickly and he drew large crowds. It is almost certain that the disciples would had heard of him in advance
3. The hero meets the Elder, who offers them initiation	Jesus directly asks young men to give up their occupation and follow him - "I will make you fishers of men."
4. The hero accepts and initiation commences, including induction into the institution led by the Elder	Numerous disciples accept the offer. Jesus names the twelve most important. They are present with Jesus for the rest of the story and are witnesses to the events
5. A Shadow Elder tries to subvert the initiation	The Pharisees and Sadducees appear throughout the story to challenge Jesus and discredit his teaching
6. There is a struggle between the hero, the Elder and the Shadow Elder	Jesus and the disciples argue their case against the Pharisees while also engaging in more dramatic actions such as the temple rebellion. Eventually, the Pharisees have Jesus arrested.
7. The Elder dies or otherwise goes missing (usually sacrificing themselves for the hero)	The most famous death of the Elder in Western culture. Jesus is crucified
8. The hero faces the Shadow Elder alone	The rest of the New Testament starting with the book of Acts. The disciples confront the twin Shadow Elders of Jewish religious authorities and the Roman imperial state

The crucial point to understand about the analysis we have just carried out is that it accords with historical fact. There are a number of things in the gospel story that we can't believe from a modern scientific point of view, however, every element of the New Testament that matches our Orphan Story template has substantial historical evidence behind it. The veracity of the resurrection, while important for theological reasons, does not affect our analysis because we know that the disciples really did go on to face the Shadow Elders in real life. Therefore, the Orphan Story that we have just summarised is based in reality, meaning the structural relation of events existed prior to the narrative of those events.

Because of the enormous cultural baggage associated with the New Testament, some may find it hard to be able to see the reading of it as an Orphan Story. Let's therefore do a second example of a world-historical relationship that fits the template, one which has the advantage that it has never been written into a complete narrative.

The historical evidence suggests that Plato would have been almost the same age as the disciples when he first met Socrates. This should be no surprise to us now because what they all have in common is that they were in the late Orphan stage of life, exactly the right time to receive initiation. Plato was twenty-years-old when he met Socrates, who was most likely in his early sixties. Just as the relationship between Jesus and the disciples was highly informal in nature, so too was the initiation that Socrates would give to Plato. Their initial meeting almost certainly occurred during one of the philosopher's famous public debates in the marketplace, an activity which was very similar to Jesus' public preaching. Just as Jesus had earned himself a number of enemies, Socrates was a controversial figure at a time of social upheaval. Jesus railed against the Pharisees; Socrates against the sophists. All of these elements should now be familiar to us because they match the Orphan Story template; Elder vs Shadow Elder.

The part of the story that we know least about in relation to Plato and Socrates was the years during which Plato was a student of the older man. Socrates had already been a controversial character before the relationship began, and he continued to be while they were together. Plato's presence as a supporter at Socrates' trial is an indication that he was willing to advocate for Socrates in public. Nevertheless, we have little information about specific events that occurred during this time. What is absolutely not in doubt, of course, is that Socrates was sentenced to death during his trial and that it was this event which shocked Plato into carrying out the set of activities that would become the foundation of Western philosophy. These represent Steps 7 and 8 of our template. Putting it all together, we can represent the relationship between the two men as an Orphan Story as follows:-

Orphan Story Template	Plato and Socrates
1. The hero is separated from his parents (becomes an Orphan)	Plato was 20 when he met Socrates. He had almost certainly just finished his study at the Ephebia and graduated to become a citizen
2. The hero hears news of the Elder or the institution to which the Elder is associated	Socrates was already well-known as an eccentric and controversial thinker as evidenced by the fact that Aristophanes has satirised him in one of his plays many years before. It's almost certain Plato knew his reputation
3. The hero meets the Elder, who offers them initiation	Plato met Socrates while the latter was conducting his public philosophising
4. The hero accepts and initiation commences, including induction into the institution led by the Elder	Sometime later, Plato became Socrates' student and studied under him for many years until the latter's death
5. A Shadow Elder tries to subvert the initiation	Socrates had a number of enemies, some of whom would later lead his prosecution. The sophists were his main intellectual enemies
6. There is a struggle between the hero, the Elder and the Shadow Elder	Plato was present at Socrates' trial indicating his public support in the battle against Socrates' opponents
7. The Elder dies or otherwise goes missing (usually sacrificing themselves for the hero)	Socrates was sentenced to death. He had the opportunity to flee but willingly chose to drink the hemlock, dying for his beliefs
8. The hero faces the Shadow Elder alone	The death of Socrates shocked Plato's worldview. He began writing his philosophical works afterwards. Socrates' enemies feature in many of the dialogues

We have now demonstrated how the Orphan Story structure accounts for the evolution of the relationship between Orphan and Elder in these major historical episodes. However, it should be easy to see that the examples we have used are not normal, everyday occurrences but exceptional in nature. One way or another, everybody goes through the Orphan phase of life and meets with Elders who help them through the process. But not everybody's Orphan Story changes history. There is one factor in the historical stories we have just recounted that we need to recognise, and that is the socio-cultural milieu in which the protagonists lived. It is the time of great tension and social upheaval that forms the backdrop to the Orphan Story and which leads the Elder to make the sacrifice that forms the crux of the structure.

Although they were very different kinds of societies, what 4th-century

Athens and the Levant in the time of Jesus had in common was that both communities were going through a period of crisis. Athens had just lost the Peloponnesian War and had experienced a number of religious scandals in the lead-up to the trial of Socrates. There was simultaneous political, economic, and religious turmoil at this time. The same was true of the Jewish communities that Jesus was born into. The main cause of their crisis was their ever-increasing subjugation under Roman imperial rule, which led to significant internal conflict. In the case of both Jesus and Socrates, it was this internal conflict which led to their deaths.

Both men had challenged the establishment of their respective societies at a time when that establishment was struggling to retain its hold on power. Socrates had been involved in two other legal matters in the years before his own trial, both of which involved individuals being sentenced to death. In each case, he had refused to participate, claiming that the proceedings were miscarriages of justice. He must have known about this corruption and that his own trial could lead to a similar result. We know from the gospel story that Jesus also anticipated his own conviction and death sentence. Jesus' Elder, John the Baptist, had already been put to death by Herod. Presumably, that was not uncommon at the time. What makes both men great is that they continued to stand for what they believed in despite knowing full well what the consequences could be. What this backdrop of social crisis brings to the Orphan Story is that it raises the stakes for all concerned. By definition, anybody involved had shown courage and strength of character. Jesus and Socrates were men who were prepared to die for what they believed in.

This is the key ingredient which demarcates the Orphan Story from a regular kind of initiation. Orphan initiation is a universal of human culture, but only special circumstances require the Elder to put their life on the line over the matter. But having an Elder who is prepared to die is not enough to complete the story. The final key ingredient in these world-historical Orphan Stories is the character of the hero. We must remember that it is the Orphan who is the hero of the story. It is the Orphan who carries on the legacy of the Elder. What distinguishes the Orphan Stories of Plato and the disciples of Jesus was how they turned the grief and despair of the death of the Elder into a historical paradigm shift. Plato went on to write the foundational texts of Western philosophy and founded the Academy, later becoming himself an Elder to Aristotle. That begins the Western philosophical tradition. The disciples went on to write the New Testament and to found the nascent Christian church, which would later unify Europe under the guidance of the Catholic Church. In both cases, what we see is that the informal relationship between Elder and Orphan is turned into formal institutions after the death of the Elder. That is the great contribution that the Orphans in the story make. In the world-historical Orphan Story, it is the Orphan who creates the new tradition that changes the world.

We can condense these considerations down into three factors that differentiate a world-historical Orphan Story: 1) a society under existential levels of stress due to military, political and economic failure; 2) a brilliant and charismatic Elder who opposes the status quo on principled grounds; 3) an equally brilliant disciple who turns their initiation into new institutions that change the world.

Now that we know all of the elements that make up an Orphan Story, we are ready to return our attention to the subjects of this book and the society in which they lived. When we apply the three factors required for a world-historical Orphan Story to the lives of Nietzsche and Wagner, we find that all are met. Germany had been in an existential crisis ever since Napoleon blew over the Potemkin façade of the Holy Roman Empire. The reactionary politics of Prussia and Austria clashed with the revolutionary ideals that still burned in the hearts of many. The decades-long political failure to unify the German states into some form of democratic or constitutional system eventually led to Bismarck imposing unification via *blood and iron*. This ushered in a new imperialist paradigm that would ultimately lead to the two world wars. Thus, the socio-cultural conditions in Germany were set up for a world-historical Orphan Story. What was needed was a brilliant and charismatic Elder and an equally brilliant disciple.

Wagner had been in the thick of the revolutionary fervour, as evidenced by his involvement in the Dresden uprising, but he was never primarily concerned with politics. This creates a parallel with Jesus, who was also uninterested in politics (*Give unto Caesar*). His battle was against the religious authorities who he saw as being corrupt. Thus, Jesus' death was explicitly not political. This is made crystal clear in the gospel story since Pilate, the representative of the Roman political system, has no care or understanding of the case before him. The case of Socrates is a little bit more complicated since, like all Athenian citizens, he was expected to participate in the political and legal systems. Nevertheless, we can still see from his life and especially the way in which Plato characterises him in the dialogues that Socrates was primarily concerned with truth, not power. In both Jesus and Socrates we have Elders who are either ignorant of or unconcerned with political realities and refuse to temper their behaviour according to pragmatic concerns.

The same was true of Wagner in the 19th century. Although he had become involved with revolutionary politics and although he certainly had political opinions, all the evidence suggests that Wagner's first and foremost concern was always art. That was true prior to Dresden, and it was even more true afterwards. During what must have been an incredibly stressful and despairing period of his life, when he was thrown back onto the core of his being, what Wagner did was to redouble his efforts and his focus on art. Although he would inevitably get caught up in politics, it is fair to say that the post-exile Wagner was single-minded in his devotion to the cause of art and the related questions of German culture. Since Wagner was undoubtedly a brilliant and charismatic advocate on behalf of the principles he believed in, he is just the kind of Elder we need for a world-historical Orphan Story. This is especially true because German culture had created the role of the heroic Artist as an explicit replacement for the religious Elders of the Christian church, and, although nobody thought about it that way, the heroic Artist was incredibly similar to the Jewish prophets of the Old and New Testaments. The Bible prophets claimed to be messengers on behalf of God; Wagner claimed to be a messenger of the German Volk. Incredibly, we find much the same thing in Socrates, who, in Plato's *Apology*, tells us that his thoughts and actions are guided by his *daimon*, which was a figure in Greek culture believed to be an intermediary between the gods and humans. Thus, the world-historical Elder is not only a charismatic and principled leader but also one who claims to speak as a messenger on behalf of something higher.

We have shown that the cultural and political milieu in Germany was under existential stress. We have also shown that Wagner was an ideal candidate for the role of revolutionary Elder. All we need now is a brilliant disciple to receive initiation from the Elder. Nietzsche's brilliance is self-evident to us now, but we have shown that he was already one of the most promising scholars of his age by the time he met Wagner. If we needed any further convincing that Nietzsche fitted the bill, we must simply point out that Nietzsche was twenty-four-years-old when he met the fifty-five-year-old Wagner, almost the same age range that existed between the young Plato and Socrates when their Orphan Story began.

As if all that wasn't enough, our analysis has already established that the first several steps of the Orphan Story template had been fulfilled when Nietzsche and Wagner first met. We know that Nietzsche was in the Orphan phase of life. He had established his independence from his family. He had made the difficult decision to drop theology and choose his own pathway, guided by his intellectual Elder in Ritschl. Step 2 of the Orphan Story template requires that the Orphan hear about the Elder prior to their meeting. We know that Nietzsche had been a fan of Wagner's for about seven years and that his appreciation of the composer's work had been growing in the lead-up to their first encounter. That first encounter gives us Step 3 of our template. We will have more to say about it later, but it happened in such a rapid and unexpected fashion that Nietzsche wrote ecstatically to his friend Rohde immediately afterwards, "On these days I felt as though I was living in a novel, and you must allow that in view of the inaccessibility of the exceptional man, the circumstances leading up to this acquaintance were somewhat romantic." What an incredible coincidence that Nietzsche would refer to his first meeting with Wagner as like "living in a novel". He was more correct than he knew. This was the beginning of the Orphan Story between the two. Step 3 of the story was consecrated just months later when Wagner wrote a letter to Nietzsche telling him to visit and show him "what kind of man you are."

As we will see shortly, Nietzsche's exclamation that he felt as if he was *living in a novel* is also borne out by the events that happened between the first meeting and when the actual relationship with Wagner began in earnest. The whole period is marked by a set of improbable coincidences that came together to allow the beginning of their bond to take place. What is also extraordinary is how fast things proceeded once the structural elements we have identified came together. That is why we will set out our subsequent analysis of the relationship between the two men using the Orphan Story template. What we will see is that the coincidences in the larger flow of events all cluster around the steps in the template and that the twist that the story takes in the end, when the two men parted ways, must also be understood against the implied background of the Orphan Story structure. Just as Shakespeare used inversions of the template to create the tragedy of *Hamlet*, the Orphan Story of Nietzsche and Wagner features several mind-bending inversions at the end. Once we understand what those are and how they affected Nietzsche's subsequent philosophy, the idea that this period of his life was a "false start" will be impossible to uphold.

For us, then, the Apollonian approach is certainly not going to be a tame or boring affair because behind it sits the proposition that otherwise unrelated events were drawn into the structure of the Orphan Story. We must stress again that this happened in reality and, therefore, that the story we are going to tell is not fictional. Every fact and record used in this book is part of the public record and is verified empirical evidence. Furthermore, there will be no intricate or subtle interpretations of historical data required. All we are going to do is apply the template to the events. We now know that this same template applies to at least two major historical relationships in Western history. There are others we could also cite, especially the falling out between Julius Caesar and Brutus (with Brutus in the role of Orphan and Caesar in the role of Elder). When we apply the template to the relationship between Nietzsche and Wagner, we will find that, just like Cinderella's shoe, it is a perfect fit that unlocks the rest of the fairy tale.

This structural, Apollonian approach to relationships and stories is a valid and necessary part of our understanding. What's more, since it is an unappreciated and relatively unknown way of looking at the world, our focus on it is justified as a way of fixing an inherent imbalance in our worldview. However, we should not lose sight of the meaning which these structures create. For the Orphan Story, the structure is there to facilitate the initiation of the hero. That is its meaning, and all the elements of the structure serve that meaning. More generally, however, stories also have a structure which serves a meaning, and that meaning is about a journey into the sacred. That is why it is perfectly fitting that the New Testament is an Orphan Story and that even Socrates understood his life from a religious point of view. Before we get into our analysis proper, let us review this highest meaning and purpose of a story.

The Journey into the Sacred

As Nietzsche knew from his philological studies, and Wagner knew from his experience with over-intellectualised, formulaic art, one of the primary risks of the Apollonian approach to art and scholarship is that it can snuff out life. Having learned the rules of the game, it is very easy to see nothing more than those rules. The world then becomes just a big machine churning out the same thing over and over again. This is a very old trap, as evidenced by the fact that we find one of its most poetic expressions in the Book of Ecclesiastes, probably written a few centuries before Christ. *There is nothing new under the sun.* This is a trap we could fall into, since we have now identified the properties of the Wagner-Nietzsche relationship and the structure of the story which will now unfold. In one sense, the rest of this book could be just the mechanical explication of that structure as we work through the Orphan Story of the composer and his disciple.

Great storytellers know how to navigate the fine line between repeating clichés that have been used a million times and creating novelty. Even though a story might be almost the same as ones that have been told before, even though we are 99% sure the hero is going to win the day, there must be the possibility that something different and unexpected can happen. This *something different* is always a combination of the slings and arrows of outrageous fortune and the internal, esoteric character of the hero, some unknown force, or some secret source of power or motivation that drives them. Great stories make us feel as if anything is possible. Nevertheless, the Apollonian cynic will point and laugh: *look, it's the same structure as every other story. The author has just tricked you into thinking it's new.*

But great authors do not trick us. On the contrary, they capture something fundamental about life, and this is where, yet again, we must insist with Wagner that the greatest stories have an intrinsic connection to what he called Life and Nature. What the great author does is to give us a hero. The hero does not know how the story is going to end because the hero is living through the story. The reason we can empathise with the hero is because we are the heroes in our own story, and, even though our lives have a fixed Apollonian structure at an abstract level, the details are never known in advance. We can learn to love these details. That's why we can read the same novel or watch the same opera time and time again. We don't resent the repetition. We forget that we know how it all ends and just immerse ourselves in the moment, enjoying the world that the artist has created for us. That's what Wagner's operas were famous for in his time, and that is why we can liken them to a religious experience of the sacred since this getting lost in the details is a feature of the magic moments in life that seem to transcend normality and point to something higher.

Aside from this enjoyment in repetition, we also know from our own lives that, through some combination of unknown forces from within and without, new and unforeseen things can happen. In such moments, we learn that we are larger than we think. We have to let go of the restrictions of our conscious mind in order to incorporate something new. We have to learn to see the world anew. There is always a risk involved in such an approach, and that is also what great stories convey to us. There must be something on the line for the hero in any great story, some risk that necessarily implies uncertainty, but also some gain, which is also not fully understood, because it cannot be understood until it has been experienced. The greatest stories make us live through the hero on a journey into the unknown where the stakes are not fully understood and the outcome is in no way fixed. A story is an exploration of both the outer and inner worlds.

Real life becomes a story again when we step into the unknown, chasing something that we are not fully conscious of, driven by deeper desires that we do not fully understand. Can it be a coincidence that Nietzsche discovered the Dionysian concept at just the time when he had extricated himself from the Apollonian rut of academic philology? Can it be a coincidence that he dedicated the book containing that concept to the man who had pulled him off a fixed and known pathway and into the unknown? Not at all. It's also not a coincidence that Nietzsche needed to find inspiration for this concept in the Greek tradition and not the Christian one because, as we have already noted, the elites of 19th-century Europe could no longer take the concepts associated with Christianity seriously. Nevertheless, it is the religious concept of *the sacred* that best encapsulates the combination of ambiguity, uncertainty, and excitement which sits at the heart of every story.

Another way to say the same thing is that every story requires the hero to make a sacrifice. One way to understand the nature of that sacrifice is as a function of the archetype of the hero. If we take the Warrior as an example, in both of Shakespeare's great tragedies, the sacrifice required of Macbeth and Othello is to give up active combat and learn to take part in normal life. At the beginning of his story, Macbeth is offered a thaneship by his king. Meanwhile, Othello has just gotten married. He needs to go on his honeymoon and then settle down into some kind of marital routine. Because these stories are tragedies, neither hero is able to make the sacrifice required, and they come to grief as a result. Both men are unable to let go of their existing Warrior identity and incorporate something new into themselves. Having no more external enemies to battle, they turn friends into foes. Both men end up killing the person who is the one asking for the sacrifice. Duncan has asked Macbeth to give up active battle and become a thane. Desdemona has asked Othello to be her husband. Othello kills his wife, and Macbeth kills his king. The two great Warriors are unable to relinquish their old identity and transition into a new one.

The hero of every story must exchange a fixed, established, and known identity for one that is new and ambiguous. This is also true of the two world-historical Orphan Stories we have analysed. At the beginning of the gospel story, Jesus asks men who already have jobs and mature identities to become his disciples. He is going to take literal fishermen and turn them into *fishers of men*. What exactly does that mean? It's not entirely clear, and that's the whole point. If it was perfectly stated in advance what the outcome would be, then it would not be a proper sacrifice. True sacrifice requires uncertainty in relation to the outcome of the sacrificial act. The disciples know what they are giving up, but they do not know what they are getting in return. The reason why religions and other institutions always become sterile is because the sacrifices they require become formulaic and devoid of esoteric meaning. For a sacrifice to be real, there must be ambiguity, risk, and uncertainty. Only then is the hero really laying something on the line. Only then does a story and a journey into the sacred occur.

At first glance, we might think things were different in the case of Plato and Socrates. Socrates was well-known as a philosopher, and the oracle had declared him the wisest man in Athens. Wasn't Plato's invitation to study under Socrates precise and well-defined? Not really. We must remember that Socrates' circle was a very informal arrangement, one that was explicitly in opposition to the formal and structured education offered by the sophists. Furthermore, Socrates' philosophy was based on his claim that he knew nothing. He was not offering answers; he was offering an open-ended search for truth. For that reason, Socrates was not offering a fixed goal or endpoint but rather a journey. We know that his fellow citizens found this approach to be deeply unsettling and therefore risky. His students must have felt the same way. By genuinely challenging people's worldview, Socrates took his students and opponents alike on a journey into the sacred.

It is precisely because neither Jesus nor Socrates offered their disciples a fixed path with a fixed outcome that their initiations can be thought of as stories because, to say it one more time, a story requires a step into the unknown. In order to take that step, the disciple must let go of their existing situation. It is clear that the disciples of Jesus were sacrificing their identities to follow the master. There was inherent danger attached to the situation given the background of social turmoil that existed and the controversial figure that Jesus was. The same was true of Athens. Socrates had powerful enemies who saw his method of enquiry as being dangerous and corrupt. In both cases, the disciples who accepted the offer of initiation were sacrificing a relatively safe position in society to pursue a risky, uncertain, and dangerous path by being associated with a controversial figure. That was especially true of Plato, who came from an aristocratic family and could have retained the relatively easy lifestyle that came with his social status.

The exact same dynamic applies to the position that Nietzsche was in when he decided to follow Wagner. By the time their relationship began in earnest, Nietzsche had attained the secure, respectable position of professor. He had earned that title after many years of hard, disciplined work. Just like the fisherman in the gospel story and just like Plato, Nietzsche had something to lose, while the question of what he had to gain is ambiguous at best. Wagner's invitation was: *Come and show me what kind of man you are. Come and rekindle my belief in German freedom.* This is equally as vague as Jesus' offer to make the disciples *fishers of men*. Nietzsche didn't know what he was getting into, and that is why his relationship with Wagner was a journey into the sacred.

Every Orphan Story is sacred from the point of view of the Orphan hero. However, we might be tempted to think that this property of sacredness does not apply to the Elder of the story since they are the ones offering initiation on behalf of the institution of which they are the leader. Therefore, they are not sacrificing their identity. That may be true in most real-life cases of an Orphan-Elder relationship, but it is the distinguishing feature of the world-historical Orphan Story that the Elder *will* have to make a sacrifice. In fact, they will have to make the ultimate sacrifice. Step 7 of the template is about the Elder choosing to die for their beliefs. Therefore, the Orphan Story is a journey into the sacred for both the Orphan and the Elder.

Note that this is true even of Jesus in the gospel story since the idea of a god manifesting in human form was deeply strange to the ancients for whom the whole point of being a god was that you did not have to die. The uncertainty and ambiguity in this case are inherent in the idea that a god was learning for the first time what it meant to be human. Therefore, we can say that the gospel story is a journey into the sacred for the Elder of the story, Jesus.

The case of Socrates is easier to understand since he was a man who claimed only that he knew nothing and therefore made no predictions about the future, even though he certainly knew the risks that existed for him in the general upheaval that was going on in Athens. Socrates was living his own hero's journey and therefore his own version of the sacred.

The same is true of the Elder in our story. Wagner had been on a hero's journey ever since he outlined the plan for his new art form in a series of essays between 1849 and 1851. This included specific details about the Ring Cycle and even the construction of a purpose-built theatre. It was both a theoretical and practical program that Wagner had been working towards ever since, and he had accumulated a core group of people around him to achieve it, including the composer Franz Liszt, his daughter Cosima and her husband Hans von Bülow. Just as had been the case for Socrates and Jesus, this core group was organised in a highly informal manner. But the informality is a feature, not a bug, when we understand that a story entails a journey into the ambiguous, the uncertain, and the unknown. Although Wagner had a relatively fixed goal in mind, he had no clear way to achieve that goal. Another way to think about the Orphan Story is that the Orphan hero is joining the Elder in order to contribute towards the fulfilment of their goal. That is what the disciples did for Jesus, what Plato did for Socrates, and what Nietzsche would do for Wagner.

It follows that both the Orphan and the Elder are on a journey into the unknown. Thus, neither Nietzsche nor Wagner understood what was going on in a conscious, rational way. However, they certainly felt that something special was occurring. This is the Dionysian or sacred element of stories. To be in a story is to feel this Dionysian force drawing you onwards to a destination that your Apollonian, rational mind does not properly understand. The feeling that this creates is one of superfluity where anything seems possible, and, indeed, anything is possible. It is one of the defining features of stories that the outcome is not clear, even when we have countless examples that we can analyse in an Apollonian fashion. We know how the story of Wagner and Nietzsche ended because we are looking at it after the fact. The two men involved did not and could not know. In the end, their story was unique not just in the details but in the structure. That is what ultimately led to the break between the two men and which determined the direction of Nietzsche's mature philosophy, not to mention Wagner's final opera.

In short, we must understand that the story of Nietzsche and Wagner was a journey into the sacred. The modern secular philosophy, which began to dominate in the 19th-century, and which completely dominates in our time, denies the sacred, meaning it denies anything which cannot be explained by cause and effect. As it happens, modern science provides us with phenomena that cannot be explained by cause and effect, and so we have reason to look for other explanations even within the hard sciences. One explanation that we are putting forward in this book is that the structure of stories explains reality.

But we must always remember that the structural aspects do not exist independently of the meaning, and the meaning is always a journey into the sacred. Thus, a story cannot occur unless the individuals feel that they are making a sacrifice in exchange for something uncertain but which they are drawn towards for reasons they don't understand. It may very well be that the formal, Apollonian structure of stories is a necessary part of the sacred. But the structure cannot, by itself, produce the sacred. What seems to be required is the combination of the Apollonian and Dionysian. Thus, there is a meta sense in which Nietzsche and Wagner couldn't have consciously known what they were doing. They had stumbled into the sacred, and the fact that they talked about it using secular terminology was part of the reason they were not conscious of it. And perhaps that is another quality of the sacred. Perhaps the sacred only ever appears in this world when our conscious mind is overridden and we are transported onto a pathway that we don't understand. That is when the Dionysian takes over, life is born anew, and anything becomes possible. That is how Nietzsche and Wagner felt during their relationship. Let's now join them on their journey into the sacred.

Part 2: The Orphan Story of Nietzsche and Wagner

The Hero Meets the Elder

Recall that Step 1 of the Orphan Story is about the hero being separated from their parents and beginning to forge an identity of their own, while Step 2 is about the hero becoming aware of the Elder usually by word of mouth from the society in which they live. We have already established that Nietzsche first heard of Wagner back in 1861 via the *Germania* club he had formed at his high school. We noted at that time that Nietzsche was interested in Wagner's music but did not seem to have been instantly captivated by it. In the collected correspondence of Nietzsche's that has survived for posterity, and on which we will rely heavily in this book, Wagner scores only a few mentions in the years from 1861 to 1868, when they first met. In a letter to his mother and sister in December of 1861, Nietzsche asks them to procure him a photograph of a famous person and lists Wagner as one possibility. Five years later, in 1866, he writes briefly of Wagner in a letter to his friend Rohde:-

> "However, I was accompanied by the piano score of Richard Wagner's *Walküre*, about which my feelings are very mixed, so I dare not express a judgment. The great beauty and virtues are balanced by equally great ugliness and flaws."

This is not exactly a ringing endorsement of the composer's work. It gives us the impression that Nietzsche was lukewarm in his attitude to Wagner at this time.

Just under two years later, in July of 1868, Wagner gets another lukewarm mention in a letter of Nietzsche, this time addressed to none other than the wife of the man under whose guidance he was forging ahead in the discipline of philology, Professor Ritschl. Nietzsche ends the letter with a cryptic reference to both Schopenhauer and Wagner's "clubfeet" (in German, *Pferdefüße*, literally, "horse's feet"). In short, there is nothing in Nietzsche's correspondence prior to July of 1868 that would lead us to believe he had become enamoured of Wagner's work. But then something changed. We get our first glimpse of that two months later in a letter he sent to another friend, Deussen. This letter, sent in September 1868, contains the dual dynamic that will dominate our narrative from this point forward.

On the one hand, we have the following sentence given in a tone of slight reproach at Deussen's apparently dissipative life situation:-

> "May I come clean right here? You're missing a man like Ritschl, someone who can direct your genius to where it can prove fruitful."

Here we have reference to what we have called Nietzsche's Apollonian Elder, the one who had guided him to his identity as one of the most promising philologists of the day. The quote itself is an implicit compliment to the work that Ritschl had done in guiding Nietzsche's own genius. But the far more important quote comes towards the end of the letter:-

> "Incidentally, I also discovered the true saint of philology, a genuine and real philologist, ultimately a martyr (every stupid literary historian believes he has the right to piss on him: this is martyrdom). Do you know his name? Wagner, Wagner, Wagner!"

This passage is supremely important for several reasons. First is the tone of the language. It is the earliest instance of what would become numerous quasi-religious expressions of admiration, bordering on worship, that would dominate Nietzsche's letters to friends over the next few years. It references Wagner as not just a *philologist* but a *saint* of the discipline. It calls Wagner a *martyr,* and it rails against the entire discipline of *literary historians* who had taken to launching openly hostile denunciations of Wagner in the press under the guise of scholarship. Something had massively changed in Nietzsche's attitude to Wagner in the space of just a couple of months. He had gone from sardonically complaining about Wagner's *clubfoot* to an impassioned declaration of his allegiance.

The second crucial point about the letter to Deussen is the timing of it. We have already presaged the appearance of improbable coincidences in the story of Wagner and Nietzsche, but another quality that will reveal itself time and again in our analysis ahead is that events in the real world will be prefigured and seemingly predicted by events in the mind of the individuals in the story. To this end, we are incredibly fortunate to have access to the extensive correspondence, notebooks, and diaries of the three main players: Nietzsche, Wagner, and Cosima Wagner. By contrast, we know nothing about Plato's inner thoughts during the time when he was a student of Socrates, and the gospels tell us almost nothing about what was going through the minds of the disciples in the years in which they followed Jesus. In these cases, what we know must be inferred from the words and actions of the master, such as Jesus reproaching the disciples, *O Ye of little faith.* In relation to Nietzsche, we have both his personal correspondence and notes and the intensely personal nature of his philosophical writings. It is the comparison of these with the objective facts of history that will form the basis of our analysis.

The facts in this case are stranger than fiction. We know that Nietzsche seems to have undergone an epiphany in relation to Wagner in the months leading up to the letter of September 1868. We also know that Nietzsche had a personal relationship and regular correspondence with the wife of his esteemed leader at the University of Leipzig in which they discussed topics that included important figures in the wider culture such as Wagner. These two facts would come together in the most incredible way to set up the original meeting between Wagner and Nietzsche, which occurred just weeks after the letter to Deussen. Nietzsche could have had no advance warning of this since the circumstances surrounding the meeting were unknown to all parties until just a couple of days before it happened. But to fully appreciate the serendipity at play, we need to go back even further in time.

Recall that Nietzsche began studying under Ritschl in Bonn in 1864. Less than a year later, in 1865, the fiery dispute between Ritschl and Jahn broke out, with the former being forced out of the university. Since Ritschl was held in the highest esteem among his colleagues of the day (Jahn excluded, of course), he quickly acquired a place at the University of Leipzig in the same role as professor of philology. Nietzsche and a number of other students followed him there to continue their studies. We can imagine that it would be perfectly natural that a distinguished professor would quickly make new friends in his adopted hometown of Leipzig. One of those new friends was a certain Hermann Brockhaus who was married to a woman named Ottilie, who just happened to be the sister of none other than Richard Wagner. Wagner had been born in Leipzig, and his sister still lived there. Over the next few years, Frau Ritschl and Ottilie Brockhaus (née Wagner) became close friends, and it was this connection which would eventually lead to the wife of Nietzsche's mentor receiving an invitation to visit the Brockhaus household on the occasion of a visit by Ottilie's brother, Richard.

Wagner was not particularly close to his sister, and so this visit was itself rather unusual. It appears to have been prompted by the depressed mood that the composer was in on account of the exact dynamic that Nietzsche had alluded to just weeks earlier in his letter to Deussen. Wagner had always been a controversial figure, and his relationship with Cosima, which was scandalous due to the fact that she was still married to von Bülow, had only given the press more grist for the mill. Combined with the usual troubles that plagued Wagner's life, such as financial problems, it seems that he desired to take a break and reconnect with his sister in Leipzig. However, since he was already annoyed with the negative press coverage he was receiving and since Cosima was joining him on the journey, the whole trip had to be done incognito. Wagner instructed Ottilie to only invite the most trusted guests during his stay.

One of those trusted guests was Frau Ritschl, and here is where the improbable coincidences begin because the epiphany that Nietzsche had in relation to Wagner in the months leading up to October had not gone unnoticed by those around him. The quasi-religious tone of Nietzsche's letter to Deussen was clearly not reserved for written correspondence. He was apparently raving to anybody he met about Wagner and had gained a reputation as a devotee of the composer among fellow students and professors in the philology department at Leipzig. This reputation extended to the wives of professors. Thus, when Wagner sat down at the piano in his sister's house in early October and regaled the company with a piece from *Die Meistersinger*, which had premiered in June that year, Frau Ritschl exclaimed that she was already familiar with the tune on account of a bright young student of her husband who was mad for all things Wagner. Wagner was interested enough to have the young man invited over for a visit before he left Leipzig.

The question that must be asked at this point is, Why would Wagner do that? He was already a famous man. It must have been a regular occurrence for him to meet his fans while out in public or at events. In addition, he regularly received letters from admirers and supporters in Germany and around the world. Furthermore, Wagner's popularity was highest among the younger generation. The fact that a student at the University of Leipzig would be a big fan of his should not have been a surprise to the composer. Why would he feel the need for a personal meeting with this particular supporter, especially since he had gone out of his way to be incognito in Leipzig and this risked breaking his cover?

The first thing to bear in mind is that the exclusive nature of the gathering at his sister's residence meant that there was a high level of implied trust in Frau Ritschl. Furthermore, she was the wife of one of the foremost philologists in Germany, and she was not just recommending any student of her husband but his best student. Wagner may have railed against the stuffy old academics who didn't care for his work, but he still held academia in the same high regard as most Germans of that era. What's more, as Nietzsche had not incorrectly pointed out in his letter to Deussen, Wagner was a kind of philologist himself, even though his approach to the subject was creative and not scholarly in nature. It's likely that the fact that Nietzsche was studying philology interested the composer.

But there's one more point to be made, perhaps the most important in this regard. For his entire career, which was now more than thirty years old, Wagner had struggled to find anybody who really understood what he was trying to do with his art. Yes, he had many supporters and admirers, but many of those were primarily interested in his musical innovations or the catchier parts of his compositions. Others would have been more interested in Wagner's theatrical inventions or his use of popular medieval stories. How many people actually understood the theory behind all this? How many had read his essays laying out the ideas behind the *Gesamtkunstwerk*? The answer is not many, and even those who had often did not understand what he was getting at. In short, Wagner was misunderstood. He believed in the idea of the heroic Artist and the duty of such a person to address the highest questions of life. What he came to realise was that the public wanted something very different from their heroic Artist, something more like rock star rebels like Byron. Wagner's art and his life were iconoclastic, not as ends in themselves, but in service to higher ideals. Wagner yearned for those who could understand these higher ideals. Viewed this way, we can start to see why Wagner might have been interested to meet one of the brightest philology students of the day who just happened to be a devotee.

We need no further clues to understand Nietzsche's interest in being introduced to Wagner or to imagine how he felt the next day when he received an invitation to a top-secret meeting with the maestro. Empirical verification of the young man's excitement can be found in the fact that the first thing Nietzsche did on receiving the news was to rush out and instruct a tailor to make him a new suit for the occasion. There followed a comedic episode in which the tailor delivered the suit late then demanded payment upfront, which Nietzsche was not in a position to provide. After attempting to prevent the man from leaving with the new garment by physically inserting himself into it, Nietzsche admitted defeat in his attempt to impress the maestro with a new outfit. He ended up visiting Wagner in the clothes he deemed most appropriate from his existing wardrobe.

In any event, the meeting went swimmingly. Wagner enquired how Nietzsche had come to know his work so well, and, presumably, the young man gave a suitable answer. The composer then played several tunes from *Meistersinger* and read from his autobiography. If Nietzsche had been enraptured before, he was now borderline ecstatic. The very first thing he did afterwards was to write to his friend Rohde, detailing the events of the meeting. We have already noted the line from the letter, "On these days I felt as though I was living in a novel…".

Nietzsche was absolutely correct to say that he was living through a story. It was, in fact, the beginning of an Orphan Story, Step 3, to be precise: *The hero meets the Elder, who offers them initiation*. The offer that Wagner gave to Nietzsche occurred at the very end of the meeting as the guests were saying their goodbyes. In Nietzsche's words, it happened like this:-

> *"At the close of the evening, when we were both ready to go, he shook my hand very warmly and kindly asked me to come and see him so that we might have some music and philosophy together. He also entrusted me with the task of making his music known to his sister and his relations, a duty which I undertook very solemnly to fulfil."*

Note that Wagner did not just invite Nietzsche to visit him; he gave the young man his first task, namely, to explain to his own sister why his music was so good! Nietzsche accepted this rather strange and pompous assignment with glee, which is not surprising given that he had already begun proselytising Wagner to everybody he met in the months beforehand. Nietzsche's initiation as a Wagnerian had begun and we can mark it on our template as follows:-

Orphan Story Template	Nietzsche and Wagner
1. The hero is separated from his parents (becomes an Orphan)	Nietzsche's father died when he was young. He left home when attending Schulpforta and then university
2. The hero hears news of the Elder or the institution to which the Elder is associated	Nietzsche had been introduced to Wagner by a friend when he was fourteen years old
3. The hero meets the Elder, who offers them initiation	Nietzsche met Wagner in secret at Wagner's sister's house. Wagner invites Nietzsche to visit in Tribschen
4. The hero accepts and initiation commences, including induction into the institution led by the Elder	
5. A Shadow Elder tries to subvert the initiation	
6. There is a struggle between the hero, the Elder and the Shadow Elder	
7. The Elder dies or otherwise goes missing (usually sacrificing themselves for the hero)	
8. The hero faces the Shadow Elder alone	

The Call to Adventure

Of all the incredible coincidences and fairy-tale qualities of just this initial evening that would begin the relationship between the two men, there is one element which stands out as unusual and which will play a crucial role in the evolution of the story we are in the process of telling. We must remember that the Orphan Story begins with the hero already having a stable identity, a base which, even though it may not be especially interesting, is solid and real. Jesus' disciples were fishermen and tax collectors, very practical occupations. Plato was a newly-graduated citizen of Athens. In fictional Orphan Stories, Luke Skywalker works on his uncle's farm at the start of *Star Wars*. Neo has a presumably well-paying and high-status job as a computer programmer in *The Matrix*. Even Hamlet has a place at university where he can escape the court intrigues of his uncle. What this means is that it is not necessity which forces the Orphan into a change; it is the promise of something more, something which exists in an unrealised and only barely-conscious part of their being. The Elder's offer of initiation is what unlocks the part of the hero that they could not reach by themselves.

All of this is true of Nietzsche, as we have already covered. Yet, what is highly unusual, perhaps even unique, in just the parts of the story we have told so far is the involvement of Nietzsche's existing Elder, Ritschl. It was Ritschl's feud with Jahn which caused the move to Wagner's hometown of Leipzig and created the connection with his sister. It was Ritschl's wife who would be directly responsible for introducing Wagner to Nietzsche. Incredibly, the next step in the story also revolves around Ritschl. What we see is that Nietzsche's existing identity seemed to be "creating" or at least "facilitating" the new identity which he would be offered by Wagner. Where it gets even weirder, though, is that aspect of the story was already present in the letter that Nietzsche sent to Deussen in September. At a time when he could have absolutely no expectation of meeting Wagner just weeks later, Nietzsche wrote: "*I...discovered the true saint of philology....Wagner!*" The order of events here is that Nietzsche dreams of Wagner as a philological *saint* and *martyr,* and then a few weeks later, he is introduced to Wagner by a philologist's wife.

The philological coincidences do not end there. On the contrary, they multiply. The initial meeting with Wagner had taken place in Leipzig at the beginning of October in 1868. Wagner invited Nietzsche to visit him at his home in Lucerne, Switzerland. The distance between the two cities is seven hundred and fifty kilometres. Not only was this a lengthy and uncomfortable journey given the train technology of the time, it was also not cheap. Nietzsche was existing at the university largely on account of his mother's purse, and that purse was not very deep since the family had never been rich. On purely pragmatic grounds, any potential visits to the Wagner household were going to be few and far between while Nietzsche was still a student in Leipzig. The young man must have been painfully aware of that fact.

And so, what are the chances that, almost immediately after the Leipzig meeting between Nietzsche and Wagner, one of the old faculty members in the philology department at the University of Basel should retire? What are the chances that the name of a promising young scholar named Nietzsche should come up for discussion on account of the several articles he had published in philological journals which had caught the attention of the professorship in Basel? Finally, what are the chances that the man who was placed in the position of providence to swing the scales one way or the other was none other than Nietzsche's Apollonian Elder, Ritschl? The philology faculty in Basel contacted Ritschl to ask for his opinion on Nietzsche's suitability for the professor role which had just opened up. Ritschl replied that Nietzsche was a genius and that the faculty should quit its search immediately and give him the job. A problem arose. Nietzsche had not yet been granted his degree and was therefore technically not qualified. After some deliberation, the Swiss decided to waive the rules and proceed anyway. Ritschl marvelled at the fact that such a thing could never happen in Germany, where it simply wasn't possible to bend the rules in this fashion no matter how badly the individuals involved might have wanted to.

Within two months of being invited to visit Wagner in Lucerne, Nietzsche was about to be offered a job in what was almost the nearest possible location. What are the odds? Meanwhile, Nietzsche's obsession with Wagner had continued to strengthen. Ritschl had told the Swiss that Nietzsche was a genius. By December of 1868, Nietzsche was referring to Wagner in exactly the same way. Here is how he described the composer in a letter to Rohde that month:-

> "I also have the firm confidence that we will fully understand one another about a genius who seemed to me like an insoluble problem and whose understanding I have made new attempts year after year: this genius is Richard Wagner."

This followed a letter from the previous month where Nietzsche recommended Wagner's essay *Opera and Drama* to Rohde. It is clear that Nietzsche had become interested not just in Wagner's music but, more importantly, in his writings. That is surely what was behind the notion that he was a *saint of philology.*

Nietzsche's use of religious metaphor may seem to be the product of enthusiasm, and yet we have already noted that the tone of Wagner's essays, especially in the period 1849-51, was biblical in nature. Wagner had taken on the role of the prophet of Germany, calling the folk to rediscover their own culture and thereby to revitalise their nation. For all their logical flaws, it must be admitted that Wagner's writings do contain the spark of genius, and it is very easy to imagine that a young man such as Nietzsche would both recognise the power of those ideas while also being carried away by the quasi-religious tone in which they were delivered. Our hypothesis, then, is that it was not primarily Wagner's music which enraptured Nietzsche but his writings. Since those writings do contain much that is somewhat applicable to the study of philology, it makes some sense that Nietzsche would come to think of Wagner as a *saint of philology.*

But all of this only makes the already incredible set of coincidences in our story even more incredible. Let's work through the chronology one more time. Nietzsche becomes enraptured with Wagner's essays, starting around the middle of 1868. We know that he wasn't shy about sharing this with his colleagues at the university since even Frau Ritschl had heard the young man's enthusiasm. The first true expression of that enthusiasm comes in the letter to Deussen in September. Then, at the beginning of October, Frau Ritschl sets up the initial meeting between Nietzsche and Wagner. Nietzsche's admiration only grows in the aftermath. We find him now referring to Wagner as a *genius* and all but instructing Rohde to go out and buy a copy of *Opera and Drama* so that the two can talk about it.

At just the same time that this enthusiasm for Wagner burst into bloom, Nietzsche's letters reveal that he was losing interest in academic philology. The earliest evidence for that is in 1867, and we see further examples of the same feeling in the lead-up to the first meeting with Wagner. In fact, Nietzsche had organised with Rohde to take some time away from academia and live in Paris for a while. Meanwhile, he had also expressed a desire to swap out of the philology department and try his hand at one of the hard sciences. In any case, around this time, Nietzsche was highly dubious about a future career in philology.

Then, incredibly, it seems that the discovery of Wagner's essays reignited Nietzsche's passion for philology. Wagner became the "saint of philology". The next thing that happens is that a philologist's wife organises for Nietzsche to meet Wagner, and then a group of philologists at the University of Basel offer Nietzsche a job with Ritschl playing a key role in making it all happen. If all of this had happened prior to the meeting with Wagner in Leipzig, it seems certain that Nietzsche would have turned down the job offer. But Basel was only one hundred kilometres from Lucerne, meaning that Wagner's invitation to Nietzsche to visit him at home would now be a real possibility. Everything had miraculously fallen into place to allow Nietzsche to pursue a relationship with Wagner. Nietzsche himself remarked in a letter to Rohde that the whole thing was like a fairytale.

The other term that Nietzsche used to describe the events at this time was one that would become a foundation of his mature philosophy: fate. On the 16th of January 1869, when the job in Basel had become almost a certainty, Nietzsche wrote excitedly to Rohde, saying, "From the very beginning, I've grown accustomed to seeing this story as a magnificent coincidence" and then, "We're truly the fools of fate..."

But the far more important statement comes at the end of the same letter: "Lucerne is no longer out of reach for me." This proves two things. Firstly, in Nietzsche's mind, Lucerne *was* out of reach before the job offer was made. Secondly, the job offer *was* his ticket to Lucerne. We do not have to speculate on this matter. We can be one hundred percent sure that Nietzsche took the job in Basel in order to pursue the relationship with Wagner. If there is any lingering doubt on this score, consider these lines from the letter that Nietzsche sent to Rohde on 12th February 1869, the same day he got news that he had been offered the job:-

"Dear friend, the leap into the inevitable has occurred: today, on this festive day on which your ¨Onos enters life richly adorned, the undersigned ¨Onos has entered the rank of sacred professor. Long live free Switzerland, Richard Wagner, and our friendship."

PART 2: THE ORPHAN STORY OF NIETZSCHE AND WAGNER

On the day in which Nietzsche became a professor of philology, he did not give a cheer for his teachers at Schulpforta or for Ritschl, the man who most made it happen; he gave a cheer for Richard Wagner.

Nietzsche's use of concepts like 'coincidence', 'fate', 'inevitability', and 'fairytale' is all perfectly consonant with our analysis based on the structure of the Orphan Story and shows that, even though he wasn't thinking about it consciously in the way that we are, he had realised that something special was happening. Some kind of higher force seemed to be guiding in the direction of Richard Wagner. The story began as a fairytale, but we know that it did not end that way, and, with the benefit of hindsight, we can identify already at this early stage a number of contradictions that would play a key role in the way that the relationship between Nietzsche and Wagner would evolve.

The primary contradiction is that Nietzsche was accepting a formal role at the University of Basel that had been organised and offered through official academic channels. That role came with high expectations and a significant workload. Nietzsche must have known that, and it seems highly likely that his attitude to academia prior to the Wagnerian epiphany would have seen him turn down such a burden and go to Paris with Rohde instead. The Wagner connection changed the calculus for Nietzsche, but it also made the professorship little more than a chore that could only get in the way of what he really wanted, which was to spend time with the composer and pursue the new ideas that Wagner had planted in his mind. We can see that the burden began to manifest almost immediately after Nietzsche had moved to Basel. On the 22nd of May 1869, he wrote to Wagner regretting a missed opportunity to visit, which he most certainly would have taken up if "the tiresome chain of my profession hadn't kept me confined to my Basel kennel". Nietzsche had been in the job for only one month when he wrote this. Right from the beginning, there was a divide between Nietzsche's Apollonian identity as a proper and upright professor of philology and his Dionysian voyages into new and exciting territory that came with his trips to Lucerne.

The second contradiction follows from the first. Nietzsche had become convinced that Wagner was the *saint of philology,* and it is clear from his notebooks at this time that Wagner's ideas really had influenced him in new and profound ways. The problem was that nobody else thought of Wagner as a philologist, least of all Nietzsche's colleagues. The idea that Wagner would have anything to teach Nietzsche about philology would have seemed absurd to them. That's why the relationship between Wagner and Nietzsche could never be understood to an outsider. He would say that Wagner was teaching him many things. But what could that mean? What would a composer teach a philologist? Nobody could have understood that the relationship really was about philology.

But even that is not exactly true. Wagner had precisely no interest in the Apollonian approach to philology. He was interested in what we have called the Dionysian and its manifestation in a true form of art that got its vitality from Life and Nature and which would nurture a new German culture. The art form that was to deliver that was none other than Wagner's. There were no other composers with whom he was working, no larger institutions to which he belonged. On the contrary, he had been in opposition to the established institutions for most of his life. Thus, the entire enterprise of creating this new, vibrant, living art form revolved around Wagner himself. It was his personality, his strength of character, his determination, and, most importantly, his ideas that ran the show. While Nietzsche was enamoured of those ideas, the relationship could proceed to grow and flourish as it soon would. But the fault lines were there from the start. Nietzsche was useful to Wagner so long as he served the Wagnerian cause. Wagner had signalled that by asking Nietzsche to advocate for his music. Thus, the contradiction between advocacy and scholarship was also there from the beginning.

In truth, what both men were doing was to extend their own domain of speciality into the higher questions of life. Wagner was not concerned with opera as such but with the *Gesamtkunstwerk*, which, for the average person, just happened to look almost identical to opera. But even his dream of the *Gesamtkunstwerk* was tied in with larger dreams around freedom and German culture and all kinds of other philosophical ideas that the average person had no interest in. It seems that Nietzsche did much the same thing. He called Wagner the *saint of philology,* but, in reality, he was conflating philology with the same set of larger questions and dreams.

PART 2: THE ORPHAN STORY OF NIETZSCHE AND WAGNER

These confusions and conflations distinguish the story of Wagner and Nietzsche from the other world-historical ones we have looked at. Jesus tells the would-be disciples to put down their fishing nets so that he can make them *fishers of men*. He is clearly offering them a new role and a new mission in life. The same would have been true of Socrates when he took Plato into his inner circle. In the story of Wagner and Nietzsche, we have no clear break with the hero's past identity. On the contrary, we have what looks on the surface to be the natural continuation of Nietzsche's Apollonian identity as one of the best philology students of his era. Due to his young age, it was highly unusual for him to receive a job as professor, but it still made sense to the average person in light of the fact that Ritschl said he was a genius. The German culture of that era was obsessed with the concept of genius and so would have had no compunction about categorising Nietzsche as such.

The real problem was not in the outward appearance of it all but in Nietzsche's inner understanding. If Nietzsche had told Ritschl that he thought Wagner was the *saint of philology*, there is not only no chance that his mentor would have agreed, there is every chance he would have seriously questioned the sanity of his student. It simply would have made no sense to him. Similarly, Ritschl would have been outraged if Nietzsche told him that the only reason he took the professorship in Basel was because he wanted to visit Wagner in Lucerne. The contradictions we have noted all boil down to a dichotomy between outward appearance and inner reality. Outwardly, Nietzsche had become a professor of philology. Inwardly, he had already started to become a disciple of Wagner. The philology professorship was the price that Nietzsche would have to pay to pursue the Wagner connection, and it is clear that he resented it as such. But even before the job was confirmed, we can see that Nietzsche could already barely distinguish the opportunity from his growing adulation of Wagner.

All this created a contradiction between Nietzsche's inner identity and his outer one. To the outer world, he was the young genius philologist who had just become the youngest professor of the classics in the history of the subject. That made him already a minor celebrity in philological circles and also in Basel, which was delighted to become the home of an academic superstar. On the inside, however, Nietzsche was doing all this for ulterior motives, and, outside of a few close friends who he was mostly in contact with via mail, nobody else knew his true motivations. For the next three years, this discrepancy would grow as the inner identity was fostered through the relationship with Wagner and the outer continued on in a seemingly normal fashion. Eventually, the contradiction would make itself public in the dramatic events surrounding the publication of Nietzsche's first book, *The Birth of Tragedy*, in 1872. But all of that was three years away.

What needed to happen first was that the relationship with Wagner needed to be officially consecrated. All Nietzsche had was an invitation to visit Lucerne and a job that gave him the opportunity to make that happen. By the time he had arrived and gotten settled in to his new home in Basel, it had been around six months since the secret meeting in Leipzig. Wagner was a famous and busy man. What guarantee was there that he would even remember either the invitation or Nietzsche? Nietzsche couldn't be sure, and so he chose a surreptitious method of approach. On Saturday 15th May 1869, only three weeks after his arrival in Basel, he decided to spend a weekend in Lucerne. He booked in with a tour group but found an opportunity to sneak away to Wagner's house, named Tribschen, which was nearby. Wagner was upstairs composing the third opera of the Ring Cycle, *Siegfried*. The servant took Nietzsche's details up to the master, who did not want to be disturbed. Nevertheless, he did remember Nietzsche from Leipzig and invited him back for lunch. As Nietzsche needed to rejoin his tour group, he had to decline. Wagner offered lunch on Monday instead, an invitation that Nietzsche was able to accept.

This brings us to the final unusual property of the beginning of the Orphan Story between Wagner and Nietzsche, which was now about to begin in earnest. Recall that the Elder's offer of initiation is not just about a personal relationship between the Orphan and himself; it is also about the Orphan becoming part of the institution of which the Elder is the established leader. For Jesus, this was the group consisting of his disciples. For Socrates, it was his students. In the case of Wagner, the institution of which he was the leader was very largely his own household, in which lived the most trusted person

PART 2: THE ORPHAN STORY OF NIETZSCHE AND WAGNER

in his life and arguably the one who, until that point, best understood the man and his art, Cosima. At that time, the two of them were not yet married. Wagner and Cosima had been having an affair while she was still wedded to one of Wagner's other main supporters, Hans von Bülow. Von Bülow tolerated the dalliance at first, even as Cosima fell pregnant to Wagner. But, eventually, he lost patience, and Cosima made the very difficult decision to leave him in order to live with Wagner; difficult because it meant separating from her children. This had created a major furore in the media.

The connection with Wagner's art was even deeper, however, since Cosima was the daughter of Franz Liszt, and it had been Liszt more than anybody who had supported Wagner during the depths of his post-exile despair. Liszt was, of course, also a famous composer and so had a thorough understanding of Wagner's talents in that respect. Therefore, Wagner's inner circle really was familial in the literal sense of the word, and the fact that Nietzsche was paying a visit to Wagner's home meant that the institution he was about to be inducted into was, in very large part, Wagner's family. The Wagner household in Tribschen was the centre of the Wagnerian world. It received all of the closest and most loyal Wagnerians, including the young king of Bavaria, whose patronage had become crucial to Wagner's ambitions and who was about the exact same age as Nietzsche. But there was another person who was almost the same age as Nietzsche, and that was Cosima. Technically, she was seven years older, but that made her far more a member of Nietzsche's generation than her husband's. Cosima was also Wagner's number one supporter in an emotional, intellectual, and logistical sense. If Nietzsche was about to join the ranks of the Wagnerians, then he would not just need Wagner's endorsement; he would need Cosima's too.

This endorsement was given immediately, and the swiftness with which Nietzsche was accepted into the household is quite startling. The lunch on the Monday (17th May) went off so well that Cosima wrote to Nietzsche just days later to invite him back for Wagner's birthday on the Saturday. It was his inability to attend this great event due to work commitments that led to Nietzsche's quip about being trapped in his Basel kennel in a letter he sent to Wagner for his birthday. The manner in which Nietzsche begins that letter is noteworthy:-

> *"How long have I intended to express, without any hesitation, the degree of gratitude I feel toward you since the best and most sublime moments of my life are truly linked to your name, and I only know one other man, your great spiritual brother, Arthur Schopenhauer, whom I think of with equal reverence."*

He goes on to tell Wagner he is a genius and laments the fact that nobody else has understood that genius (implying that he himself had). Nietzsche had only met Wagner twice in his life when he wrote this letter and he already says that Wagner had caused the most sublime moments of his life. It may sound as though Nietzsche was being obsequious, and, in one sense, that is perhaps true. But there is no doubting the sincerity of what he writes and also the radical openness of it, a quality that is only shared with Nietzsche's letters to his closest friends at this time. This reveals that there was an immediate intimacy with Wagner. Moreover, that intimacy and openness were reciprocated.

It was in response to this letter that Wagner wrote the line we have already mentioned: "Now let me see what kind of man you are". In the context of the Orphan Story, this line consecrated Steps 3 and 4 of our template. It was the official call to adventure that the Elder gives the Orphan. But it should be clear now that, by this point, the acceptance of the offer was already a *fait accompli*, since Nietzsche had taken the job in Basel with the express hope of joining with Wagner somehow. There were no further problems from Nietzsche's side, and, apparently, there were none from the Wagners either. With Nietzsche unable to attend the birthday, another visit was set up. This time Nietzsche was to stay an entire weekend, from June 5 until June 7. He had gone from a casual lunch guest to an overnight guest in the space of a week.

As if all that wasn't enough, another improbable coincidence was about to occur. On the first night of Nietzsche's visit, Cosima would go into labour. At about four in the morning, she would give birth to Wagner's first son,

Siegfried. Several times in the letters exchanged between the two men over the following years, Wagner would tell Nietzsche that he considered him a son. For his part, Nietzsche referred to Wagner as his *Pater Seraphicus*, his Holy Father. If Wagner was the father and Nietzsche the son, then Cosima was the Holy Spirit. Some commentators have claimed that Nietzsche was romantically or sexually in love with Cosima. That is certainly possible. But it also seems just as possible that the love he felt for her was similar to that which he felt for his master, i.e., it was a spiritual kind of love, a love born out of the fact that three highly intelligent and accomplished people had found in each other somebody who could truly understand.

But the word *understand* here is wrong because it is far too Apollonian. What was going on here was Dionysian in nature. It was the feeling that something had happened, the feeling which Nietzsche called *fate*, *inevitability*, or *living in a fairytale*. It is clear that all three of them felt the same way. Even though so much about the whole dynamic is uncertain and ambiguous from a logical or empirical point of view, there was an inner certainty to it. Only that can explain how Nietzsche, who was little more than a stranger, went from lunch guest to overnight guest in an instant. In doing so, he became part of the family, the Holy Son to a Holy Father and Mother. His induction into the *institution of Wagner*, the Tribschen household, was officially sanctified.

With this, Step 4 of the Orphan Story template is also sanctified, and we can add this to our template as follows:-

Orphan Story Template	Nietzsche and Wagner
1. The hero is separated from his parents (becomes an Orphan)	Nietzsche's father died when he was young. He left home when attending Schulpforta and then university
2. The hero hears news of the Elder or the institution to which the Elder is associated	Nietzsche had been introduced to Wagner by a friend when he was fourteen years old
3. The hero meets the Elder, who offers them initiation	Nietzsche met Wagner in secret at Wagner's sister's house. Wagner invites Nietzsche to visit in Tribschen
4. The hero accepts and initiation commences, including induction into the institution led by the Elder	The professorship at the University of Basel allows Nietzsche to become a regular visitor at Tribschen
5. A Shadow Elder tries to subvert the initiation	
6. There is a struggle between the hero, the Elder and the Shadow Elder	
7. The Elder dies or otherwise goes missing (usually sacrificing themselves for the hero)	
8. The hero faces the Shadow Elder alone	

If Nietzsche's acceptance of the Basel professorship had been done with his express desire to enable a relationship with Wagner to proceed, then the consummation of that plan had occurred with incredible rapidity. But, then again, so had all the events leading up to this moment. If we reckon the middle of 1868 as the time during which Nietzsche had the epiphany that led him to regard Wagner as a *genius* and *saint*, then it had taken less than a year for a personal relationship to begin. But we must remember that there was nothing overt or consciously created in all of this. Nietzsche hadn't tried to make contact with the composer. As a student in Leipzig, he had no prospect of ever meeting Wagner and no personal or family connections he could call on to make it happen. And yet it did happen. It happened by the most extraordinary set of "coincidences". As a result, it all felt like a wonderful dream.

We mentioned earlier the contradictions that were inherent in the dynamic right from the beginning. Another way to understand them is in terms of the archetypes. Nietzsche was still in the Orphan phase of life when he first met Wagner in Leipzig. But that had now changed. With the professorship in Basel, Nietzsche had officially taken the step into a mature Adult identity. If we remember back to our archetypal overview, the Orphan archetype graduates into the Adult. One of the most important aspects of Adult identity is our economic contribution to the society in which we live. That is what Nietzsche had attained with his professorship in Basel, and we shouldn't underestimate what that meant for a young man who had grown up in a household which was stable but not rich. Nietzsche's scholarship at the Schulpforta had brought him into contact with families who were all far wealthier than his own. His university studies had needed to be conducted on a shoestring budget since his sole source of income was a stipend from his mother. With the Basel professorship, Nietzsche had an income for the first time in his life. He proudly boasted of it in the excited letters he sent to his friends and family upon landing the job.

The fact that it was Ritschl who organised the position in Basel is fitting because the older man had been Nietzsche's Elder during the preceding years. In fact, if we wanted to talk about the concepts of destiny and fate, it must have seemed from an outside observer's point of view that Nietzsche had been destined to become a professional philologist ever since receiving the Schulpforta scholarship. It was the goal that he had been working towards for ten straight years and for which everything seemed to have fallen into place. We know better, of course, but the only reason is because we have access to Nietzsche's inner thoughts via his letters and notebooks. Those were private at the time, and so even a man such as Ritschl, who was very close to the young Nietzsche, could have no idea about the change in inner motivation that had occurred and which was the true driver in Nietzsche's ambition from that point onwards.

Thus, another way to look at the contradiction between the inner and outer identities of the young man is that, at the exact same moment that Nietzsche appeared to have graduated from the Orphan-Elder relationship with Ritschl and taken a firm step into the Adult phase of his life, what had actually happened was that he had really stepped into a new Orphan-Elder relationship with Wagner. It is perfectly fitting that nobody else could have any clue what had happened, since it all began with a secret meeting in Leipzig. That is what made it Dionysian and esoteric in nature. The tension between Nietzsche's Apollonian identity as a professor of philology and his Dionysian one as a disciple of Wagner would only grow from now on. Back at the start of January, when the professorship seemed certain but had not yet been confirmed, Nietzsche wrote in a letter to Rohde, "Now the devil 'Fate' is beckoning with a professorship in philology." Perhaps Nietzsche had some presentiment of the Mephistophelian bargain he had signed. But, as of June 1869, he was still riding high like Faust on the magic carpet.

Initiation Begins

In one of the final things he wrote in the lead-up to his mental breakdown in the first days of 1889, at a time when his attitude to Wagner had completely reversed from the worship of the early days, Nietzsche asserted that he would swap anything else in his life but never the time he spent at Tribschen, Wagner's house in Lucerne. This period of his life would end up lasting almost a full three years, and Nietzsche would visit approximately twenty-three times over the period, usually for an extended stay of a weekend or more. Tribschen was the centre point of the Wagnerian empire, and we have a detailed understanding of the life that was lived there courtesy of the meticulous diary kept by Cosima. It is worth noting that the house was paid for by none other than King Ludwig of Bavaria, who, alongside Nietzsche and Cosima, was perhaps the main admirer of Wagner's art. The generosity of the king's purse waxed and waned over the years, but for the time being, it remained open to keep Wagner in the luxury for which he had always strived but rarely been able to afford.

The hard days may have seemed to be over in 1869. Not only was Ludwig able to lend his support, but Wagner's fame had been on the rise for some time, and performances of his operas were now commonplace in Germany. With *Die Meistersinger* completed and premiered in the previous year, Wagner was now concentrating on composing the remaining music for the Ring Cycle. Tribschen was far enough away from town, and Lucerne was far enough away from Germany to offer Wagner the peace and quiet required to fulfil his task. Nevertheless, the household was a busy one, receiving regular visitors, not just Nietzsche. The arrival of the mail also provided a share of drama on a more or less daily basis. One of the main topics of discussion was the still illicit relationship between Wagner and Cosima on account of the fact that Cosima was still married to von Bülow. The birth of Siegfried had only added complication in this respect. Negotiations were ongoing with von Bülow to finally grant a divorce to Cosima, a request that had remained unfulfilled for several years. Von Bülow had originally agreed to keep up the façade of the marriage to protect Cosima from public approbation, but now that she was openly living with Wagner, the emphasis had shifted to the two getting married as speedily as possible so that her honour might be restored.

The other main source of tension in the household came from the regular reports of smear campaigns in the media and various hijinks from the audience that were taking place during the performances of Wagner's operas, especially *Die Meistersinger*. Apart from the controversy around Cosima's marital status, the other main scandal at that time was related to the accusation that Wagner had inserted an anti-Semitic trope into *Meistersinger* by apparently basing the main song of Beckmesser (the Shadow Elder of the story) on an old Jewish tune. Wagner rejected this idea, but the story grew legs largely because the composer's increasing fame had drawn attention to his non-fiction writings, including a pamphlet titled *Judaism in Music*, a deeply strange piece of work whose main theme appeared to be that *the Jews were somehow responsible for suppressing the emergence of a true German culture*. Since Wagner's attitude to his own ideas bordered on messianic, there was no chance of him disowning, or even just remaining quiet about, these less popular opinions, and the result was that it had become fashionable for audiences to hiss during the parts of *Meistersinger* deemed to be anti-Semitic, all of which was further material for the gossip pages in the press.

The other main daily activity that took place at Tribschen was the one which certainly must have appealed to Nietzsche. Wagner and Cosima were not just interested in art; they were interested in ideas about art and ideas in general. In the evenings, both when they had company and when they were alone, they would read and discuss famous works from the Western canon, including everything from Plato and ancient Greek tragedy through the Renaissance and Shakespeare and into Goethe and modern pieces. In his dedication to Wagner in the preface of *The Birth of Tragedy*, Nietzsche would write about the "seriousness of art", and that was certainly the environment that he found at Tribschen. Ideas were not passively reviewed but passionately discussed. We can safely assume that they were discussed in the same manner in which Wagner wrote his essays, which came with a number of virtues and vices, the latter of which was that Wagner much preferred to make bold, categorical statements rather than nuanced argumentation. But since Nietzsche had already developed a taste for Wagner's writing style prior to their initial meeting, he seems to have had no problem with that.

Given the belligerent tone of Nietzsche's mature philosophy, written after the break with Wagner, it may seem hard for us to imagine, but Wagner dominated the discussion that went on at Tribschen. For the vast majority of the time that Nietzsche visited the household, their discussion time would have been spent in the evenings after the children had been put to bed. It would have been just the three of them: Nietzsche, Cosima, and Wagner. The job of Nietzsche and Cosima was to agree with the master, or at least disagree in the most inconspicuous way possible. We shouldn't mince words. Wagner was a narcissist and a bully. He certainly had his virtues, but these were his main vices. None of this was a problem at this time since we know Nietzsche thought of Wagner as a saint, Holy Father, and genius. That's pretty much exactly how Cosima felt too. More important for Nietzsche was that the ideas of Wagner's that he was exposed to stimulated his own. In the evenings at Tribschen, he had direct, unfettered access to the sermons of the master. It was this environment which would eventually give rise to Nietzsche's first published book, which was inspired by Wagner in more ways than one.

There is one other vice of Wagner's that is worth briefly touching on at this point, and that is hypocrisy. The issue of the relationship between Nietzsche and Cosima, specifically whether Nietzsche had romantic and sexual feelings for her, has been raised by many commentators. The main piece of evidence in favour is the fact that one of the first things Nietzsche wrote after losing his mind was a letter to Cosima declaring his love. There seems to be no evidence that Cosima reciprocated any such feelings. But the fact is that Wagner had stolen Cosima from von Bülow, a younger and less powerful man. Earlier in the book, we mentioned how a power differential between a younger and an older man appears in every single one of Wagner's mature operas. In *Tristan and Isolde,* this dynamic sits at the core of the plot since the love between the younger man and woman is destroyed because of an older man, King Marke.

Wagner wrote that opera just years before his relationship with Cosima had begun in clandestine fashion. Von Bülow had walked in on Wagner and Cosima while the two were in Wagner's bedroom, but such was his regard (or should we say religious-like devotion) for Wagner that he did not make a fuss or ask them to stop. Nine months later, Cosima gave birth to a daughter assumed to be Wagner's. The daughter was named Isolde. Just two months later, von Bülow would conduct the premier performance of *Tristan and Isolde* in Munich. He agreed to register Isolde as his own child to avoid controversy. As if all this wasn't bad enough, Wagner, Cosima and Von Bülow were kicked out of their residence in Munich due to Wagner's meddling in Bavarian politics through his influence on King Ludwig. He would eventually end up at Tribschen, where he invited Von Bülow and Cosima to stay. After an initial visit, von Bülow left with the children, and Cosima remained.

Not only did Wagner not practice what he preached, but his own actions were even more outrageously over-the-top than even the characters in his operas. We almost get the idea that Wagner was using his operas as a form of apology for his bad behaviour in life. While the affair with Cosima was still in its early stages, Wagner was putting the finishing touches on *Meistersinger.* As we have already discussed, the plot of that opera involves the older man, Hans Sachs, refusing to seduce the younger woman, Eva, so that the man of her own age, Walther, can have a chance. *Tristan and Isolde* is a tragedy brought about by the older man coming between the younger pair. *Die Meistersinger* explicitly avoids the same fate, and Wagner even throws in a reference to *Tristan* to drive home that exact point. Nevertheless, when it actually mattered in real life, Wagner behaved exactly like King Marke and not at all like Hans Sachs. He was a hypocrite of the first order.

It is the presence of such obvious vices in the character of Wagner which leads to the question of how it came to be that he nevertheless had the capacity to inspire genuine devotion on the part of the small but impressive group of people who had become his foremost supporters. Perhaps one of the reasons can be found in the fact that most of Wagner's operas were tragedies. In tragedy, the hero strives for what he cannot achieve, and one of the results of this is that the tragic art form concentrates more on the striving and the underlying emotions that come with it. In the hands of Wagner, the tragic form takes on this esoteric, Dionysian mode that shares much with Shakespeare. Wagner's operas became an exploration of these deeper emotions, and, as we have already noted, this was something that he had explicitly incorporated into the form, insisting that "feeling" should be at the centre of his art. All of this has the effect of foregrounding the desires of the characters above and beyond what would normally make sense in a story.

As the audience, we empathise more with the desires of the characters than with their fulfilment. We do not blame the hero of a tragedy for his failings; we admire his courage and determination. Wagner provides an extra dimension by encouraging us to feel what the tragic hero is feeling as opposed to understanding him intellectually. And that is the way that Wagner lived his own life. His non-fiction writings give us a useful window into that because they are infuriating from a logical and rational point of view. Wagner uses vague terminology without providing any firm definitions and then strings his terms together in whatever fashion he chooses, barely ever pretending to create any kind of argument. He then simply asserts his conclusions, making up in passion what he lacks in reason. All of this earned him a frosty reception at the hands of the academics whose support he desired and then resented when it was not forthcoming. Academia at that time was very uptight, with strict rules in the presentation of arguments meant precisely to prevent the kinds of intellectual leaps and bounds that Wagner preferred. How boring and unfeeling these stuffy old scholars were. Wagner had no such problem in his writings, which, whatever else we may want to say about them, were written with great emotion and which, to be fair to Wagner, did contain a number of interesting and thought-provoking ideas.

Nietzsche had spent the previous ten years receiving a first-class initiation into the field of scholarship. We know that he had thrived in that environment, receiving recognition for his talents from his peers and his superiors, including the foremost exponents of the philology of his day. None of this could have happened if Nietzsche had not shown the utmost ability to construct rigorous argumentation backed by observable facts. The facts in this case were almost all to be found in books, both the original texts which formed the backbone of philological study and the extensive secondary literature which interpreted those texts by cross-examining against other data sources such as findings from archaeology and anthropology. The bread and butter of this kind of scholarship was the kind of low-level detailed analysis that only those who have attempted to obtain a doctorate degree need bother themselves about. In modern language, we have invented words like *'nerd' and 'geek'* to describe the type of person who has the discipline bordering on obsession required to spend long hours on such minutiae. At least in terms of his academic career, Nietzsche was one of the *nerds* of his time.

The trouble with all this, as anybody who's taken a peek behind the curtain of academia knows, is that the scholar finds themselves down various rabbit holes for much of their career, and it can happen very easily that one gets stuck down there and forgets to find one's way back up again. This severs the connection between the low-level truths and the bigger questions of the discipline itself and how those bigger questions relate back to the even bigger questions facing humanity. For most of Nietzsche's schooling, it would have been left to the Christian religion to address those bigger questions of life. However, the day-to-day activities of his education were of a very different manner. They were about drilling the students in the discipline and techniques required to burrow down into rabbit holes. To the extent that those rabbit holes were focused mostly on the Greek and Roman traditions, the connection back to the Christian theology was always problematic, if not actively contradictory. A bright young man like Nietzsche must have seen that.

When Nietzsche renounced Christianity in 1864, he told his sister that he was now becoming a devotee of "truth". That made sense given that he was embarking on a career in a discipline that was concerned with truth. But the truths in question were these low-level issues of classical scholarship, and what was lacking was a connection back to the bigger issues of life. Nietzsche had always been devout as a child. Another way to say the same thing is that he had always been concerned with the bigger questions, and that was something that philology simply didn't deal in as a matter of the day-to-day tasks required of the discipline. Thus, there was a gap in Nietzsche's life which he partly filled by the discovery of Schopenhauer in 1865. Finally, he had stumbled across somebody dealing with the bigger questions in a way that resonated with him. But, still, there was no obvious connection between Schopenhauer and philology, and therefore the insights of the philosopher were not of relevance to Nietzsche's daily work.

We can now see why Wagner emerged as such a powerful force for Nietzsche, even before they ever met in person. He filled the gap between the bigger questions and the low-level ones. This may seem strange because Wagner was neither a philosopher nor a scholar. But those are just official titles. Wagner had never received the title of philosopher or scholar; the sneering of the "real scholars" and their laceration of him in the press reminded him of that. They called him a pretender, a dilettante. The exact same attitude can be found in our time, and it comes from those inside official institutions, who always have a vested interest in defending the walls of the ivory tower from barbarous intrusions. What Nietzsche found in Wagner's essays were reasons why philology was worth studying in the first place. Why study medieval myth? Because it was the true representation of a German culture that was struggling to find expression. Why study the Greeks? Because the Greeks were an example of a vibrant, energetic culture, the kind that Germany should strive for. Why study tragedy? Because tragedy was the highest expression of the feeling modality of human existence, a modality that Enlightenment reason had all but snuffed out.

There were more specific examples. The use of music in Greek tragedy was indicative of the Schopenhauerian will because the philosopher had asserted that music represented will in its purest form. The point is that Wagner offered to Nietzsche what had been conspicuously absent from his education. In the bluntest terms, it was meaning and purpose. The young man, who had just months before been contemplating giving up philology altogether and pursuing the study of chemistry, was now reinvigorated not just for the study of philology but with all the larger questions of German culture and heroic art. It is another one of Wagner's quirks that, although he was in most respects the ideal manifestation of the artistic genius, and he had the ego to match, he was firmly convinced that something else was speaking through him. That something was the German culture of the German folk. That is why, to reiterate our point made earlier, Wagner belongs to the archetype of the prophet.

But Wagner also belongs to the other major archetype from Western history that we have mentioned. Why was Socrates hauled before the courts of Athens? *Corrupting the youth.* Most of Wagner's operas were, in a metaphorical sense, about an older man corrupting the younger. That was what was about to happen with the young Nietzsche. The promising young scholar had been cooped up in his academic cage for ten years. Wagner offered him a way out. More specifically, it was through Wagner that Nietzsche could reconnect with the bigger questions of life. In that way, Wagner really was a philosophic mentor to the younger man. He was not just able to capture the deepest inner desires of his characters and place them on the stage for an adoring audience; he had the ability to do that to the people he met in his own life. That was his charm and his magnetism, and that is why people forgave him all his vices. The initiation that Nietzsche received in his many blissful evenings at Tribschen was the expression of his own inner desires. He no longer had to converse with Schopenhauer in his mind; he had flesh-and-blood interlocutors in Wagner and Cosima. It was in this way that Wagner set Nietzsche on the path to fulfilling his "destiny" of becoming a philosopher. But, first, the young scholar needed to be "corrupted".

THE INITIATION OF NIETZSCHE

* * *

We have made our preliminary analysis of what the initiation meant for Nietzsche as an individual, but we also know that the Orphan's induction into the institution led by the Elder entails them beginning to contribute to that institution. The institution in this case is the Wagnerians, the group of people dedicated to Wagner's art, which included Cosima, Cosima's father, Franz Liszt, King Ludwig of Bavaria, and a number of other people who were regular visitors to Tribschen and correspondents with the Wagners via post. Since this was not a formal institution, there were no clearly defined roles or expectations. Rather, these were people who Wagner could call on when he needed something. In less pecunious times, this might have involved a request for a loan, although Ludwig had been a reliable financial backer of the enterprise for some years, and this has reduced Wagner's need to go cap in hand to his supporters.

The primary criterion for admission to the inner circle was an admiration for Wagner and his art. That is what had captured the composer's attention when he first heard about Nietzsche. But what specifically interested Wagner was Nietzsche's understanding of not just his music but the ideas behind it as expressed in his various essays. We see a prime example of this from the diary entry that Cosima made about Nietzsche's first visit to Tribschen, the one where he showed up unannounced and was invited back for lunch. Cosima notes that Nietzsche was a professor of philology who "knows R's works thoroughly and even quotes from *Opera and Drama* in his lectures." Here is an interesting question. Was Nietzsche really quoting Wagner in the lectures he gave at the University of Basel? It would seem unlikely that Wagner's work could be of relevance to technical philological subjects. On the other hand, it is true that professors in 19th-century Germany had complete freedom to lecture about whatever they liked, so there was certainly no institutional impediment if Nietzsche had desired to throw in the occasional Wagner reference.

Could it have been that Nietzsche was telling the composer what he wanted to hear? If so, it worked. As we have already mentioned, Wagner had been shunned and pilloried by the academics of the day, and it's fair to say that he had a rather large chip on his shoulder about it. Here was a brilliant young man, who had attained some minor fame as the youngest professor of classics and who not only understood Wagner's ideas but was communicating them to the next generation of up-and-coming scholars at the university. Everything about this would have been music to Wagner's ears. More importantly, in terms of our Orphan Story template, it showed that Nietzsche was already contributing to the Wagnerian cause, and he had been doing so without Wagner's express instruction. If we marvelled earlier at how quickly Nietzsche seemed to be accepted into the group, here we have one of the surest reasons why.

What followed in the just under three years during which Nietzsche was a regular visitor at Tribschen was, in most respects, a match made in heaven. Nietzsche was genuinely inspired by Wagner's ideas and had been since before they met. Meanwhile, Wagner and Cosima were already the kind of people who sat around the fireplace in the evenings discussing intellectual topics. Now they had a brilliant young man who not only could grasp Wagner's concepts in full but expand on them in interesting and unforeseen ways. Because all of this was happening in person, a rapid exchange of ideas could take place where Nietzsche would suggest something and Wagner and Cosima would provide their own perspective. One of the ways that happened was that Nietzsche began to read his university lectures to them in the evenings. At Basel, Nietzsche would read, and his students would listen. At Tribschen, he could count on instant feedback, especially from Wagner, who was not exactly known for keeping his mouth shut. One of the things discussed was his inaugural address to the faculty at Basel, about which he received praise from Ritschl but, more importantly, from his new Elder. As he put it in a letter to Rohde:-

"...my friend Wagner...read it to Frau von Bülow. He agrees, which strengthens me greatly, with all the aesthetic views presented and congratulates me on having correctly posed the problem, which is, after all, the beginning and perhaps the end of all wisdom and which is

mostly not even considered."

It's fair to say that Cosima and Wagner were supremely happy with this new arrangement. Cosima, as always, was primarily interested in what it meant for the advancement of Wagner's art. In her diaries, she refers to Nietzsche as "a gifted man imbued with R's ideas in his own way". Later, when Nietzsche would transition from presenting lectures to bringing entire essays to Tribschen for review and discussion, Cosima remarked, "My greatest pleasure is in seeing how R's ideas can be extended in this field." For his part, Wagner was also delighted to see his earlier writings be taken up by somebody who was clearly passionate about them. Cosima writes that he once said to her about Nietzsche, "He is the only living person, apart from Constantin Franz, who has provided me with something, a positive enrichment of my outlook." When we consider how many accomplished and intelligent people Wagner must have met over the course of his life, this is high praise indeed.

If Cosima and Wagner were very happy with the situation, Nietzsche was nothing short of ecstatic. Since we are blessed to have records of most of his correspondence during this time, we can let him speak of his experiences in the words he wrote to his most trusted friends and family. Here are just a few of the more relevant examples.

In mid-June 1969 to his mother:-

> *"This is Richard Wagner, who, as a human being, is as great and unique as he is as an artist. I have spent several happy days with him and the brilliant Frau von Bülow (Liszt's daughter), for example, the last one again, Saturday and Sunday. Wagner's villa, situated on Lake Lucerne, at the foot of Mount Pilatus, in enchanting lake and mountain solitude, is, as you can imagine, superbly furnished. We live there together in the most lively conversation, in the most amiable family circle, and completely removed from the usual social triviality. This is a great discovery for me."*

To Rohde, in June 1869:-

"I recently stayed with him [Wagner] again for two days and felt amazingly refreshed. He makes everything we could wish for come true: the world is completely unaware of the human greatness and singularity of his nature. I learn a great deal from his company: this is my practical course in Schopenhauer's philosophy. — Wagner's company is my consolation."

To Gersdorff, 4th August 1869:-

"Such unconditional idealism reigns in him [Wagner], such deep and touching humanity, such sublime seriousness of life, that **I feel in his presence as if I were in the presence of the divine**. How many days have I now spent on the charming country estate on Lake Lucerne, and this wonderful nature is ever new and inexhaustible." (emphasis mine)

To Deussen, 25th August 1869:-

"Recently, I've enjoyed a delightful rapprochement of the warmest and most affectionate kind with Richard Wagner—that is to say, **the greatest genius and greatest man of our time, absolutely incommensurable!** Every two or three weeks, I spend a few days on his estate on Lake Lucerne and **consider this rapprochement the greatest achievement of my life, next to what I owe to Schopenhauer**." (emphasis mine)

To Rohde, 3rd September 1869:-

"By the way, I also have my Italy, like you; only I can only escape there on Saturdays and Sundays. It's called Tribschen, and I already feel completely at home. I've been there four times recently, in quick succession, and almost every week a letter flies the same way. Dearest friend, **what I learn and see, hear, and understand there is indescribable**. Schopenhauer and Goethe, Aeschylus and Pindar are still alive, just believe it." (emphasis mine)

To Wagner, 21st May 1870:-

> "Please allow me to define the scope of my wishes today as narrowly and personally as possible. Others may dare to offer their congratulations in the name of sacred art, in the name of the most beautiful German hopes, in the name of your own most personal wishes; for me, the most subjective of all wishes suffices: **may you remain what you have been to me over the past year, my mystagog in the secret teachings of art and life**." *(emphasis mine)*

We could continue with such quotations, but the point should be well and truly clear. Nietzsche was genuinely enraptured, and we have no reason to believe that his constant use of religious terminology in the highlighted quotations was hyperbole. This should not surprise us in the slightest because we have already noted that the Orphan Story is about a journey into the sacred. At the time in which these letters were written, Nietzsche could have had little intellectual or rational understanding of what that meant, but it is clear that he felt very deeply that something special was happening.

But a journey into the sacred is not just about pleasant afternoons spent in idyllic locations. There must also be uncertainty, ambiguity, and risk. We get our first sign that these attributes were also present, even in the early days of the relationship, from a letter that Nietzsche sent to Rohde in early 1870:-

> "On the other hand, through him, the bond with my friends in Tribschen has become even closer. **I am becoming a walking hope: Richard Wagner, too, has revealed to me in the most touching way the destiny he sees preordained for me. This is all very frightening.** You know well what Ritschl said about me. But I will not let myself be challenged: I really have no literary ambition at all, and I have no need to adhere to any prevailing stereotype because I do not aspire to brilliant or famous positions. On the other hand, when the time is right, I will express myself as seriously and frankly as possible. Science, art, and philosophy are now growing so closely together within me that I will certainly give

birth to centaurs one day." (emphasis mine)

It seems certain that Wagner was already encouraging Nietzsche to publish a book of what must have been the ideas they were discussing in Tribschen. The tone of the letter suggests that Nietzsche was reticent about the idea. Indeed, it frightened him. He had good reason to be wary, and we will examine later the dramatic events that occurred when he did eventually publish the book in 1872. The key point for now is simply that Wagner was instrumental in the publication of that first book from an intellectual, emotional, and, as we will see later, practical point of view. This is exactly what we would expect from an Elder in relation to the Orphan. The Elder's role is to force the Orphan into doing things that they wouldn't otherwise be able to. If there is nothing on the line, no sacrifice to be made, then the relationship exists in the Apollonian world and not the Dionysian. To the extent that there does exist a Dionysian element, it is natural for the Orphan to feel fear. Knowing how powerful a personality Wagner had and his ability to charm as well as chide, it is clear that he had this effect on Nietzsche.

We have corroborating evidence for this in a couple of Cosima's diary entries. On 5th August 1871, she writes of Nietzsche:-

"The latter is certainly the most gifted of our young friends, but a not quite natural reserve makes his behaviour in many respects most displeasing. It is as if he were trying to resist the overwhelming effect of Wagner's personality."

Once again, we see here Cosima's one-eyed devotion to Wagner's cause. If Nietzsche was genuinely trying not to be overwhelmed by Wagner's personality, what could be wrong with that? Reading between the lines, it seems certain that what was really going on was that Wagner was bullying Nietzsche and Nietzsche was refusing to yield, hence Cosima's displeasure. In truth, Nietzsche had noticed this unpleasant tendency in the master right from the beginning. In a letter to Krug on August 4th, 1869, he writes:-

> "Once again I have spent the last few days with my esteemed friend Richard Wagner, who has kindly granted me the unrestricted right to frequent visits and who is angry with me for not making use of this right after taking a break of four weeks."

Even at this very early stage of the relationship, Wagner's prima donna ways were on full display. While Nietzsche was bewitched by the charms of Tribschen, he barely felt these small barbs, but they would later become a source of growing resentment.

A final, more light-hearted example of the influence which Wagner had over Nietzsche at this time can be seen from a lunch held at Tribschen in September 1869. Nietzsche declared to the table that he had become a vegetarian and stated his reasons for doing so. Wagner erupted that this was *nonsense* and *arrogance*. Ironically, Wagner himself had been vegetarian earlier in his life, but, as we have already seen, hypocrisy was not the composer's strong suit. In any case, Nietzsche claimed eating only vegetables was the morally right thing to do, to which Wagner responded that life was a compromise and that the way to expiate a wrong was by ensuring you more than balanced the scales by doing right elsewhere. Nietzsche held to his convictions for the rest of the lunch, much to Wagner's anger. However, in a long letter to Gersdorff only days later, Nietzsche said he was giving up vegetarianism and explained in detail his reasons for doing so. As he puts it, Wagner "demonstrated to me, not without the warmest sympathy of his heart and with the most forceful discourse, all the inherent perversities of that theory and practice." It is fair to imagine that Wagner changed the younger man's mind on a great many things during the three years spent together at Tribschen. That is what initiation is all about.

* * *

A new plateau in the initiation process was reached during the Christmas of 1869. It's indicative of Nietzsche's confirmed place in the family that he was invited to stay at Tribschen for the entire Christmas-New Year period. He brought along gifts not just for Cosima and Wagner but for their children also. Noteworthy, too, is that Cosima had by this time taken to giving Nietzsche errands to run, such as purchasing various items in Basel for the household. But the crowning gift of the festive season was that a room at Tribschen had been converted into a permanent bedroom for the young professor. As Nietzsche wrote to his mother on 20th December, "I myself am now leaving for Tribschen on Friday morning, the day my vacation begins; where, in Richard's words, I am awaited with 'jubilation'. A new room has also been set up for me, with a library, etc., the newly christened 'thinking room'". Tribschen now had its *Philosoph-in-Residenz.*

With the benefit of hindsight, we can see what all of this was leading towards, namely, the publication of Nietzsche's first book, *The Birth of Tragedy*. But this way of thinking is still far too Apollonian. We know how the story ended, and so all we see is inevitability. We have to remember that Wagner was a famous man whose work and life were constant subjects of public debate, with regular articles in the press stirring the pot. He was also a genuine hero in the eyes of Nietzsche and many others, and now Nietzsche was all but living in his home. It's worth recounting one more time the series of events that led up to this.

The process had begun with Nietzsche's sudden epiphany sometime in the middle of 1868 in relation to Wagner's non-fiction works. Let's remember, Nietzsche had no prospect of ever meeting Wagner at this time, let alone of having an intimate relationship with him. Put yourself in Nietzsche's shoes. You discover something special in Wagner's writing, something that triggers a flurry of your own ideas while also promising great things for the future of German culture. While these new ideas are formulating in your mind, you get offered a secret meeting with the man himself. In the nervous excitement, you go out and buy a new suit, even though you really don't have the money for it. The meeting with the maestro goes well, and you hold your own. But even Nietzsche knew that the invitation to visit given at the end was little more than a pleasantry. Thus, he could still have had no expectation of an ongoing relationship at this time, not least because Wagner lived seven hundred kilometres away in a town that Nietzsche had no other reason to visit. All he had was the slightest chance.

At the time, Nietzsche had no way to capitalise on this chance. That's when the second set of impossible coincidences arrive on the scene. A Swiss university had heard about his work and was prepared to bend the rules to make him the youngest professor of classics in the history of the university system. Again, this is highly improbable. Academia at this time was ultra-conservative, and there was really very little that the faculty in Basel had to gain from this move. In any case, the job was offered and would allow Nietzsche to reside in Basel. Suddenly, he had the money and the opportunity to visit Tribschen.

He still needed a pretext to take up Wagner's invitation, and he created that by taking a weekend trip to Lucerne and *accidentally* getting himself separated from his tour group. The result was a lunch with Wagner and Cosima alone, without the additional social pressures and constraints that had come from the first meeting. Imagine the delight that Nietzsche must have felt to be able to impress the master directly by showing that he knew all his ideas inside out and was even incorporating them into his curriculum at Basel. Imagine the additional delight when he received a letter from Cosima days later inviting him for Wagner's birthday. Within the space of one year, Nietzsche had gone from the excited discovery of Wagner's ideas in written form to being invited to the famous composer's birthday party. Six months after that, he had his own personal room at Tribschen.

A final fascinating parallel here is the fact that the dynamic at play matches almost exactly to the beginning of what was at that time probably the most famous work of German literature, Goethe's *Faust*. Wagner had even mentioned Goethe in his letter to Nietzsche referencing the concept of *German freedom*. The story of *Faust* begins with a man who is a disillusioned intellectual who seeks something more from life. That's exactly the position that Nietzsche was in when Wagner appeared on the scene. Just like Faust, Nietzsche's wishes had been fulfilled and he was swept up in a great adventure. Is it any wonder that he would have believed at this time that something biblical was occurring, as if some higher power were intervening to fulfil his deepest desires? But he also felt that the higher power was leading him towards something, something that was going to require a major sacrifice.

At this point, we need to raise a subject that has been the source of many different theories over the years from Nietzsche commentators, and that is the issue of his persistent ill health. The two main theories to explain this have been some kind of neurological problem that he inherited from his father and the notion that Nietzsche's symptoms were consistent with syphilis, which he may have contracted from a visit to a brothel during his two stints in the army. A third option that is less talked about but which seems equally plausible is that Nietzsche suffered from mercury poisoning derived from the fact that many medications at that time contained the chemical due to its antibacterial properties. Mercury is now known to cause neurological disorders, including so-called Mad Hatter's Disease, a name derived from the condition that afflicted medieval hat makers who doused hats in mercury to make them last longer. But the pathogenic effect of the chemical was still unknown in the 19th century, hence its continued use in medicines. Nietzsche was regularly ill and just as regularly medicated. It seems at least possible that his illnesses were the result of mercury poisoning.

The question of the cause of Nietzsche's illnesses will never be answered definitively. However, there is one more possible explanation that we need to cover, one that accords with Nietzsche's writings, although it goes against modern materialist science and medicine. In his very last books, when his attitude to Wagner had turned sour, Nietzsche referred to the maestro as a "sickness". He labelled the relationship with Wagner an illness that he had needed to overcome. In his very last book before going mad, *Nietzsche contra Wagner*, Nietzsche notes more generally that illness is the "answer" whenever we doubt our mission in life. Putting the two ideas together, we could conclude that the break with Wagner and the illnesses that Nietzsche suffered were caused by him doubting his "mission". We will provide a great deal of evidence for this interpretation later on when we get to the subject of the famous split between the two men. For now, we simply point out that there is strong evidence that the cause of Nietzsche's illness was *psychosomatic* in nature. We might even go a step further and create a category of *existential-somatic* illness, i.e., illness caused by spiritual or religious imbalances.

Nietzsche was incredibly sensitive to such psychological and spiritual matters. We must also remember that he had been trained as a scholar. He was a bookworm who spent most of his time in the inner, esoteric realm of human existence. That is a big part of the reason why Tribschen worked so well for him, because it was just himself, Cosima, and Wagner. There were no extra social dynamics to get in the way and derail the conversations. It was a pure exchange of ideas, hopes, and dreams. But it seems that the potency of these exchanges was itself a risk to Nietzsche's psychic equilibrium. That is what Cosima had intuited when she criticised Nietzsche's "reserve" as if he was trying to protect himself from Wagner's personality. One of the ways Nietzsche protected himself was through illness since illness gave him an excuse not to visit Tribschen during the times when he needed his own space. These absences enraged Wagner, who demanded that his followers do *as* he wished *when* he wished. Nietzsche was extremely sensitive to this and lamented several times in his letters over this period that he was always "upsetting the master".

Given the ecstatic tone of most of Nietzsche's correspondence during this time, we can surmise that what he was actually doing was protecting himself from a kind of overloaded psychic energy that he was receiving from Wagner specifically and the situation more generally. Cosima was correct, but her devotion to Wagner led her to see his as a failing in Nietzsche rather than a failing in her husband. Anything that angered or otherwise stood in the way of the Wagnerian program was a problem that she needed to solve. Thus, we can also be certain that Nietzsche also received a more subtle and esoteric form of "correction" from Cosima, which his sensitive nature would have understood perfectly well, especially since he had grown up in a household full of women.

All of this is highly psychological and esoteric in nature, but we must remember that these were people whose lives were lived in the realm of ideas and for whom these matters were of the utmost seriousness. It's for this same reason that all the major turning points in the story are very largely invisible unless we understand the inner lives of the main characters. If we didn't have access to the diaries, letters, and notebooks of Nietzsche, Wagner, and Cosima, our knowledge of what was going on would be hopelessly shallow and incorrect. In fact, as we will see in the pages ahead, some of the most important upheavals in the relationship were not about things that were done but things that were *not* done and words that were *not* said. The fact that all this took place in a family household is perfectly fitting since an understanding of what was going on requires a level of intimacy normally only visible in family settings.

There is evidence to suggest that Wagner was cognisant of the influence he had on Nietzsche and Nietzsche's broader psychic struggle. This will also become an important aspect of the story as we proceed because it's easy to write Wagner off as a megalomaniac for whom every person in his life and every issue revolved around his own personal conception of the world and his own goals. Those criticisms are valid for the most part, and yet, Wagner was not completely ignorant of those he cared for, and he did genuinely care for Nietzsche. In Cosima's diary entry on 17th February 1870, she notes that Wagner had said that Schopenhauer's philosophy might turn out to be a bad influence on young men such as Nietzsche because "they apply his pessimism, which is a form of thinking, contemplation, to life itself and derive from it an active form of hopelessness." This would be a theme that would recur in Wagner's attitude towards Nietzsche over the next several years. He thought that the young man was too wrapped up in thinking and contemplation at the expense of "life". And, yet, Wagner had himself given Nietzsche a "thinking room" at Tribschen and was clearly cultivating the young man as a vehicle for the expression of his own ideas.

Thought about in another way, the dynamic at Tribschen was, in some sense, a microcosm of the macrocosm of Germany more broadly. Wagner had all but renounced political activity in the aftermath of Dresden and had focused all his energy into art, philosophy, and culture. Meanwhile, the political issues facing the region were slowly being resolved in favour of the militaristic nationalism that would blow up in everybody's faces in the 20th century. Wagner, Nietzsche, and Cosima all lamented this state of affairs as the bourgeois philistines took over the institutions of society, and the state increasingly operated not with a view to creating a grand *German culture* but with the expediency and utilitarianism of monied interests. This was what was mostly behind Wagner's famous anti-Semitism. In reality, he was railing against the capitalist class for whom the Jews had long been the scapegoats. As charming as the scene in Tribschen was, it was also far away from what was becoming the dominant force in German society, and that meant that *German culture* was not moving in the direction that Wagner, Cosima, and Nietzsche desired.

By necessity, the day-to-day work at Tribschen was deeply personal and introverted in nature. Wagner was the heroic Artist sitting at the piano, being a conduit for whatever forces were working through him. The Ring Cycle needed to be finished, and nobody else could do it but the master. Most of the Wagnerians who were helping the cause were doing so from an intellectual point of view by publishing pamphlets and articles in newspapers. Wagner's other main activity was conducting, but this was also something that he and he alone could do. In short, there was very little in the way of tangible, overt, constructive jobs to be done, something that would have lifted Nietzsche out of his esoteric inner life and into the outer world. This schism was part of the larger one that had grown up in German life more broadly between the *doers*, who gravitated to the world of business and state, and the *dreamers*, who gravitated to the arts and universities, often, it must be said, as an escape from the world of action. Since Wagner's art was supremely intoxicating, he attracted more than his share of fans from this group of people who were looking for a quasi-religious experience.

It must also be said that Nietzsche's character was already supremely introverted in nature. We get a crucial insight into his attitude in a letter to Rohde from 22nd February 1869 where he writes:-

> *"You wish me to participate in your literary interests, but I, for one, have not the slightest desire of clucking in public like a hen. And what's more, my fellow Wagnerians are mostly too stupid and write disgustingly. This means that, fundamentally, they are not at all related to that genius*

and have no eye for depth, but only for the surface."

Two things stand out here. Firstly, Nietzsche has no desire to argue his case in public. Secondly, he already considered himself the foremost disciple, the only one who had truly grasped Wagner's genius. Wagner would actively encourage this attitude in the years ahead. In a letter sent to Nietzsche in 1872, he wrote, "You are the only real gain that life has brought me, and second only to my wife in that respect..." We can only guess the effect this kind of thing had on a young man who already considered himself the only one who understood Wagner properly.

All of this relates back to the primary contradiction that existed right from the start of the relationship. Nietzsche had created for himself an esoteric, Dionysian identity that was separate from his exoteric, Apollonian one. Throughout these blissful years spent in Tribschen, Nietzsche's esoteric identity grew and developed at an incredible pace while his exoteric identity remained unchanged. Partly, this was caused by the fact that there was a complete absence of any formal or exoteric manifestation of the Wagnerian cause, any proper institution for which organisation and leadership were required. In the absence of this, there existed what was essentially a kind of religious cult atmosphere, and Nietzsche was the foremost true believer in that cult. The irony is that there were forming at this time various Wagner societies, and these were becoming an important component in the emerging push for what would eventually become the *Festspielhaus* in Bayreuth. Nietzsche could have become a member of one of these. He could have run one himself. But that would have drawn him into contact with exactly the kinds of people he had already derided as too stupid to understand the great genius of the master. Thus, Nietzsche's expression of his hopes and dreams for German culture took place mostly through the letters he exchanged with his two friends Rohde and Gersdorff, both of whom were almost equally infatuated with Wagner. The tone of these letters is rather morbid and sickly, mostly framed in terms of wild ecstasy but also swinging to the other extreme at times.

As we have noted, Wagner was not blind to the fact that there was an unhealthy aspect to what was going on in Nietzsche. Wagner had spent his early adult years living a life of action and adventure with plenty of wine, women, and song. He looked on Nietzsche, Rodhe, and Gersdorff and saw a group of over-intellectualised and under-sexed youth who were living far too much inside themselves. In his letters to Nietzsche from after the Tribschen period, Wagner often took on the tone of the concerned uncle, even stating directly in a letter that he thought the young men "lacked women".

Still, it's clear that Wagner was excited to finally have a small group of intelligent young men from the next generation who could carry on his ideas. Whatever characteristics Wagner lacked, self-belief was not one of them. He genuinely saw his art and the *Gesamtkunstwerk* concept as the future of German culture, and he had real plans to create an institution that would safeguard it. He would eventually achieve those goals with the building of the *Festspielhaus*, but that part of the plan had not been realised in 1869 when the relationship with Nietzsche began in earnest. Thus, what Wagner seems to have hoped for in Nietzsche was a "son" who could safeguard his legacy and transmit it to posterity in the realm of ideas. That was also what he would have seen in Rohde and Gersdorff. As much as he might have wished that the young men would get their act together in the other aspects of their lives, he had been gifted a group of bright, young, enthusiastic scholars who were able to give him the admiration he had always longed for while also doing justice to his ideas. Wagner had named his *Gesamtkunstwerk* the *art of the future*. Nietzsche, Rohde, and Gersdorff were his *men of the future*, the torchbearers to whom he would hand the *new German culture*. All of this was itself highly esoteric and intellectual, but that's how it had to be at the time.

* * *

We are now ready to understand how this whole dynamic led to Nietzsche's first published book, *The Birth of Tragedy*. By Christmas of 1870, the work was taking shape. Nietzsche had gifted the first draft to Cosima, which, at that time, was titled *The Birth of the Tragic Concept*. On Boxing Day evening, they sat together in the Tribschen drawing room while Wagner read passages from the text. Cosima commented in her diary, "...the depth and excellence of his survey, conveyed with a very concentrated brevity, is quite remarkable; we follow his thoughts with the greatest and liveliest interest." The full text would be published just over a year later, at which time Wagner wrote to Nietzsche, "Never have I read anything more beautiful than your book."

The support of Wagner and Cosima follows straightforwardly from the description of their relationship that we have just undertaken. But in order to understand the monumental episode in the broader arc of Nietzsche's life that the publication of *The Birth of Tragedy* was to engender, we now need to zoom back out again and recall that Nietzsche had been living two lives during this time. Under the guidance of Wagner, he had been developing an esoteric, Dionysian identity formulated entirely within the confines of the Tribschen household. It has been very easy to forget that, while all this was going on, Nietzsche had been living out his exoteric, Apollonian identity as a professor of philology at Basel University. The workload there was not insignificant, and it had prevented Nietzsche on a number of occasions from being in the place he would have preferred to be, i.e., Tribschen.

Life at the university was dull and uneventful in comparison to what Nietzsche was experiencing with Wagner. But he was doing his job well, and there appear to have been no complaints about his performance. In fact, he received several pay raises during this time. Meanwhile, he also kept up a warm and respectful correspondence with the man who had landed him the job in the first place, Ritschl. Although the subject of Wagner was always the primary topic, Nietzsche often shared his professional activities with Rohde, who was also a philologist.

We have kept the distinction between Nietzsche's two identities clear from the beginning of our analysis, and we have been justified in doing so because that's how they really were. Nietzsche was more than happy to share his innermost feelings with friends like Rohde and Gersdorff, and he even occasionally mentioned Wagner in his letters to Ritschl, but none of his colleagues or the wider philological community could have had any inclination of what had been brewing at Tribschen. These are crucial facts because what was about to happen was that Nietzsche's exoteric, Apollonian identity and his esoteric, Dionysian one were about to collide in the most spectacular fashion. The blame for this lies squarely with Nietzsche himself because it was clear that he had lost track of the difference between these two identities.

Of course, this had been the case right from the beginning, even before he met Wagner. He had called the composer the "true saint of philology" after reading Wagner's essays, especially *Opera and Drama*. If Nietzsche had shared this opinion with his fellow students or especially with Ritschl, he would have either been laughed out of the room or considered to have gone mad. Ironically, the latter of these two options is not far from the truth. We have already shown ample evidence that Nietzsche was experiencing what Jung would later call *psychic inflation*. He was projecting deep, inner desires through Wagner, who had become a semi-divine being in his eyes. All of this had become entangled in the new and exciting ideas that Wagner had opened up for the young man. Nietzsche seemed unable to keep these ideas separate in his mind, thus his belief that Wagner could be the *saint of philology*. Philology was a rigorous, serious discipline. The flights of fancy on which Wagner led Nietzsche were every bit as thrilling as those on which Mephistopheles had led Faust. But, whatever they were, they were not rigorous scholarship, and therefore they were not acceptable to Nietzsche's Apollonian identity as a professor of philology.

It does seem that Nietzsche was trying to balance the two identities he had created for himself. But it's clear he was struggling and not fully conscious of the matter. In itself, this struggle was in the Dionysian realm and it played out in the various forms of psychic inflation we have seen. We start to see in his letters strange premonitions of danger ahead. We have already mentioned a couple of examples. Another is a letter to Gersdorff on 12th December 1870, where he writes:-

> *"But what enemies are now growing up for our faith on the bloody ground of this war! I am prepared for the worst in this regard, at the same time confident that, amidst the excess of suffering and terror, here and there the night flower of knowledge will bloom. Our battle is still*

> *to come—therefore we must live! Therefore, I also have good faith that you are immune; The bullets that are meant to kill us are not fired from rifles and cannons!"*

This all sounds rather over the top, yet a war was not far away, and its weapons would be those which Nietzsche had spent his whole life learning how to use: words, ideas, and books.

The sequence of events that would trigger the battle was as follows. Nietzsche had been building up a set of ideas based on his discussions with Wagner and Cosima at Tribschen. Those ideas had coagulated into the form of the manuscript Nietzsche gifted to Cosima for Christmas in 1870, and the admiration they won from the Wagners led Nietzsche to redouble his efforts towards producing a book-length version. During an extended leave of absence from university, where he journeyed to Italy, nominally due to ill health, Nietzsche dedicated himself to the task of finishing the book. His sister, Elizabeth, had joined him for moral support. According to Elizabeth's record of events, Nietzsche believed he had all but finished the work, and he excitedly stopped by Tribschen on the return trip to show it to Wagner. The response from the composer should not surprise us, although the directness with which Elizabeth relates the matter is perhaps less subtle than the manner in which the news was delivered to Nietzsche. Wagner was disappointed that the book contained very few references to his own work. In Elizabeth's words, Wagner hoped the work would "glorify his own art".

From our point of view, this makes total sense. Wagner is the Elder in the relationship, and we have shown ample evidence that both he and Cosima were primarily interested in Nietzsche's work to the extent that it furthered his own. It seems that Nietzsche's draft of the book had, indeed, been more scholarly in nature. Thus, Nietzsche's attempt to balance his two identities had already failed at this point, and Wagner was tilting the scale back towards his own interests. Nietzsche now had a dual allegiance to the Wagnerian cause but also to his scholarly identity. In any case, he spent the next months rewriting the text and inserting Wagner into the last part by reflecting on the similarities between opera and Greek tragedy, thereby creating the link to his own work that the composer desired.

While Nietzsche was still making the necessary edits to placate Wagner, he wrote to a publisher named Engelmann on 20th April 1871. Engelmann had previously shown interest in Nietzsche's scholarly work, and the professor was writing to offer him the rights to *The Birth of Tragedy*. The letter is highly revealing because Nietzsche presents the book concept as follows: "As you will see, I am trying to explain Greek tragedy in a completely new way, by disregarding for the time being any philological treatment of the question and keeping only the aesthetic problem in mind". Nietzsche was explicitly stating that the work was not philological in nature, even though he would be quite specific later in the letter that it was a scholarly work. All of this must have confused Engelmann, who knew Nietzsche as a professor of philology. Why would a professor of philology be writing a book on "aesthetics"? If Engelmann was not already confused, however, Nietzsche muddied the water even further with this line: "The real task, however, is then, Richard Wagner, to illuminate the strange riddle of our time in his relationship to Greek tragedy."

All of this makes sense to us because we understand the personal circumstances surrounding the matter and Nietzsche's desire to somehow combine two versions of his own identity, which the outside world had no knowledge of. Ironically, the "strange riddle" in this case really was Richard Wagner since Engelmann could have no clue what the composer's connection was to a scholarly work about the origins of Greek tragedy. We don't have any record of what Engelmann thought about this weird proposal, but we do know that he passed on Nietzsche's offer to publish the book.

This might have been Nietzsche's wake-up call that what he was trying to do did not make sense to the world outside of the Tribschen drawing room. We can imagine what the master would have thought about the idea of giving up on the concept. Fortunately, the master was in a position to exert his influence to ensure that the manuscript would see the light of day. Wagner had recently signed his own work over to a new publisher who specialised in the field of music. Recall that Nietzsche's original exposure to Wagner was via sheet music purchased by his friend Krug. That had taken place ten years prior, and Wagner's fame and popularity had only grown since then. The new publisher, Fritzsch, had agreed to re-release all of Wagner's sheet music and his non-fiction writing as well. Presumably, this was very good business for the man, and so when Wagner reached out to him and recommended the work of one of Germany's foremost young philologists, Fritzsch eagerly got on board with the proposal. *The Birth of Tragedy* was going to be published after all, not through a scholarly institution but a music publisher.

With the publishing deal signed, the race was on to get the book released in time for Christmas. In the end, this was not achieved partly due to miscommunication and partly because Nietzsche's professional duties got in the way of getting the proofreading done in time. It seems somewhat fitting that the discipline of philology appeared to be tugging at Nietzsche's sleeve and telling him one more time to be careful about what he was doing. By the middle of 1872, the metaphorical sleeve tugging would turn into a real tug of war as the philological battle spilled out into the open. But, before then, Nietzsche was to go through a private, psychological battle that was arguably even more distressing. Deep down, he must have understood what was about to happen, and the manner in which his anxiety found an outlet is deeply revealing.

Once the proofreading was done, Nietzsche asked Fritzsch to send a complimentary copy of the book to a small group that consisted of Rohde, Gersdorff, Elizabeth Nietzsche, Wagner's sister Ottilie, and Nietzsche's old professor Ritschl. From the first three names on the list, Nietzsche could count on a positive reception. But it was the last name that he was most concerned with. We know that Ritschl was Nietzsche's Apollonian Elder. He represented the official, exoteric, professional life path that Nietzsche had studied for and then consecrated when he took the professorship in Basel. It was Ritschl who went above and beyond to get Nietzsche that job. It was Ritschl who had allowed Nietzsche to submit scholarly articles to professional journals and to have them accepted even though Nietzsche was still just a common student. In the words of Nietzsche from 1868, prior to the whole Wagner business, it was Ritschl who had "guided his genius".

It is not surprising, then, that Nietzsche would want to hear Ritschl's opinion of his first book. After all, he had sent some of his lectures to the old master for feedback. But what occurred as the month of January 1872 wore on and Nietzsche had received no word from Ritschl was an almost existential angst in the young man. It is clear that, deep down in the darker parts of his psyche, Nietzsche knew that *The Birth of Tragedy* was not a scholarly book in any sense that Ritschl had educated him to understand the meaning of that word. It was not the product of his ten-year philological education in the highest institutions of that profession; it was the product of two years in the Tribschen drawing room listening to what surely were the inspiring and uplifting sermons of Richard Wagner. But we shouldn't place the blame solely on Wagner here. It is clear that Nietzsche was projecting onto Wagner his own deeper desires, the ones that he dared not let see the light of day. Well, now they had seen the light of day. Now they were in published book form. Not only that, the book bore a title that sounded for all the world like the debut performance of Germany's most promising young philologist. Anybody who saw the cover must have assumed the interior contained a scholarly work.

Nietzsche was hanging by the post box waiting to hear what Ritschl thought about it in the same way that a guilty murderer waits to hear the verdict in a courtroom. We get a glimpse into the effect the stress was having from his letters in early January 1872. First, there is a letter to Wagner which contains the following lines:-

> *"Meanwhile, I feel with pride that I am now marked and that I will always be mentioned in connection with you. God bless my philologists if they don't want to learn anything now."*

Note that this letter makes direct reference to Nietzsche's two identities. It almost reads as a confession. On the one hand, he states that he will be forever "marked" in connection with Wagner. On the other hand, he already anticipates that the philologists will not want *to learn anything new*. Not only is this a reference to his dual identities, but it is also our first taste of the psychic inflation that was about to manifest in the most extraordinary manner. Until now, Nietzsche had projected that psychic inflation onto Wagner. Now that he had his own name on a book, the projection would become personal.

Wagner had travelled to Berlin in early January. By the 24th of that month, Nietzsche appeared to be getting more and more anxious, as is evidenced by a letter he sent to the master. It was a very short letter. This is the entire text of it:-

> *"It seems now is the moment when the bow is finally being drawn—after hanging there for so long with slack strings. But that it should be you who does this! That everything ultimately comes back to you! I consider my current existence a reproach and sincerely ask you if you can use me. Apart from this request, I have nothing to report at the moment—but much, very much to wish for and to hope for, my esteemed master!"*

The penitential tone here is quite extraordinary. Nietzsche considers his existence a "reproach" and asks if Wagner can *use him*. It is almost a cry for help. What had caused this sudden collapse of confidence? We find out in a separate letter four days later sent to Gersdorff. "Bitterness is said to reign again in Leipzig. No one writes me a word from there. Not even Ritschl." Ritschl was the only one in Leipzig who had received the book and so this sentence gives the whole game away. The problem was that Nietzsche hadn't heard from Ritschl. It had now been one month, more than enough time for a distinguished scholar to digest a book of little more than one hundred pages. In Nietzsche's mind, the silence could only mean one thing: Ritschl did not approve. How did he try to escape this terrifying prospect? By writing to Wagner to ask for forgiveness and to be put to work! He was writing to his new Elder in penitence for an anticipated rebuke from his old one. Again, this is evidence that, during times of high stress, Nietzsche was unable to keep things separated in his mind. All this comes back to the contradiction between his Apollonian and Dionysian identities that we have noted was there right from the start.

But there is something else in the letter to Rohde that is important precisely because of the psychic stress that Nietzsche was under and the effect it had on the tone of his correspondence, which had become shrill and borderline hysterical. He writes:-

> "I announce to you, quite discreetly and demanding secrecy, that, among other things, I am preparing a memorandum on the University of Strasbourg, as an interpellation to the Reichsrat, for Bismarck's attention: in it, I intend to show how shamefully an enormous opportunity has been missed to establish a truly German educational institution for the regeneration of the German spirit and the destruction of what has hitherto been called "culture." Fight to the knife! Or to the cannon!"

Those familiar with Nietzsche's mature writings, especially the last few works written in 1888 before he went mad, will recognise this tone and style of writing. Once again, it is a prime example of psychic inflation. To suppose that Bismarck would care to read his letter in the first place or that the statesman would have any idea what was meant by the *destruction of German culture* reveals a conflation with Wagner. Wagner was the one who had always asserted that German culture was in dire straits. This is the exact same dynamic as that which played out in Nietzsche's letter to Engelmann. Nietzsche was struggling to maintain control of his own psyche. He had lost track of what was "real" in the sense of the shared knowledge of external reality that other people would understand and what was internal to his own world, and specifically the Wagner relationship. In modern terminology, Nietzsche really appears to have been on the verge of a mental breakdown at this time, and it all revolved around the fact that he must have known deep down that his book was not something that Ritschl could ever assent to.

Finally, he couldn't take it anymore. On 30th January, Nietzsche wrote a letter to Ritschl. It is worth reading in its entirety:-

> "You will not resent my astonishment that I have not heard a

single word from you about my recently published book, nor, I hope, the candour with which I express this astonishment. For this book is something of a manifesto and least of all calls for silence. Perhaps you will be surprised when I tell you what impression I assumed it would make on you, my esteemed teacher: I thought that if anything hopeful had ever happened to you in your life, it would be this book, hopeful for our ancient studies, hopeful for the German character, even if a number of individuals should perish because of it. For I will at least not fail to put my views into practice, and you will guess something of this when I tell you that I am giving public lectures here "on the future of our educational institutions." I feel—as you will believe—quite free of personal intentions and precautions, and because I seek nothing for myself, I hope to contribute something to others. My main concern is to gain a foothold among the younger generation of philologists, and I would consider it a shameful sign if I were to fail. Now, your silence worries me somewhat. Not that I doubted for a moment your sympathy for me; I am convinced of that once and for all—but I could certainly explain a personal concern for myself precisely from this sympathy. I am writing to you to dispel this.

I have received the register of the Rhenish Museum. Have you perhaps sent my sister a copy?

I answered a question as to whether I would accept an eventual call to Greifswald with a negative answer without a moment's hesitation.

Please remain in my best interests, my esteemed Privy Councillor, together with your wife, and best regards from"

In one respect, the tone and content of the letter is a continuation of those Nietzsche had sent to Rohde, Gersdorff, and Wagner during January. It contains the same psychic inflation, the same overblown expectations of future glory, and the same penitential tone at the prospect of failure. But what is extraordinary about this is that he sent it to Ritschl. We must remind ourselves that Ritschl lived in the über-Apollonian world of 19th-century German academia. He was Nietzsche's professional teacher, and Nietzsche had always addressed him by his formal title. The content of all of Nietzsche's prior letters to Ritschl adhered strictly to the formal requirements dictated by the social conventions of their relationship. The letters were warm but always professional. For the entirety of the time that Nietzsche had spent at Tribschen, during which he was writing the most ecstatic things to Wagner, Cosima, and Rohde, he had always kept his professionalism when writing to Ritschl and to other members of his profession. He had always known how to maintain the Apollonian façade as a proper philologist.

Thus, the letter to Ritschl shatters the boundaries between the two identities that Nietzsche had managed to keep mostly separate. Incredibly, he refers to *The Birth of Tragedy* now as a "manifesto", some kind of revolutionary guide for the next generation of philologists. But the truly extraordinary sentence, one that must have really made Ritschl think there was something desperately wrong with his best student, is this one: "*I thought that if anything hopeful had ever happened to you in your life, it would be this book, hopeful for our ancient studies, hopeful for the German character, even if a number of individuals should perish because of it.*" With this, Nietzsche breaks all bounds of propriety. He presumes that his little book would be the greatest thing to ever happen to Ritschl, as if the older man should bow down and kiss the feet of the prophet of philology who has come to save the *German character*. It even contains the ludicrous idea that somehow people's lives are on the line over the matter.

It's hard to understate how inappropriate this was. We must remember that we are here referring to Victorian-era Germany, a society that had become excessively formal and rigid, in short, Apollonian. The true irony here is that Nietzsche really had captured something important about 19th-century Germany in his distinction between the Dionysian and Apollonian, and he was in the process of manifesting exactly that by projecting the Dionysian depths of his own psyche into what should have been a perfectly Apollonian letter to Ritschl. What really distinguished *The Birth of Tragedy* was that it achieved a kind of shattering of the Apollonian façade of German scholarship, and so, in some sense, it is fitting that Nietzsche was living through that exact experience with his own Apollonian Elder.

But what hope on earth could Ritschl have had of understanding any of this? Just over two years earlier, he had sent the young scholar to Basel with high hopes. All the letters and reports he had received in the meantime must have led him to believe everything was going fine and Nietzsche was settling into his new role. The news of Nietzsche's first book must therefore have been incredibly welcome for the old man, and the title, presentation, and style of the work must have led him to believe it was a piece of philological scholarship. Ritschl must have been dumbfounded when he read the work, and it seems certain that he would have remained respectfully silent about it. This is another thing about the 19th century culture in which these two men lived. Silence had meaning. Sometimes, silence had more meaning than anything one could have said. Nietzsche knew it, and that's why the first sentence of his letter all but reproaches the old professor for saying nothing. He was forcing Ritschl to pass judgement on him. But we know from his behaviour that Nietzsche already knew the verdict. He was guilty. It would be another six months before the philological jury would reach the same conclusion.

The Confrontation with the Shadow Elder

It may be apocryphal, but it has been said that Freud decided to stop reading Nietzsche because he realised that so many of the concepts he was developing in his *depth psychology* had already been prefigured by the philosopher. Nietzsche described psychology as the queen of the sciences in his 1886 book *Beyond Good and Evil,* and there can be no doubt that his mature works do not just deal with psychology as a subject, but they are, in some sense, extended exercises in applied psychology in that Nietzsche manipulates the psychology of the reader. We can now start to see how Nietzsche's psychological journey during his relationship with Wagner would form the inspiration for his mature writings. The ironic nature of his latter works is a wink at the experiences he had gone through as a younger man, and his specific ability to rile up his young male readers derives from the same source.

Given this background, it would seem fitting to apply a psychological lens to the relationship between Nietzsche and Wagner to try and explain its evolution in those terms. Many commentators have done just that. The character of Nietzsche lends itself to this perspective precisely because Nietzsche internalised so much of the drama of his own life, and, as Cosima had rightfully noted, he seemed to do that instinctively as a kind of defence mechanism. It is impossible to understand Nietzsche without reference to his inner world, and any analysis of the man that only took an external, objective point of view would be comically wrong. The same is not true of Wagner. In fact, the two men present us with almost directly opposite characters, one the supreme introvert and the other an extrovert of the first order. Wagner did not bottle up his emotions, feelings, or thoughts. He laid them out on the table in all their beauty or ugliness. This won him both fanatical support and equally intense hatred depending on whether the man's ideas, art, and lifestyle resonated or repulsed. Of course, Nietzsche would learn this trick from the master. His philosophy lays out many ideas that, even to this day, revolt many readers instantly and instinctively. The point Nietzsche makes by incorporating this technique into his writing is that a great deal that passes itself off as "reason" or "logic" is nothing more than inherent prejudice and is therefore subjective in nature. Which is to say that, when it comes to ideas, most people are more concerned with how those ideas make them look and feel than whether they are "true".

While the psychological perspective is crucial for an understanding of what was going on with Nietzsche throughout his life, especially in relation to Wagner, we get a more complete understanding when we think about the issue in terms of *identity*, which also includes the exoteric aspects of life. That is what we have already discussed by noting that Nietzsche had an officially recognised exoteric identity as a professor of philology at the University of Basel. That is how the average person at the time would have thought about Nietzsche as an individual. It is also how people even relatively close to him, such as his mother and sister, must have thought of him. For most of us, our exoteric and esoteric identities are tightly in sync since we simply don't have the time, inclination, or opportunity to have a secretive lifestyle separate from our public one. In addition, we would need to find others who can also share that secret identity. For Nietzsche, it was primarily his friends Rohde and Gersdorff who facilitated that part of the initiation he was going through, and it is his letters to them as well as Wager and Cosima that form the backbone of our analysis in this book. While not quite as fanatical about it as Nietzsche, both Rohde and Gersdorff believed in Wagner as a kind of saviour of German culture. Nietzsche had convinced both men to write to Wagner and had taken them to visit at Tribschen.

We should also note here that Nietzsche was in regular correspondence with a number of other Wagnerians. These were all people who were drawn to Wagner for esoteric, personal reasons. They were not earning a pay cheque or receiving any official title or social status for their troubles. It follows that Nietzsche was not unique among the Wagnerians in pursuing the association as an esoteric identity. Accordingly, the rituals involved in being a Wagnerian were also esoteric in nature, including visits to Tribschen, letters to the master and fellow Wagnerians, attendance at performances of Wagner's operas, and fighting for the Wagner cause in the press. None of this is to say that the identity was not "real", only that it was heavily skewed towards the esoteric with no exoteric component to formalise the association. (There did exist the aforementioned Wagner Societies, which were growing in number, but which seemed almost like a separate institution from the inner circle of true believers).

It was this esoteric identity which Nietzsche had been forming for more than two years by the time that *The Birth of Tragedy* was published. Until that time, it had been almost entirely hidden. To the extent that the average person would have been aware of it at all, the association with Wagner must have seemed like a hobby. Being interested in fine art was the kind of thing you would expect from a professor. Thus, a casual observer could only have drawn the wrong inference about Nietzsche based on external observation. They would have assumed that his job was the most important thing in his life and the Wagner association was a bit of entertainment or relaxation on his off days. As we know, the exact opposite was true. Nietzsche barely cared for his job. He had only taken it in the first place in order to be close to Tribschen. Nobody could have known that since Victorian society was completely preoccupied with the formalities of life, such as correct behaviour and dress. Nietzsche's feelings towards his job were practically irrelevant as far as the general attitude of the era went. As long as he showed up to work on time and did what was expected of him, he was fulfilling his duty. A side hobby as an opera enthusiast could be nothing more than a pleasant diversion from the real business of life.

In this way, Nietzsche's life story and his philosophy really were a precursor to the psychology of Freud and Jung because the latter's client base was almost entirely made up of the educated elites of Victorian society for whom the stifling cultural rigidity led to what would later be called *mental illness*. Nietzsche's contrast between the Apollonian and Dionysian perfectly captured this imbalance between a rigid external identity and the unfulfilled desires that lurked beneath the surface. Although he expressed it in relation to his own personal circumstances, Nietzsche would declare war on this dynamic in the preface to his first book. Naturally, that preface was a dedication to Wagner. We have already quoted the relevant section, but it should now take on a deeper meaning:-

> *"But perhaps those same people will find it distasteful to see an aesthetic problem taken so seriously, if they can see art as nothing more than an entertaining irrelevance, an easily dispensable tinkle of bells next to the 'seriousness of life': as if no one was aware what this contrast with the 'seriousness of life?' amounted to. Let these serious people know that I am convinced that art is the supreme task and the truly metaphysical activity of this life in the sense of that man, my noble champion on that path, to whom I dedicate this book."*

This was a rousing call to action not just for Nietzsche as an individual but for all the Wagnerians. It is no coincidence that the book's primary audience was the inner circle and the hardcore fans of the composer. Those who had experienced the Dionysian through Wagner's operas understood the concept immediately, and that same group were almost universally part of the wider cultural movement in Germany that felt that something important was missing in the life of the nation.

Thus, *The Birth of Tragedy* received immediate recognition and support from Wagner and his followers, in other words, from those who shared Nietzsche's Dionysian identity. The same could not be said for those who shared his Apollonian identity, the philologists. They were expecting a disciplined, rigorous work of scholarship. What they found was something completely unexpected and unfathomable. That is why the book received a kind of stunned silence from Ritschl. The old professor still lived in Leipzig. What he knew about Nietzsche's time in Basel was only what the young man had told him in the polite letters they exchanged or what he heard from the academic grapevine. Ritschl could have had no clue what the Wagnerians were up to because he was not himself a Wagnerian. The same was true of anybody else who did not have access to the inner goings-on at Tribschen. Ironically, perhaps the main purpose of *The Birth of Tragedy* was to announce to the world what it meant to be a Wagnerian. Wagner had done that in his own way through his non-fiction writings, but those were, at least nominally, written about technical matters to do with composition and art. Nietzsche had just made the exact same mistake. Rather than just come out and say, *Look, this is what Wagnerism is*, he wrote a book that appeared to the casual reader as a work of philology. The Apollonian and Dionysian meanings of the book were just as out of sync as Nietzsche's own identity.

Thus, there was a multi-faceted miscomprehension that took place. Wagnerians took the work as a scholarly treatise that just happened to show the virtues of Wagner's art. Professional philologists like Ritschl saw that the book had nothing to do with scholarship and assumed it was really about Schopenhauer or aesthetics. Meanwhile, members of the general public could not understand either the Wagnerian or the scholarly references and assumed that the book was all part of the secret, esoteric world of academia which, as non-initiates, they were not supposed to understand.

All of this confusion stemmed from the fact that Nietzsche had been unable to keep clear in his own mind the boundaries between the various aspects of his identity. We have the seen that the conflation of philology and Wagner was there right from the beginning even before Nietzsche ever met the composer. No doubt, this was because Wagner's writings had opened up a genuinely new way of thinking for Nietzsche, a way of thinking that, at that time, he associated with philology. And, of course, some of it really was about philology. But there was a whole other dimension to it which we have given the label of *psychic inflation*. Wagner's bombastic, belligerent, and abrasive writing style sparked something in Nietzsche. Here was a man who thundered down truths like an ancient prophet. The fact that there was no logical or rational argumentation to justify those truths didn't really matter. On the contrary, it was to a tonic to Nietzsche who had already lamented at having to grind through a hundred and one books just to make an argument about some minor detail of Greek culture. So much work for so little outcome. Wagner didn't care a jot for any of that and, yet, there was a kind of truth in Wagner. It was a very different kind of truth, but it was a truth nevertheless.

There is no doubt that the attraction of Wagner was partly because he spoke to something deep inside Nietzsche. He became a hero and an archetype of the kind of man that Nietzsche wanted to be. This is practically the definition of the Orphan-Elder relationship and we have already shown that this relationship is always based on imitation. The trouble for Nietzsche was that he already had exactly that kind of relationship with Ritschl and he had already attained the identity of philologist. That was not a dream or a deep desire, it was an external, objective fact. Thus, Nietzsche's use of war metaphors in his letters to Rohde and Gersdorff was accurate in at least two respects. There was about to be a mini-war in the philological community over *The Birth of Tragedy*. But the war was also going to be an inherently personal one for Nietzsche since his new identity as a Wagnerian that was now publicly emerging for the first time was about to go into battle against his existing identity as a philologist. Nietzsche felt the approach of this battle deep within himself. Let's recall the letter of 15th February 1870 sent Rohde:-

"*On the other hand, through him, the bond with my friends in Tribschen*

> has become even closer. I am becoming a walking hope: Richard Wagner, too, has revealed to me in the most touching way the destiny he sees preordained for me. This is all very frightening. You know well what Ritschl said about me. But I will not let myself be challenged: I really have no literary ambition at all, and I have no need to adhere to any prevailing stereotype because I do not aspire to brilliant or famous positions. On the other hand, when the time is right, I will express myself as seriously and frankly as possible. Science, art, and philosophy are now growing so closely together within me that I will certainly give birth to centaurs one day."

Wagner had revealed a destiny to Nietzsche; one that was very frightening. Nietzsche even puts up some kind of defence against this Wagnerian *destiny*: "I will not let myself be challenged." What was this destiny? It was nothing other than to write a book. We know that this is true because of a letter that Wagner sent to Nietzsche only nine days before the one just mentioned. On 4th February 1870, he wrote to the young man about his manuscript on *Socrates and Tragedy*. Wagner gives it the highest of praise but notes that others are unlikely to understand it. "Even those people who are initiated into my ideas are bound to be shocked when they find out how much your ideas conflict with their own belief in Socrates and even Aeschylus." A couple of sentences later, Wagner advises Nietzsche to "collect your thoughts together for a longer and more comprehensive work on the subject." Thus, *The Birth of Tragedy* was born as an instruction from Wagner to Nietzsche, an instruction that Nietzsche found "frightening" because he knew that the ideas presented would not be accepted.

This might all seem rather silly. Why would Nietzsche be scared of ideas? But Wagner had warned him in the same letter of what he also knew was true. These ideas were dangerous because they were not appropriate to be expressed by a scholar. They were guaranteed to get him into professional trouble. So, why did Nietzsche do it? Why publish a book that he knew was only going to cause him so many problems?

The answer to that can be found in another question: why did Nietzsche become a disciple of Wagner? Of course, there is no single answer, and that is the whole point. Nietzsche was on a journey into the sacred. Part of that journey is that you don't consciously know what you are doing. All you know is that you are being driven on by some deeper desire that you don't fully understand. Nietzsche went ahead with the publication despite the risks that were entailed because he was following a more fundamental calling. That deeper calling involved him becoming a disciple of Wagner and that *The Birth of Tragedy* was the direct product of that relationship. None of this had come out of nowhere. The book was published two-and-a-half years after his first visit to Tribschen. It was, in every respect, the product of those years. Wagner had offered Nietzsche initiation, and Nietzsche had accepted. Right from the very first meeting, Wagner had given Nietzsche the task to advocate for Wagnerian music. Nietzsche had eagerly agreed. By becoming a Wagnerian, Nietzsche had implicitly, informally, we might even say, *unconsciously*, accepted the burden of furthering the cause of Wagnerian art and all of the associated meanings that came with that: *German freedom, German culture, the artwork of the future.* Wagner did not give explicit instructions because he was not an official leader. But Nietzsche had learned very early on that when Wagner made a "suggestion", it was really an instruction. If Wagner invited Nietzsche to attend Tribschen, that meant Nietzsche had to attend. If he did not, the master would become angry. When Wagner "suggested" that Nietzsche write a full-length book, the same principle applied. Nietzsche knew it, and that is why the tone of the letter sent to Rohde on 15th February 1870 reveals both excitement and also a deep anxiety. Nietzsche's Dionysian identity was forcing its way to the surface, and it was about to go into battle with his Apollonian one.

More generally, a clash of identities is all part of the Orphan Story template. However, it must be said that, in relation to the other Orphan Stories we have covered, it had taken an extraordinarily long time for this event to finally occur in Nietzsche's story. Jesus asks the disciples to immediately give up fishing and become fishers of men. In other words, he asks them to swap their official occupation for an informal one. There is no mention of it in the gospel text, but we can safely assume that this would have caused some friction for the disciples in their relationships with friends and family since Jesus was a dangerous man and an unknown quantity. Why give up a stable, secure occupation to follow such a man? The average person wouldn't understand. Similarly, when Plato became a student of Socrates, we can surmise that some of his friends and families would have objected since Socrates was a polarising figure. It is a normal part of the Orphan Story that the time comes for the disciple to face the inevitable backlash that comes from their decision to follow the master. This backlash occurs in relation to their exoteric identity.

The big difference in the case of Nietzsche is that he managed to hide the relationship with Wagner for more than two years. Unlike the disciples of Jesus or Plato, he had protected himself from any personal consequences that might have come from his support of a controversial figure. That is why so much of this story takes place in the psychological realm. The attempt to keep his two identities separate and balanced had gone on for a long time, but it was all now coming to a head with the publication of *The Birth of Tragedy*. The time had come for Nietzsche to face the music.

* * *

Let's pick up the story where we left it. Nietzsche had included Ritschl in the initial list of those who would receive a copy of *The Birth of Tragedy* directly from the publisher before it was made available to the general public. Ritschl would have received the book in the post either in late 1871 or the first days of 1872. As the month of January rolled on, it is evident from his personal correspondence that Nietzsche's anxiety was growing by the day. He sent a very strange letter to Wagner and then another to Rohde where he directly referred to Ritschl's failure to say anything. In the same letter, he wrote the words:-

> "For everything that is on my mind now and what I am preparing for the future cannot even be touched upon in letters. — I have formed an alliance with Wagner. You can't imagine how close we are now and

how our plans overlap."

The absence of Ritschl's judgement seems to have led Nietzsche to conclude that it was all over with his philology career and that he would throw in his lot with Wagner. What that exactly meant is highly unclear. There was certainly no formal alliance with Wagner because what would such an alliance have even meant in the circumstances? In the stress, we find Nietzsche reverting again to psychic inflation, projecting grand plans and hopes for the future.

The letter to Rohde containing the grand plans was written on the 28th of January. By the 30th, Nietzsche couldn't take it anymore. He wrote directly to Ritschl, asking him for his feedback on the book. This was the letter that also included grandiose pronouncements about how Nietzsche's book would be the "most hopeful" thing that ever happened in Ritschl's life. Nietzsche could not have known it, but Ritschl had indeed already passed judgement on *The Birth of Tragedy*. We are fortunate to have access to his notes where, in relation to the book, he had simply written the word "megalomania". If Ritschl had already formed that opinion based on a reading of the text, the letter he subsequently received from his former top student could only have confirmed it. Nevertheless, now that Nietzsche had asked him explicitly to comment, he could no longer remain silent.

The letter that Ritschl would send to Nietzsche two weeks later with his opinion on *The Birth of Tragedy* was a beautiful piece of understatement, although also candid in nature. Included in it were a couple of generous servings of self-deprecation. Ritschl claimed to be too old to go off and study the philosophy of Schopenhauer. Therefore, large sections of Nietzsche's book were off limits to his understanding. Related to this problem, he insisted that philological problems must be addressed by philological scholarship, not by reference to vague metaphysical theories. As to Nietzsche's claim in his letter that he hoped the book would become a guide for future philological students, Ritschl noted that any such students would do well to follow the process that Nietzsche himself had been initiated into by learning how to establish facts and draw conclusions from them. He concluded that the "poetic" form that Nietzsche had taken in *The Birth of Tragedy* could only lead genuine students astray, while the intermixing of poetry and scholarship also detracted from the artistic merits of the work. All in all, it was a restrained but clinical takedown by the older man, who must have been wondering what on earth had happened to his brightest pupil.

Nietzsche received Ritschl's response on the 14th of February, but we get more insight into his mindset at this time from a short letter he sent to Gersdorff on the 4th. The plan had been for Rohde to publish a proper review of *The Birth of Tragedy* in a scholarly journal. However, Rohde's piece had been rejected. How did Nietzsche respond to this news which, while it was a setback, was hardly the end of the world? The letter speaks for itself:-

> *"My book will have difficulty spreading: an excellent advertisement that Rohde had made for the literary Centralblatt was rejected by the editorial staff. That was the last chance for a serious voice in a scholarly journal to declare its support for my book: now I expect nothing—or malice or foolishness. But I am counting on a quiet, slow progress— through the centuries, as I tell you with the greatest conviction."*

Based on a single piece of bad news (and Ritschl's continued silence), Nietzsche concludes that the matter is hopeless and turns his attention to the centuries ahead in which the book will eventually find its audience! This is exactly what Wagner had done in the aftermath of Dresden. His *Artwork of the Future* was born out of the dejection he felt that his operatic innovations had gone unappreciated. All he could hope for was that things would turn around in the future. Of course, Wagner's situation at that time had been far more dire. He had been in genuine fear for his life. He had lost his official position, and he had even been kicked out of his country. He had genuine cause for despair. By contrast, Nietzsche's despair was largely a product of his own identity crisis. If no support came to him from the philological community, then that side of his identity came under threat. Nietzsche's career might have been harmed, but that was not a foregone conclusion, and the extent of the damage was unknowable at that time. The reason Nietzsche was on edge was because he knew that *The Birth of Tragedy* was simply not a proper work of philological scholarship, and yet he had passed it off as one.

The confirmation of that came with the receipt of Ritschl's letter on the 14th. As was always the case during this time of his life, we learn of Nietzsche's reaction through a letter that he immediately wrote to Rohde. The crucial point in this letter is that Nietzsche does have some good news to tell. The book had received a lot of positive reviews, but all of them were from Wagnerians! Meanwhile, there had been nothing from the philological community. As Nietzsche put it, "In short, a small community is forming for it—but I hear nothing from the worthy philologists—". Once again, the battle is between Nietzsche's two identities. The Wagnerians were supportive. The philologists were not.

It took Nietzsche three weeks to reply to Ritschl. The letter is strange because it mostly reverts back to the formal and polite tone that he had always taken with his former master. But he could not hide his hurt:-

> "I absolutely wanted to know how you would feel about my book. Now I know and am reassured: not completely, though. But I don't want to write about that. Later, what I want will become clearer and more illuminating to you, when my essay "On the Future of Our Educational Institutions" is published. In the meantime, I express my conviction that philologists have several decades to go before they can understand such an esoteric and, in the highest sense, scientific book. Incidentally, a second edition will be published very soon."

Once again, we see the megalomania that Ritschl had noted. Nietzsche asserts that it will take philologists several decades to come to grips with the work. This is his former teacher he is talking to, one of the foremost philologists of the day. The man has just explained the problems with the book, all of which were perfectly valid and correct, yet Nietzsche politely informs him that it's a work that only future generations will be able to understand, the implication being that Ritschl will not. Nietzsche may have been writing to his former Elder but he was now doing so in the language of his new Elder. This kind of tone and these kinds of bold pronouncements presented without evidence or reason were exactly the kind of thing that Wagner specialised in. Nietzsche was very much emulating his new master in that respect.

But it is the final letter of this dramatic period that is the most telling and reveals the true turmoil that Nietzsche was going through. Only days after the letter to Ritschl, he wrote to Rohde. We must remember that Rohde was himself a philology graduate at this time but had not yet achieved a professorship. With that context in mind, the beginning of Nietzsche's letter speaks for itself:-

> *"I am thinking about how you can assume all the honours and emoluments of my Basel professorship as my full successor around Michaelmas. I myself intend to spend the next winter travelling around Germany, that is, invited by the Wagner societies of the larger cities, to give lectures on the Nibelungen Festival—everyone must do what is their duty, and, in the event of a collision, what is their duty more. But once I have separated myself from the university for a winter in this way, I will certainly take advantage of the vacuum that has arisen to go south for two years. For the purpose of this venture, I am resigning my position here so that you will then become my successor in every respect."*

Nietzsche now proposed to resolve the conflict between his Dionysian and Apollonian identities by giving up the latter entirely. This may seem like an overreaction to the negative feedback he had received for *The Birth of Tragedy*, yet we must remember the meaning of that work to the young man. He had told Ritschl it was a *manifesto*. There is little in the actual text that would lend itself to this reading, but the preface most certainly takes this form, specifically the part about art being the highest metaphysical task in life. It was that call to arms which Nietzsche was now proposing to embrace whole-heartedly. It was a declaration of war against the Philistines, the businessmen, and the militarists. Nietzsche had been a Dionysian disciple for almost three years by this point. Now he was going to become an Apollonian one by taking his Wagnerian identity public. In truth, this would really have resolved the conflict between his two identities.

The publication of *The Birth of Tragedy* had forced Nietzsche to finally reveal his hidden, Dionysian identity that had been incubating in Tribschen. And just like Nietzsche described it in his book, this dangerous subterranean energy had the potential to rise up and destroy the Apollonian identity that the professor held in Basel. The rebuke that Ritschl had given the work confirmed Nietzsche's fears, but the impudent response Nietzsche had given was also important because it made clear he was not going to back down. He was prepared to take the fight even to his old teacher. If academia could not handle Nietzsche's new identity, then he would renounce it. "Everyone must do their duty", he writes. Nietzsche was pledging himself to the Wagnerian cause. He would travel around Germany advocating directly for it by lecturing on the Ring Cycle. Note that this was not merely bluster. Nietzsche mentions that his tour would be at the invitation of the various Wagner societies that really did exist around Germany by this time. In fact, many of them received copies of *The Birth of Tragedy* in due course. The societies were filled with the kinds of people who constituted the main demographic of Wagner supporters. Therefore, they were the kinds of crowds that would actually turn up to hear a distinguished professor lecture on the subject of their favourite composer. A couple of the societies were even dabbling in a kind of scholarly approach to Wagner. Therefore, Nietzsche wasn't just blowing hot air. He really could have done this.

Had Nietzsche followed through with this proposal, the parallels with the gospel story would have been directly relevant since we would have seen the young professor renounce his occupation in order to travel the land advocating on behalf of the master. Just as Jesus sent the disciples out to spread the word around the Levant, Nietzsche really would have become a travelling apostle spreading the good news of Wagnerism throughout Germany.

However, "fate" had other ideas, and it worked them through the arrival of yet another improbable coincidence. Just days before Nietzsche sent his letter to Rohde offering him the Basel professorship, Rohde had been offered the same role by the University of Kiel and had accepted. Therefore, he was no longer able to agree to Nietzsche's terms even if he wanted to. This was important for two reasons. Firstly, it meant Nietzsche's plan of handing his professorship to Rohde could not happen. More importantly, however, it changed the calculus of the whole idea. With Rohde as a fully recognised professor, Nietzsche would now have a powerful ally from within philology itself. Not only would he no longer be completely alone, his main supporter was essentially his best friend, who was also an avowed Wagnerian. This seems to have convinced Nietzsche to continue the academic fight a little longer. He informed Rohde that "I will endure the university for the next few semesters and reserve my blessed escape to the south for when my position becomes unbearable and disgusting." A stay of execution had been granted to Nietzsche's Apollonian identity.

However, this was a small silver lining in the increasingly darkening skies over Nietzsche's academic life. He was not being paranoid. The aberration of *The Birth of Tragedy* had been noted within philological circles, and the results were starting to come in. In a letter to Rohde, he writes:-

> "On the other hand, I have advertisements that say I already seem ridiculous to my actual colleagues, ridiculous and impossible, which is why, for example, the usual courtesy is no longer shown in letters. Now the Index of Rhenish Music has also been published—just imagine that neither Ritschl nor Klette has said a word of thanks to me for this free, silly work! My essay on Homer (although unpublished) already provoked the remark, 'One more step like that and he's ruined!'"

It seems apparent that Nietzsche still firmly believed at this time that his "new philology" was something worth fighting for within the academy, even though it had precisely two exponents. Still, most of the "attacks" on the work had so far come in the form of Ritschl-like silence and other gossip. These were difficult to combat. Fortunately, things were about to become a lot more overt, and it seems almost to have been a relief to Nietzsche when a real opponent stepped up and challenged him directly. The days of silence and innuendo were about to end and be replaced by a good old-fashioned academic scrap of the kind that both Nietzsche and Rohde knew how to fight.

* * *

The man who was about to take to the philological barricades was a certain Ulrich von Wilamowitz-Moellendorff (Wilamowitz for short), and a writer of fiction couldn't have scripted a more fitting opponent for Nietzsche. Wilamowitz was an old boy of none other than the Schulpforta. The two would have been students at the school simultaneously, although Wilamowitz was several years below Nietzsche. Just like Nietzsche, Wilamowitz then went on to study philology at the University of Bonn, which was now the domain of Ritschl's old nemesis Jahn. Since Nietzsche had slipped a barb against Jahn into *The Birth of Tragedy*, and since he was a student of Ritschl, it was natural that Wilamowitz would be an opponent.

We need not pay attention to the details of the attack that Wilamowitz lodged against Nietzsche's first book, which were tailored to a professional philological audience. The mode of attack he used does, however, give us an insight into the kind of atmosphere that prevailed in 19th-century academia in Germany. Volume was Wilamowitz's weapon. He picked up countless low-level arguments that Nietzsche had made and rubbished them, often with direct reference to the established literature or to the original texts themselves. This method not only aims to wound the target; it is also a demonstration of scholarly muscle that establishes the author as a man who knows the literature inside out. In addition, Wilamowitz also made extensive use of the original Greek orthography when referring to various concepts. This practice that was common in the philological scholarship of the day, but Nietzsche had conspicuously not used it in his book (probably because Wagner could not read Greek). The implication was that Nietzsche's scholarship was sloppy.

All of this was par for the course, and Nietzsche would have expected nothing less in a scholarly rebuttal. Where Wilamowitz's manuscript departed from scholarly convention was in its belligerent and even mocking tone. He repeatedly denigrates Nietzsche as somebody who hadn't even done the basic reading. He even managed to slip in a reference to Schulpforta:-

> "What a disgrace, Mr. N, to alma mater Pforta! It must appear as if you were never given Iliad or the corresponding passage in Lessing's Laokoon to read; and Schneidewin's introduction to Sophocles's Oedipus Rex is also part of the wisdom which a first-year student at Pforta picks up during his first semester."

The main body of Wilamowitz's argument reads like this with endless name-dropping. The sardonic tone was considered impolite by the standards of the day but not entirely out of bounds. Nevertheless, it does seem to have heightened Nietzsche's offence at the text.

From our point of view, however, by far the most interesting parts of Wilamowitz's paper are the introduction, conclusion, and title, because it was here that he stepped outside the scholarly frame and addressed the broader themes of the work. It turns out that the young philologist had, to a very large extent, grasped the true meaning of Nietzsche's book, perhaps even more than Nietzsche himself in some ways.

The title is the first piece of evidence for that. We know that Wagner had called his *Gesamtkunstwerk* the *artwork of the future*, and there was a common variation on this called *zukunftsmusik* (future music). Thus, Wilamowitz was signalling that he understood the Wagner connection in Nietzsche's book when he titled his critique "Zukunftsphilologie" (future philology). What is incredible about this, however, is that it is exactly how Nietzsche had been talking about the work in his letters to Rohde and Ritschl, i.e., the idea that it would take philologists several decades before they could understand what he had written.

What Wilamowitz was doing, of course, was imputing that the connection with Wagner was what had motivated such sloppy scholarship on the part of Nietzsche. He implied this in the title and then rammed home the point in the body of the work:-

> "Thanks to R. Wagner (Mr. N's "sublime predecessor," to whom

the book is dedicated), tragedy and the tragic myth are now reborn. Euripides killed them; Shakespeare, Goethe, Schiller seem...to have composed merely "dramatised epos"; other dramas of utterly natural origin, such as those of Kalidasa and Calderon are not even mentioned."

The key fact here is that these ideas that Wilamowitz references really were Wagner's, especially the reference to the failings of mere literature, which Wagner had expressed in the *Artwork of the Future*. It seems certain that Wilamowitz was familiar with Wagner's non-fiction writing or maybe went off and read it in order to write his criticism of Nietzsche. In any case, the point he is making is one that other professional philologists would have agreed with, which was that any ideas in the book which had come from Wagner were, by definition, non-scholarly in nature and therefore unworthy of consideration.

But by far the most interesting criticisms that Wilamowitz makes are his references to the quasi-religious tone of *The Birth of Tragedy*. He correctly asserts that the book is not scholarly in nature but prophetic:-

> "Mr. Nietzsche by no means presents himself as a scholarly researcher. Insights garnered by intuition are presented part pulpit-style, part journalistic logic — all-too-closely related to the "paper slave of the day" (20, 122/130). As an epopt of his god, Mr. N announces miracles already performed and those still to come — doubtless quite edifying for his faithful 'friends'."

Wilamowitz had hit the nail on the head. The work was not really a scholarly one but had been written for the Wagnerians (the "friends"). And the work had been motivated almost entirely by intuition rather than the usual scholarly practices of evidence and reason. In this respect, *The Birth of Tragedy* really was inspired by Wagner since that was the manner in which Wagner had always operated. Meanwhile, Wilamowitz even refers to Nietzsche as an "epopt", which means disciple! He had correctly guessed exactly what was really going on. The conclusion to his work contains an exact diagnosis of the two identities that Nietzsche had found himself wedged between. Wilamowitz notes that if Nietzsche had claimed his book was not a work of scholarship but a work of art, then he would readily withdraw all his arguments against the book since they would then be irrelevant.

> *"Then I would gladly let his gospel be since it is not addressed by my weapons."*

He continues:-

> *"But one thing I demand: that Mr. N be faithful to his word. Let him seize the thyrsos; let him move from India to Greece. But let him step down from the lectern from which he is supposed to teach knowledge."*

Incredibly, we know that this is exactly what Nietzsche had decided to do when he told Rohde he would quit the professorship at Basel! In every respect, Wilamowitz had hit the nail exactly on the head. If the younger man had written to Nietzsche privately and in a more polite tone a few months earlier, it's possible that Nietzsche would have agreed with many of these points. But the Basel professor had lifted himself up from the depths of his earlier despair by this time, and the uproar that ensued after the publication of Wilamowitz's paper seems to have had the effect of reinvigorating him by way of a scholarly brawl.

It would not be Nietzsche who would do the fighting. That would not be proper. Instead, Rohde was engaged to "publicly punish" the younger scholar. Indeed, Nietzsche now assumed the psychic inflation tone we saw earlier as a matter of course. The battle with Wilamowitz was written about in Biblical language, as in this line to Rohde, "...and if Wilamowitz bears a stigma for it until his death, let it always remind him of how shamefully he misled, seduced, incited, and poorly educated." In another place, he states that Wilamowitz will need to be "executed" (metaphorically, of course).

Once again, the details of Rohde's reply and then the follow-up arguments that were made need not concern us here. There is, however, an important fact to be listed in this respect. Recall that Nietzsche had not managed to get *The Birth of Tragedy* released by a scholarly publisher but had to rely on Wagner's publisher, Fritzsch. Wilamowitz's book, by contrast, was published by a reputable house, and Nietzsche hoped to have Rohde's reply also be released by a recognised publisher of scholarly works. To that end, he wrote to Ritschl to try and use the older man's connections to have Rohde's reply published by a respectable scholarly journal. The journal refused. Whether Ritschl was involved in that decision is unclear, although Nietzsche certainly seems to have blamed him for it. In the end, it was left up to Fritzsch to once again step into the breach and release the work. Thus, even the publishing houses involved in the dispute split along party lines, with the philologists on one side and the Wagnerians on the other.

In light of all this, it was fitting, although still somewhat embarrassing, when Wagner himself waded into the debate by way of an article he got published in a music journal of all places. His essay was called an *"Open letter to Friedrich Nietzsche, Professor of Classical Philology at the University of Basel"*. It was classic Wagner, all bombast and bluster and little to nothing in the way of reasonable argument. In fact, he decided to take the opportunity to berate the entire profession of philology, who he claimed were "of no use to anyone but themselves". All of which just proved Wilamowitz's point that the true inspiration behind Nietzsche's first book was not a man interested in scholarship but in prophetic intuition, of which he himself was the supreme point of reference.

With Wagner's entry to the fray, the battle lines were made clear and explicit. It was the Wagnerians vs. the philologists. The difference was that everybody else in the dispute was fighting on behalf of their own official, exoteric identity and therefore had no internal contradiction to deal with. It was only Nietzsche who had a foot in both camps. Thus, the battle was now very much a fight over Nietzsche's identity. Even Wilamowitz had realised that. More specifically, Nietzsche's Dionysian identity, led by his Dionysian Elder, was at war with his Apollonian.

* * *

The comedic tone of the Wilamowitz incident seems fitting in hindsight, given the rather absurd nature of the way the debate played out, especially since nobody, not even Wagner and Nietzsche, had really grasped what was going on. It seems that even Wilamowitz, though he hit the nail on the head in most respects, was driven more by a mischievous desire to defeat his opponent than any attempt at constructive criticism. The reality was, however, that Wilamowitz was right on several of the most important points of our story. He was right that Wagner was the real influence behind *The Birth of Tragedy*. He was right that Nietzsche had taken to copying Wagner's *modus operandi*, relying no longer on scholarly rigour but on intuitive insights. By implication, he was also right that Nietzsche needed to decide whether he wanted to be a scholar or a quasi-religious prophet.

We know that Nietzsche was on the cusp of making that exact decision in April when he wrote to Rohde offering to gift him his professorship. It is another one of the incredible coincidences in our story that Nietzsche wrote that letter on the 11th of April, and Rohde's professorship in Kiel began only nine days later. Had the stars not aligned in such a fashion, it's possible that Nietzsche would have followed through, and this would have had the effect of bringing his Dionysian identity into alignment with his Apollonian. What would have happened in the aftermath is anybody's guess, but Nietzsche would have taken a decisive step to becoming a full-time Wagnerian. That obviously did not happen. What happened instead was that the institutions and individuals who were responsible for recognising his Apollonian identity as a professor of philology turned on him. Bitterly, for Nietzsche, that was true even of Ritschl.

Nevertheless, Ritschl, Wilamowitz, and the others were perfectly justified in their actions because Nietzsche really had broken his unspoken oath to his profession by releasing a book that purported to be a work of philology when it was not. Despite all of the feedback he had got from the real world, including the initial rejection by Engelmann and the other scholarly publishers who refused to support either his or Rohde's work on this matter, Nietzsche was still unable to sort out even in his own mind the difference between his scholarly work and his new method of operation that was inspired by Wagner.

The battle with Wilamowitz had the effect of only hardening his resolve that he was in the right and the entire profession of philology was in the wrong and that it would take decades, if not centuries, for everybody else to catch up.

What all this represents, of course, is Steps 5 and 6 of our Orphan Story template, and at this point we need to be clear about what these steps entail. Remember that the socio-cultural background of the Orphan Story is a time of tension, if not crisis. The identity that each of us develops in life does not come out of nowhere. It is intimately tied in with the culture to which we belong. When the broader culture is having an identity crisis, that means individual members of that culture will also be going through the same thing. A big part of the dynamic that sits at the core of the Orphan Story is the playing out of this identity crisis as different groups in society battle it out in whatever way is appropriate to the context.

The one thing that was missing in our earlier accounts of the two world-historical Orphan Stories centred around Plato and the disciples of Jesus is the inner struggle that the Orphan heroes must have gone through. The New Testament focuses almost entirely on the external events that occurred, with only brief attention given to the inner, esoteric, or psychological world of the hero. Thus, the gospel focuses mostly on the actions and teachings of Jesus, although there are hints at the inner difficulties facing the disciples, such as Peter's denial of Jesus and, of course, Judas' betrayal.

As a result of this, a major part of these world-historical Orphan Stories that we did not cover in any detail earlier is the exact difficulties we have now seen in Nietzsche's life. But we have every reason to believe that these same kinds of difficulties must have affected Plato and the disciples in their own time. The Orphan hero is not leaving their home and travelling to a completely different community. They are joining a side in an internal battle within their own culture, and they are doing so while physically present in their own society. That means that they are becoming enemies with their fellow citizens, and that fact brings with it a great deal of psychological stress, which may manifest in any number of ways depending on the individual in question.

PART 2: THE ORPHAN STORY OF NIETZSCHE AND WAGNER

We must remember that the Elder in the Orphan Story is offering something new and therefore something unknown and untested. The established powers always have on their side the inertia of tradition and the fact that they are a known quantity with a proven track record. The track record may not be very good, and there may be enormous problems that the powers that be are not addressing, but human psychology on this score is very conservative. People prefer the devil they know. That is why the Elder in the Orphan Story always receives a hostile response from large sections of the community.

A big part of the Orphan's journey is that they must make the decision to join the Elder and put themselves in the firing line to face the same hostile response from their fellow citizens. That is what Nietzsche had done by publishing *The Birth of Tragedy*. Wagner had been at war against the academics for many years, and we should remember that a number of different professors had specifically targeted him in the media. There is no evidence that the philological community had any specific grudge against Wagner prior to the events of 1872, but that community still belonged to academia more broadly, and academia was part of the excessively Apollonian nature of German society as Wagner saw it. Therefore, they were enemies.

It's clear that Nietzsche knew deep down what he was bringing on himself by publishing his first book. The fact he wasn't fully conscious of it is all part of the nature of a story. We must remember: a story is a journey into the sacred. That means the hero is not fully conscious of what they are doing, but they feel a strong inner necessity to do it anyway. That is the situation that Nietzsche found himself in, and the reason to go into detail about his inner state during this time is precisely because it gives us a unique window into what it means to take a journey into the unknown. It's not rational. It's not logical. But it is a part of human life, one that doesn't get much attention because we cannot fit it easily into conceptual boxes.

Having said that, Nietzsche's story is still unusual in the fact that the battle he needed to fight cut right down the middle of his exoteric and esoteric identities. What had happened is that Nietzsche's former Elder, Ritschl, had now become the Shadow Elder and the philological community had become opponents. We don't need to hypothesise that this was the case because we have Nietzsche's letters to prove that he now explicitly thought about Ritschl as the enemy. What's more, that's exactly how it started to play out in real life. The very next time that Nietzsche met Ritschl and his wife, there was a verbal altercation. As Nietzsche put it, "Ritschl had a lot of unpleasant things to report about me, for example, that I was supposed to be a bad lecturer (he didn't put it that strongly, but he meant it). I asked him to put this in writing and will send you the document."

In addition to this, Nietzsche had to face a further embarrassment when the new semester started in the second half of 1872. By now, news of the Wilamowitz dispute had spread not just in philological circles but in the wider media. As an associate of Wagner, the press took an interest in Nietzsche and began running the same kinds of hit pieces on him that they normally ran on the composer. The result was that student numbers at Nietzsche's lectures dropped precipitously, which made a further dent in his reputation, not to mention raising question marks about his future in Basel and the profession more generally. To say it again, Nietzsche was not just being paranoid. He had very real reasons to be worried about what these setbacks entailed.

On a positive note, all of this was exactly the kind of fight that Wagner loved to take part in, and he was no doubt delighted by the extra media attention the incident garnered. Both he and Cosima lent their full support to Nietzsche, and it has to be said that Nietzsche also took heart in the opportunity to now publicly advocate for the Wagnerian cause. His Wagnerian identity was no longer hidden away in the drawing room at Tribschen but was out in the open for all to see. The other Wagnerians also showed their support through numerous letters praising *The Birth of Tragedy,* and we should note that the concepts of the Dionysian and Apollonian really did strike a chord with a great number of people.

In the fight against the enemy forces, which takes place in Step 6 of our template, Nietzsche had stepped onto the battlefield for the first time in the Wagnerian colours. The fact that he needed to sacrifice his relationship with Ritschl and his relatively easy life in the faculty at Basel is all part of the dynamic of any true Orphan Story. It's what the journey into the sacred is all about.

Thus, this episode marks the next major turning point in our story, and we can now fill in Steps 5 and 6 of our template accordingly:-

Orphan Story Template	Nietzsche and Wagner
1. The hero is separated from his parents (becomes an Orphan)	Nietzsche's father died when he was young. He left home when attending Schulpforta and then university
2. The hero hears news of the Elder or the institution to which the Elder is associated	Nietzsche had been introduced to Wagner by a friend when he was fourteen years old
3. The hero meets the Elder, who offers them initiation	Nietzsche met Wagner in secret at Wagner's sister's house. Wagner invites Nietzsche to visit in Tribschen
4. The hero accepts and initiation commences, including induction into the institution led by the Elder	The professorship at the University of Basel allows Nietzsche to become a regular visitor at Tribschen
5. A Shadow Elder tries to subvert the initiation	Ritschl rebukes *The Birth of Tragedy*
6. There is a struggle between the hero, the Elder and the Shadow Elder	The public furore over *The Birth of Tragedy* including Wilamowitz's rebuttal, Rohde and Wagner's answer to it and other ongoing media stories that occurred
7. The Elder dies or otherwise goes missing (usually sacrificing themselves for the hero)	
8. The hero faces the Shadow Elder alone	

* * *

While all of this was going on, there was another monumental change taking place that must have contributed to Nietzsche's manic state of mind and which was to have unforeseen ramifications that would change everything in the years ahead. It had been more than twenty years since Wagner boldly predicted that he would construct a custom-built opera house in which to perform a cycle of operas based on the medieval epic poem of the Nibelungenlied. At the time he made that prediction, Wagner was struggling even to put food on the table, let alone build opera houses. It was a mad, bold, outrageous thing to say, and, yet, he had slowly bent reality to his will. When we noted earlier that Nietzsche had begun making equally outrageous predictions at just this time, it's certain that he was following in the footsteps of the master. The inspiration to do so may have come from the fact that it was at just this time that Wagner's crazy plan was actually coming to fruition. The composer had already tried and failed a couple of times to find a location to build his new opera house. However, he had finally found a suitable place for it and negotiated with the local authorities to begin construction. That was the monumental event that was about to take place. The foundation stone for the new *Festspielhaus* would be laid in the town of Bayreuth in May. Behind this incredible achievement, however, lay a poison dagger. Wagner and Cosima were going to move to Bayreuth to oversee the construction. The Tribschen days were coming to an end.

Is it too hard to imagine that this fact was in his mind when Nietzsche had considered quitting his job in April? There is an irony to this that Nietzsche might have appreciated. Bayreuth is much closer to Leipzig than to Basel. Nietzsche had moved from Leipzig in order to be close to Wagner, and now Wagner was moving to be closer to Leipzig. Even the direction of travel was a reversal of that which originally brought them together. This geographic inversion would eventually lead to an inversion in the entire Orphan Story. But that was years in the future, and any lingering sadness that Nietzsche might have felt at the end of the Tribschen years, as well as any continued anxiety over the future of his philological career, appear to have been completely extinguished by a feeling of jubilation at the great event that was about to take place.

Preparations had been made for a ceremony to mark the laying of the foundation stone with local dignitaries in attendance and, more importantly, all of the inner circle of Wagnerians. In several letters leading up to the event, Nietzsche wrote to Rohde imploring him to attend, knowing how important this would be for Rohde's entry into the inner circle:-

> *"Fifty years later, we would consider it unforgivable, even crazy, not to have been there—so let's overcome the deliberate inconveniences—*

PART 2: THE ORPHAN STORY OF NIETZSCHE AND WAGNER

> *Basel and Kiel will likely have their centre in Bayreuth. I truly implore you by our holy of holies, art—come there! We must experience this together, just like next year's "Bühnenfestspiele." Write to me very soon, my dear, faithful friend, and think of me as someone calling out to you with an enormous trumpet: Bayreuth!"*

As always, what might seem like exaggerations or hyperbole in Nietzsche's writing reveal the actual truth of the matter. What "god" does Nietzsche invoke to convince his friend to come to Bayreuth, the god of art, our "holy of holies". This shouldn't surprise us in the least. Nietzsche had written in the preface to *The Birth of Tragedy* that he considered art the most supremely serious topic, the true metaphysical task of life. If art was God, then it must follow that Wagner was its prophet and Bayreuth was about to become Mecca, the holy land. Because of our modern secular bias, we don't take this religious language seriously, but we absolutely should. We must understand that Nietzsche believed it. Cosima believed it. So did the rest of the inner circle.

The religious terminology was also justified to the extent that this was a time of intense transition in multiple different ways. In Wagner's life, it was the end of the Tribschen era and the beginning of the Bayreuth one. It was to be the final decade of his life; his last stand. He would die almost exactly ten years later. Although there were many challenges ahead, this final decade would be Wagner's triumph, not just in the sense that he really did achieve the peak of his influence and popularity, not just because of the incredible event that was the premiere of the Ring Cycle, but because both of these things were the fulfilment of his prediction from decades earlier. To take another biblical analogy, he had led his people to the promised land. The *art of the future* had arrived. The prophecy was about to be fulfilled.

To reiterate, when Wagner made his original prophecy, he had precisely no prospect whatsoever of bringing it to realisation. In fact, Wagner's situation was so dire that he had considered giving up on music altogether. He had been exiled from Germany for what must have seemed like a lifetime. All of the contacts he had there had been irreparably severed. In theory, there were London or Paris as alternatives, but Wagner had only met with failure in those two cities, and, with the exception of *Rienzi*, all his operas had been failures at that time. He was in a genuine existential crisis. Poverty was rampant across Europe, and the only thing stopping Wagner from falling into it was the charity of a few friends and some petty wages he collected from doing odd musical transcription jobs. It was during this time of genuine despair that Wagner wrote his prophetic pamphlets. He had spent the next two decades clawing his way up from the bottom to realise the vision he had laid out. Even those who despised the man and hated his art would have had to acknowledge that this was an incredible feat of determination and discipline in the face of all odds.

For the Wagnerian inner circle, it was clear evidence that their cause was righteous and true, and therefore it galvanised support and heightened the intensity of emotion around the laying of the foundation stone in Bayreuth. What was true for the Wagnerians in general was extra true for Nietzsche. What had occurred over the last three years, and what had been consecrated with the publication of *The Birth of Tragedy*, was Nietzsche's position as the foremost disciple. Once again, the Bible provides us with the template here because we see that Jesus elevates Peter above the others and says that he will build his church upon him.

This is almost exactly what Wagner had done with Nietzsche. It is certainly another reason for Nietzsche's heightened emotional state at this time. But to focus purely on his inner battle is to trivialise the matter. Something was happening in the real world , and Nietzsche was a core part of it. It's fitting that this would all happen just months after the publication of his first book. Wagner's push to have him publish *The Birth of Tragedy* was certainly done with the intent of glorifying Wagner's art, but it also forced Nietzsche to commit to the cause because he was putting something on the line. Sacrifice is a core part of religion for this very reason, but, in our secular age, we are inclined to view sacrifices as trivialities, especially when they are about "unserious" matters like art. That is the utilitarian point of view that Nietzsche spent most of his life fighting against. Life becomes meaningful only when we make sacrifices. Wagner had sacrificed an enormous amount over the years, and now Nietzsche had done the same.

In this respect, we can usefully contrast Nietzsche's relationship with his two Elders. Ritschl had gone above and beyond to give Nietzsche every opportunity. We might think of that as a good thing, except we have already established that Nietzsche was dissatisfied with academia and philology even very early on in his university degree. It would never have occurred to Ritschl to ask the young man what he really wanted in his heart of hearts. That was not Ritschl's role. He was an Apollonian Elder, concerned only with outward appearances. By contrast, Wagner became the Dionysian Elder not just to Nietzsche but to numerous others because he had the ability to get beyond the rational, surface appearances of life and unlock something much deeper. He did that with his music, with his writings, and with his personality and lifestyle. That was the intoxicating environment that Nietzsche had experienced. It was the revelation of his true, deeper desires which the Victorian-era culture required to be locked away and never allowed to see the light of day. Wagner knew how to open the lock.

This is the dynamic that drove the relationship between Wagner and his followers. It's the same dynamic that history shows us with Jesus and with Socrates. These kinds of paradigm shifts in individuals and cultures cannot be understood rationally and logically during the time they are happening. That is why they cannot be Apollonian in nature but only Dionysian. With the concepts he had introduced in *The Birth of Tragedy*, Nietzsche had actually begun to give Apollonian form to what was going on. Of course, it was all absurdly mixed up with all kinds of issues that seem to have nothing to do with each other. Into the boiling cauldron was thrown the old European worship of the Greeks, modern scholarly philology, Schopenhauerian philosophy, Wagnerian art, all the political and cultural problems of 19th-century Germany, and whatever else was at hand. All of this served to shatter the Apollonian façade and allow the deeper Dionysian drives to come forth. The older generation, of which Ritschl was a prime exponent, simply couldn't understand, but Nietzsche's contemporary, Wilamowitz, could. Even in his objection, Wilamowitz had still grasped what was really going on. If Nietzsche hadn't been so blinded by his old scholarly adversarial spirit, he might have realised that Wilamowitz had actually given some useful advice that might have been worth considering. But perhaps it was better this way. Wilamowitz's advice would have defused the tension and made things orderly, sensible, and Apollonian.

In any case, we can now see that what had happened with *The Birth of Tragedy* was that Nietzsche had become a disciple no longer in the esoteric, psychological sense but in a public, exoteric fashion. The book was both a declaration of his personal commitment to the cause and genuinely provided something which the other Wagnerians could rally around, not necessarily because they understood it rationally, but because they felt it in their stomachs. The other virtue of the book was that it gave form to a movement which was defined by its informality. Until that time, it had been left to Wagner to write the holy books. Nietzsche was the first among the Wagnerians to add to the ideas and ideals of the group in a meaningful and lasting way. The fact that it came just months before the laying of the foundation stone in Bayreuth only served to heighten the feeling that everything was coming together. Wagnerism was finally manifesting itself in the Apollonian world. Meanwhile, the number of Wagner societies continued to grow. It must have been a genuinely thrilling time for all involved.

The foundation stone of the *Festspielhaus* was laid on Wagner's birthday, 22nd May 1872. It was three years exactly since Cosima had invited Nietzsche to the birthday party at Tribschen, an occasion he desperately wanted to attend but could not due to work commitments. In those three years, the two men went from complete strangers to the prophet-disciple relationship that was to be symbolically consecrated at Bayreuth. Nietzsche's position as head disciple was sanctified by the fact that he rode in the lead carriage with Wagner and Cosima on the short journey to the site of the future opera house.

With this, we arrive at a new appreciation for the point we made right back at the start of the book. We said that Nietzsche had identified a bias of judging people, relationships, and events based on their end state, which predisposes us to look for evidence of that end state in everything that happened beforehand. Another way of thinking about the same dynamic is that the end state is very largely the formal, exoteric, Apollonian state.

It is the final product manifested in the "real world". What comes before it is not just incomplete but also intangible, esoteric, and Dionysian. The relationship between Wagner and Nietzsche provides a uniquely detailed case study to understand this because we have access to the inner thoughts of those involved and because there was such a long incubation period which took place almost entirely in the private household at Tribschen and therefore could never have been visible to the outside world. The casual observer could never have known what was going on. Even the individuals involved did not fully understand it. The implications of this would go on to play a central role in Nietzsche's philosophy. For anything that is in the process of becoming, we cannot understand it rationally or logically; we can only understand it esoterically or empathetically. But that is exactly what Wagner had set out to achieve with his art. He wanted to move away from the contrived Apollonian conventions and capture the inner feelings of his characters. He wanted to show the parts of Life and Nature that he believed had been ignored not just by artists but by society in general. This was one of the main lessons he would teach Nietzsche. But the education was not an academic one, it occurred in real life, and the laying of the foundation stone in Bayreuth was one of the most important parts of the lesson because it proved that great things could be achieved over long periods of time if the will was strong enough.

Thus, the events of early 1872 were proof that Wagnerism was finally moving out of its Dionysian phase and into the Apollonian world. Wagnerism now had its own Mecca. It also had a more formal organisational structure since the construction of the *Festspielhaus* and the nascent preparations for the premiere of the Ring Cycle required real things to be done in the real world. Most importantly for our story, Wagnerism had now consecrated its foremost disciple. Nietzsche had already achieved that role with the publication of *The Birth of Tragedy*, but he was now presented to both the other Wagnerians and the townspeople of Bayreuth by way of the ceremonial occasion that took place on 22nd May. Nietzsche's Apollonian identity as a Wagnerian was also beginning to take form. Nobody could have known at this time exactly what form it would take, but that was all part of the thrill.

Amidst the rightful jubilation that came with the personal and collective triumph of this time, it probably never occurred to Wagner or Nietzsche how the move to Bayreuth was going to affect the underlying dynamic of their relationship. Nietzsche had seriously considered quitting his job in Basel, and Wagner had given him a room in Bayreuth with an invitation to stay any time. In fact, Nietzsche could simply have lived with the Wagners in Bayreuth permanently if he so wished. Why did he not do so? Several reasons come to mind.

The first is that much of the value he brought to the Wagnerian cause came from his position as a professor and his reputation as a brilliant scholar. To give that up would be to lose the authority and influence that came with the role. Once again, we should remind ourselves that this was 19th-century Germany, a society which venerated the role of professor. Even if Nietzsche no longer cared about the personal benefits he obtained from his position, it was clear that he hoped to use the position to further the Wagnerian cause.

This leads to the second point, which is that there was no other formal role to step into. There were things Nietzsche could have done for the cause, such as a travelling lecture tour, but these would not be paid, and there was no real guarantee that the idea would work anyway. It was pure speculation to suppose that crowds of people would show up to listen to lectures about an opera that had not yet even been performed. The choice Nietzsche had was to give up his formal identity, including the salary that came with it, and in exchange to receive no obvious identity. Moreover, to move in with the Wagners would have made him a permanent part of the family instead of just an honorary member. For a grown man who was now twenty-seven-years-old, this would have been a very strange move and would have constituted exactly the kind of story that the newspapers would be able to twist into something insalubrious, as was their want when it came to Wagner.

On top of all this is the aforementioned issue that Cosima had noted in her diary. Nietzsche had always had a reserve in his dealings with Wagner as a kind of protection against exactly the scenario that we have just outlined, i.e., that he would become fully dependent on or dominated by the older man. That was true in multiple different ways. Everybody knew that Wagner dominated social events and conversations. That was just taken for granted.

PART 2: THE ORPHAN STORY OF NIETZSCHE AND WAGNER

We also know that Wagner dominated people in a more psychological sense to the extent that he became angry and combative when people did not do what he wanted. Nietzsche may have believed fervently in the Wagnerian agenda, but that didn't mean that he wanted to give up all his individuality to the cause. In fact, it is certain that Nietzsche had originally been excited by Wagner's ideas to the extent that they stimulated his own. At this time, Nietzsche thought of those ideas as belonging to the discipline of philology, and he saw a future in which he would develop and nurture those ideas within his existing identity as a philologist. It's for this reason that the negative response from the philologists had shaken him because it threatened his plan to try and retain the best of both parts of his identity. Ironically, it was the attack of Wilamowitz that finally gave him something to bite on. He now had a stated enemy within the ranks of philology, and he and Rohde could get to work fleshing out the *philology of the future*. This meant Nietzsche could both retain his existing identity as a philologist and incorporate the Wagnerian side at the same time. The price to be paid was that almost all of his professional colleagues were against him, including his one-time Elder, Ritschl. However, in terms of our Orphan Story template, that is perfectly fitting because Step 6 of the story involves a battle between the hero, Elder, and Shadow Elder. Nietzsche had finally found an external enemy to fight against. That was actually a great psychological relief for him since it pulled him out of his introversion and into the real world.

Still, the contradictions in the situation were not resolved. Wagner might be able to join in the battle in the public discourse more generally, but he couldn't be involved in the technical philological questions. Therefore, Nietzsche was still quite alone within his faculty in Basel and in the discipline more broadly. That was one problem. A second problem was that his main source of moral support had just left him. Wagner and Cosima now lived five hundred kilometres away in Bayreuth. This represented a fivefold increase in travel time and a proportional rise in the cost of a train ticket. Wagner had not wanted to create this distance between himself and his main disciple; in fact, he used all his usual tactics to get Nietzsche to visit or even stay permanently in Bayreuth. But, as we have already pointed out, the master had nothing to offer Nietzsche other than a place in his household, an offer that Nietzsche couldn't accept for all the reasons we have just outlined.

Thus, a new phase of the relationship had just begun, one that was going to involve a lot less direct, physical contact between the two men. Nietzsche had visited Tribschen twenty-three times in the previous three years. In the four years ahead leading up to the premiere of the Ring Cycle in 1876, he would only visit Bayreuth on several occasions. At just the time when Nietzsche's identity as a Wagnerian seemed to have become more established as a public as well as private fact, it began to wane as contact with the master dried up. What had been so intoxicating about the time at Tribschen was its intimacy. *The Birth of Tragedy* was the fruit of those years. That Nietzsche later referred to them as the happiest time in his life already tells us that what was about to come next would produce a very different result. Perhaps ironically, the family analogy would turn out to be apt after all. While Nietzsche was safely ensconced in the "family home" of Tribschen, all was well. But now he was "moving out" of that home, and he would have to find his own way. Eventually, he would do that. The beginning of the end of the Wagner relationship was also the beginning of the beginning of Nietzsche becoming the great philosopher. But there was much pain and suffering to go through first.

Wagner's Betrayal

As we proceed into the final two steps of how the Orphan Story played out in the relationship between Nietzsche and Wagner, it will be worthwhile to reiterate and reflect on the fact that the majority of our analysis so far has rested on the esoteric aspects of that relationship. Back at the start of the book, we criticised the majority of commentators for their use of the friendship frame of reference when talking about the pairing between the composer and his protégé. That criticism is valid in that the generation gap and other factors that existed when the two met should have prompted at least some analysts to dig deeper. But it's also true that a focus on the external, objective aspects of the relationship really would lead one to conclude that the men were friends, if only because no other option presents itself. A casual, objective observer in the 19th century would have reached the same conclusion as an external observer in our time. It is only by getting down into the esoteric aspects of the relationship via letters, diaries, and notebooks that we have been able to understand what was happening.

To demonstrate that, let's put ourselves again in the position of a third-party observer of the Nietzsche-Wagner relationship. Even an omniscient observer with a god's eye view of all the events of the relationship would have misunderstood. That person would have observed Nietzsche visiting the Wagner household on multiple occasions. That makes sense. Nietzsche was an up-and-coming professor with a prestigious job, and Wagner was a famous composer with a significant interest in the wider cultural and political issues of the day. A friendship would be natural between two such men, and, for the entirety of the first couple of years, that's really all it could have been when viewed externally. To be sure, it would have had to be an incredibly close and intimate friendship since Nietzsche was staying for entire weekends and was present for almost all major holidays, including Christmas-New Year's Eve and Easter. But there was no evidence of anything else going on. It was a small group of intellectuals sitting around reading, playing music, going on walks and doing all the other pleasant activities that were nothing out of the ordinary for that class of people in the 19th century.

Similarly, even the publication of Nietzsche' first book and its dedication to Wagner would not have seemed particularly unusual. Nietzsche was a scholar, and the book was ostensibly about philology. That Wagner would publicly defend a book that had been dedicated to him was also nothing unusual. It's the kind of controversy he clearly enjoyed, and he was a friend of Nietzsche anyway. Finally, there is the laying of the foundation stone at Bayreuth and Nietzsche's position at the head of the party. Again, nothing unusual for our third-party observer since Nietzsche had clearly been the most popular visitor at Tribschen in the preceding three years and seemed to be the closest friend of the family. Nietzsche was supporting Wagner in his work just as Wagner had supported Nietzsche in his; perfectly sensible, normal, and rational behaviour.

It is one of the most important aspects of the Wagner-Nietzsche relationship that there is such a sharp contrast between this objective viewpoint and the subjective one we have relied on in our analysis. Nietzsche's letters have been our number one source of evidence, alongside Wagner's letters and Cosima's diary. Sadly, most of the letters between Nietzsche and Cosima have been lost, largely because she destroyed all the correspondence in her possession in the aftermath of Wagner's death when Nietzsche really began to attack the composer in his writings. Still, this book has been mostly about Nietzsche, and it could never have been written without knowledge of his letters and especially the fact that he was so open and forthright in his correspondence with Wagner and his two main friends during this time, Rohde and Gersdorff. It is because of those letters that we know that Nietzsche had already concluded that Wagner was the saint of philology prior to their first meeting. It is from the letters that we know that Nietzsche thought of Wagner as the Meister, not just as a polite form of address but in the numerous examples of ecstatic expressions of admiration. It is clear that Nietzsche worshipped Wagner. It is also clear that the pressure and influence Wagner exerted on him forced him into a genuine existential crisis with the publication of his first book by making him lay on the line his reputation as a professional scholar. Perhaps most important of all, it is from the letters that we know that Nietzsche fully intended to quit his job as a philologist and devote himself full-time to the cause of Wagnerism.

This final step didn't happen, of course, and so our third-party observer who had no access to Nietzsche's letters could never have known that it was even a consideration in the first place. From their point of view, everything was perfectly normal, logical, and rational. Nietzsche visited a friend during an important turning point in that friend's life and then went back to his day job. In the months that followed, Nietzsche engaged in what appeared to be a robust scholarly debate over the merits of his first book, and if that debate seemed excessively personal, well, our third-party observer might also have known that Nietzsche had earlier been involved in a very public scholarly argument between Ritschl and Jahn way back at the University of Bonn. This was 19th-century Germany. Academia was a serious business.

Not only has our analysis relied on an esoteric information source, but it has also relied on an even more esoteric template that we have called the Orphan Story. Here we run up against another set of problems because the idea behind our template goes against the innate biases of modern Western culture. We separate the world into fiction and fact, and ne'er the twain shall meet. We began this book by attempting to bridge that gap by pointing out that two of the greatest stories in Western history fit the Orphan Story template (the gospels and the Socrates-Plato relationship). But even if people were to accept this reading, there is still an inherent problem because we are used to thinking of "truth" in terms of scientific cause and effect based on objective, external evidence. However, we have just pointed out that all the objective, external evidence in the relationship between Wagner and Nietzsche lends itself to the conclusion that they were friends; a conclusion which is wrong. Because our analysis here has not been based on cause and effect explanations, and because it has relied on subjective matters, our society treats it as, at best, an inferior form of truth and, at worst, nothing more than a psychological problem. Yes, Nietzsche worshipped Wagner. Yes, Wagner loved having a devoted disciple around. But that doesn't make it "real". It's all *just psychological* in the same way that it's all *just a story*.

Ironically, this is almost the exact argument that Nietzsche made in one of the books he wrote in the incredibly productive final sane year of his life (1888). *The Antichrist* applies a psychological lens to the disciples who wrote the gospels and then uses that framework to triangulate a new interpretation of Jesus. According to Nietzsche, the disciples were "little bigots" and "three-quarters madmen", while Jesus was an anarchist idiot who accidentally got himself crucified. It is not necessary for us to critique Nietzsche's argument here except to point out that his use of the psychological perspective does not follow our own in that it is not based on actual evidence (letters, diaries, etc.). Rather, Nietzsche constructs an interpretation of the psychology of the disciples and then extrapolates from that. This allows him to essentially rewrite the gospel story because it means that the facts of that story can no longer be taken at face value. After all, they were written by madmen and bigots. Why would we trust them to be truthful witnesses? But even if that were true, where does that give Nietzsche the right to then completely reinterpret the story? His new version is not based on evidence. It is nothing more than speculation; interesting speculation, to be sure, but just speculation.

A question now arises: Why would it have occurred to Nietzsche that the disciples of Jesus were "three-quarters madmen" who made up the story about their master? Maybe it was because Nietzsche himself had made up a story about Wagner. In other words, Nietzsche might agree with our hypothetical critic who claims that the idea that Nietzsche was a disciple of Wagner was all in the younger man's head. It's *just psychology*. It's *just a story*. The mature Nietzsche would have criticised the analysis in this book because, by then, he had constructed a philosophy based around materialist science where stories were just fiction and everything else could be explained by psychology. He would have said of our analysis so far: *yes, it was all in my head. I turned Wagner into a prophet. But he also led me astray. The whole thing was a falsification of reality to be explained psychologically.*

We will see later in the book why Nietzsche came to these conclusions. For now, the point to make is that none of this is *just psychology*. Yes, the majority of our analysis has been focused on the psychological aspects of the story. But we know that those psychological aspects were not imaginary. They were based on real things that happened. The relationship that developed at Tribschen was very real. It gave rise to the very real phenomenon of Nietzsche's first book which subsequently triggered a major dispute between him, Ritschl, and the rest of the philological community. Nietzsche was targeted in the media as a result of his association with Wagner. The laying of the foundation stone in Bayreuth was a very real event that had significance for all those who were concerned, many of whom, including Nietzsche, saw it as a major milestone in the history not just of Wagner's art but of German culture. Since the Festspielhaus is still standing in Bayreuth to this day and still hosts performances of Wagner's operas every year, this is not a figment of anyone's imagination. What's more, as we showed earlier in the book, when we analyse the gospels from the point of view of our Orphan Story template, all the major turning points in that story have significant historical evidence to show that they really happened. Therefore, the gospel story is also based in reality, as is the relationship between Socrates and Plato.

The reason why we must emphasise all of this is because what we are about to see is that what "went wrong" in the relationship between Wagner and Nietzsche is that, at just the time when things were becoming official, external, and objective, the template was broken. A story which was on the verge of becoming "real" suddenly fell back into the realm of psychology. Nietzsche's later objections that everything is just *psychology* became true of his own relationship with Wagner. But this descent into the psychological is also a normal part of the Orphan Story. It seems that a journey into the sacred always involves a time of despair when all seems lost. The gospel story of Jesus and the story of Socrates' death as portrayed by Plato do not go into the details about the psychological state that accompanies genuine despair. That does not mean that Plato did not feel such despair when Socrates died or that the disciples also did not feel the same despair when Jesus was crucified. It just means that they didn't feel it appropriate or necessary to relate that despair in the stories they told about the events.

As we are about to see, the main thing that differentiates the story of Nietzsche from that of Plato and the disciples was not the despair that comes with the death of the Elder and the inherently psychological struggle that is implied by that. On the contrary, Nietzsche's despair would arise out of what is perhaps a far more difficult thing to deal with, and that is that he would be betrayed by his Elder. Even worse, the circumstances of that betrayal were also esoteric in nature. Thus, what was about to happen was not just psychological in the sense of feelings and emotions but philosophical in the sense that Nietzsche would have to re-evaluate his entire worldview. It is the event which perhaps more than any other gave birth to the great philosopher.

**

A distinguishing feature of the evolution of the Nietzsche-Wagner relationship is the way in which definitive and dramatic moments signify a paradigm shift that then slowly escalates towards the next major turning point. A seasonal metaphor works to explain this. The "spring" of the relationship began with the initial secret meeting in Leipzig and then the strange series of events that led to Nietzsche becoming a professor in Basel. The "summer" would then be the Tribschen years, which we know built up slowly towards the publication of *The Birth of Tragedy*. The laying of the foundation stone in Bayreuth signifies the shift into autumn since, even though it was nominally a high point in terms of Nietzsche's public recognition as the lead disciple of the Wagnerian cause, it also broke the basis of the relationship that had existed by placing a physical barrier in the way of travel. Wagner and Cosima were now more than five hundred kilometres away. The days when Nietzsche could drop over for a weekend of intimate discussions were over.

Nevertheless, for the next almost two years, the Orphan Story continued on in the mode we have called *Step 6: There is a struggle between the hero, the Elder and the Shadow Elder*. For the rest of 1872 and into '73, the battle with Wilamowitz took place in the public sphere, with Rohde and Wagner flying the flag on behalf of Nietzsche and the Wagnerians. In addition, the newspapers picked up the story. Nietzsche was caricatured as the composer's "literary lackey" in one article, and there were variations on the theme eagerly shared between the Wagnerians, who were used to various academics using their platform to target the master (another article around this time used a well-known psychologist to prove that Wagner was clinically insane). All of this was good fun and served to unify everybody around the cause.

Less fun were the difficulties Nietzsche was having with Ritschl, who had now become the Shadow Elder. We have already mentioned the tense letters exchanged between them and even an argument that occurred when they met in person in early 1873. Later in the year, there was an even more tense personal meeting where both the professor and his wife "unleashed a barrage of quickly spoken words against me, from which I remained largely unhurt and felt that way too; in the end, they insisted that I was arrogant and despised them." It is curious that Nietzsche continued to meet Ritschl during this time when such animosity had been introduced into the relationship, but he still believed that he had a revolutionary new philological system to impart to whichever future generation could understand it. It made sense that he would at least try to maintain relations with his old mentor.

All of which is to say that Nietzsche was paying a heavy personal price for his support of Wagner during this time, but this is all exactly what the Orphan Story requires of the initiate who must make a sacrifice of their old identity in order to transition towards the new. The trouble now for Nietzsche was that he was stuck in the middle of two distinct identities and there were problems emerging for both of them. Although the news was mostly positive on the Wagnerian side, there were the first signs of the fallout from the move to Bayreuth. The first eruption in this respect was the fact that Nietzsche failed to spend New Year's Eve in 1872 with Wagner despite the latter's explicit invitation. Nietzsche must have known by now that such "invitations" were not optional, and yet his failure to attend and the inevitable anger that resulted produced a subtle but crucial change in attitude that can be found in a letter to Rohde:-

"I simply cannot imagine how one could be more loyal to W. in all fundamental matters and more deeply devoted than I am: if I could imagine it, I would be even more so. But...I must preserve a certain freedom, really only in order to be able to maintain that loyalty in a higher sense."

Reading between the lines here, it's clear that Nietzsche deliberately did not travel to Bayreuth in order to preserve his "freedom". In one respect, this was the same "reservation" that Cosima had noted a couple of years earlier, but whereas Wagner's anger could be quickly extinguished by a follow-up visit to Tribschen at that time, a short personal visit was no longer an option, and this resulted in the master's mood remaining sour well into the new year of 1873. It seems that this personal issue became tied in with a larger problem that was now threatening the viability of the entire Bayreuth project. As had happened so often in his life, Wagner found himself in financial straits. This time, the entire construction of the *Festspielhaus* was under threat.

It is worth mentioning here that quite a large amount of funding had been secured via what would nowadays be called a crowdfunding operation. The various Wagner societies that had sprung up in the preceding years were at the forefront of this, but all the Wagnerian inner circle, including Nietzsche, had been selling patronage certificates in order to raise money. This was a task that Nietzsche had carried out eagerly for some time, even though the amount of money that one person could raise was minimal. The goal had been to fund the construction in Bayreuth entirely from this income. It was a plan that was very much in keeping with Wagner's dreams that his art would be based in a true folk culture that would not rely on aristocratic patronage as had been the case with almost all opera before that time. Nevertheless, it had become clear in late 1872 that the money raised in this fashion was not going to be enough, and so Wagner had set off on a concert tour which had raised a significant amount but still left a major deficit in the budget. It was in the aftermath of that tour that the realisation sank in that the whole project was now under threat.

Nietzsche walked right into the middle of this dynamic when he visited Bayreuth in April 1873, and the whole thing was made worse by the fact that Wagner was still upset about his absence at New Year's. We can get a feel for how bad the mood was by the fact that Nietzsche wrote to Wagner immediately after returning to Basel as follows:-

> *"If you did not seem pleased with my presence, I understand only too well, without being able to change anything about it, for I learn and perceive very slowly, and then at every moment I experience something with you that I had never thought of and which it is my wish to imprint on my memory. I know very well, dearest master, that such a visit can be no rest for you, indeed must at times be unbearable. I have so often wished for at least the semblance of greater freedom and independence, but in vain. Enough, I beg you, take me only as a pupil, if possible with a pen in my hand and a notebook in front of you, and also as a pupil with a very slow and not at all versatile ingenuity. It's true, I become more melancholy every day when I feel so strongly how much I would like to help and be of use to you in some way, and how completely incapable I am of doing so, so that I can't even contribute anything to your distraction or amusement."*

Note here that Nietzsche explicitly references his desire for freedom and then begs Wagner to take him as a "pupil" so that he may be of some use. Here we get a genuine insight into the dynamic that must have been at play since the start of their relationship. Nietzsche genuinely wanted to please Wagner, and it seems that almost everything he did, including the writing of *The Birth of Tragedy*, was with that goal in mind. The whole trouble was that Wagner didn't actually have anything for Nietzsche to do. He was already doing his best by selling patronage certificates, and that was really the extent of what could be asked, short of having him quit his job and travel the country, as Nietzsche had once considered. What Nietzsche did in the aftermath of this dramatic meeting in Bayreuth is highly instructive because he fell back to the thing that had won him favour with Wagner and Cosima in the first place, i.e., writing essays. He couldn't do anything practical for the Bayreuth project, but Nietzsche could boost Wagner's spirits with a controversial new piece of writing that would hopefully stir the pot in the same way that *The Birth of Tragedy* had done.

The result was a pamphlet attacking one of the thinkers who had been highly influential on Nietzsche's intellectual development and was considered one of the foremost intellectuals in Germany at that time, David Strauss. Nietzsche would target Strauss specifically, it seems, because Wagner had disliked the man after he wrote a piece critical of Schopenhauer some years earlier. Thus, although this attack didn't directly benefit the Wagnerian cause, it did take aim at a tangential "enemy". It's also true that the essay was written using a number of conceptual weapons that Wagner himself had constructed over the years, including the ideas around German culture, the sterility of academia, and the use and abuse of the German language among writers of the time, including Strauss. One of the properties that stands out about the essay is the highly accomplished style and structure of the work. It's a beautifully written piece, and we get a glimpse at another reason why Wagner adored Nietzsche because the young scholar was able to copy Wagner's ideas without copying his woeful prose style. At this time, Nietzsche was presenting Wagner's ideas with a degree of thoroughness and sophistication that the composer never achieved in his written works.

Wagner showed his delight when Nietzsche sent the essay to him some months later: "I've read it again and I swear to God that I consider you the only one who knows what I want!" Nietzsche had once again made himself useful.

The Strauss essay did cause a minor stir in the public discourse and served to provide a much-needed morale boost for the Wagnerians. However, by the end of the year, Wagner would finally have a real use for Nietzsche, one that was directly tied in with the future of the Bayreuth project. With the financial problems still unresolved, a committee of the various Wagner societies had decided to make a plea to the music-loving public of Germany as a way to raise funds. The idea was to try and get as many people as possible to buy patronage certificates with the explicit understanding that the money raised was going towards the construction of the *Festspielhaus*. A public appeal would need to be written, and it would be printed off and sent to as many music-related businesses as possible. Wagner agreed to the idea and asked Nietzsche to write the text of the appeal.

Nietzsche may have been a brilliant writer in the scholarly domain, but a marketing pamphlet was something very different, and he seems to have been well aware of the fact that he was not really the man for the job since he immediately wrote to Rohde asking for help with the composition. Nevertheless, the final product was almost entirely Nietzsche's doing. The primary tactic he chose was to try and shame the public into action. He pointed out that in Britain, France, or the United States, a heroic individual such as Wagner who stood against the corrupt establishment could count on support from the general public as a matter of patriotism. But, in Germany, such support had not been forthcoming. The public now had an opportunity to put the matter right by standing up in the hour of need and doing what was necessary to ensure the construction of the *Festspielhaus*, which would stand as a monument to German culture for future generations. In November of 1873, Nietzsche made the journey to Bayreuth to attend a specially convened meeting of the committee and present his proposed text. It was rejected by a vote, and another member was instructed to draft a new version, which was ultimately accepted. Nietzsche does not seem to have been disappointed with this outcome since he had been sceptical of his own ability to communicate with the common man.

We should point out once again that this occurrence was evidence for Nietzsche's active and formal involvement in the wider Wagnerian cause. The fact that he was prepared to travel to Bayreuth for such a meeting shows that the desire he expressed in the letter to Wagner months earlier had been legitimate. He really did want to contribute and make himself useful in a way that was not just pleasing the master with essays. But just as the laying of the foundation stone in Bayreuth has been, on the surface, a big breakthrough that established Nietzsche's identity as a Wagnerian but which was immediately followed by the tensions caused by the physical separation between Bayreuth and Basel, Nietzsche's participation in the crowdfunding campaign would have a paradoxical outcome that would once again cause a major reconfiguration in the nature of the relationship.

To cut a long story short, the campaign was a complete flop. Barely any money was raised. Wagner blamed the committee for not choosing Nietzsche's version of the appeal, but that did not change the reality that the financial problems were not going to be solved in this manner and Wagner had to once again face up to the prospect of the failure of the whole project. As he had done several times in the past, he turned to the one card he had left in the deck: King Ludwig of Bavaria. It had been Ludwig who paid for Wagner's accommodation in Tribschen, and Wagner had almost got the young king to fund a specially constructed opera house in Munich about ten years earlier. The project had fallen through due to the fact that Wagner was deeply unpopular among the king's advisers. We have already noted the commonalities between Ludwig and Nietzsche in terms of their age and temperament, but there is one more incredible parallel. Nietzsche had been prepared to quit his job to devote himself to the Wagnerian cause. Ludwig had done exactly the same thing when the original opera house project collapsed. He was so disappointed that he resolved to abdicate the throne, and it was only a personal visit by Wagner that convinced him to stay on (a cynic might point out that Wagner had a vested interest in the matter since a Ludwig without his royal purse was of no use to him).

Although the king had previously stated that he would provide no more funding for the Bayreuth project, Wagner's desperate assurance that he had exhausted every other avenue convinced the king to loan the one hundred thousand thalers needed to finish construction and fund the premiere of the Ring Cycle, which Ludwig, like all the other Wagnerians, was incredibly anxious to witness. In one fell swoop, the financial problems were over. Nietzsche received the news early in 1874. Initially, he was pleased that it had all been sorted out, but his mood quickly changed. Once again, another major turning point in the story had occurred, and, just like all the others, what it looks like on the surface hides a set of deeper meanings that would change the entire nature of the relationship.

* * *

One of Wagner's main character failings was hypocrisy. We have previously noted several examples. A more abstract one comes from his non-fiction writing, where he praised the Volk as the only true source of a culture in distinction to the aristocracy or academy, which were always derivative. Wagner was alternately an anarchist or socialist in his younger days, and yet his radical activities came during a time when he worked for the establishment as a conductor. Furthermore, far from desiring a simple and plain life for himself, such as those he portrayed in *Die Meistersinger*, for example, he continually went into debt in order to surround himself with luxury and then defaulted when the bills came due. For a man who extolled the virtues of the common folk, he showed a singular desire to avoid becoming a member of that class of society at all costs.

But Wagner's exultation of the Volk and his vision of decentralised artistic communes as the saviour of German culture were most absurd when compared against his own art and the manner in which it was produced, which revolved entirely around the man himself and his incredible determination and willpower. Wagner's art was absolutely not the production of a commune-style form of organisation. It evolved out of the imperial demeanour of a man who knew how to bash heads together and scream and shout in order to get his way. Wagner commanded respect in much the same way as a monarch. Otherwise independent and accomplished people desired to please him and happily fell into line when he told them they had not. His was the antithesis of a folk art. It was the art of a great individual, reminiscent of the Renaissance heroes. That was true in its vision, and it was also true in its organisation. Wagner reserved the right to determine every aspect of the production, not just the music but the sets, the costumes, the performance, and everything else.

Despite all this, Wagner had been prepared to experiment with the committees that arose out of the various Wagner societies, which did, after all, represent a kind of decentralised and bottom-up form of organisation. He went along with the idea despite the fact that it caused him enormous frustration. Wagner was used to getting results instantly through force of will. The idea of sitting back waiting for a committee to meet and vote in a rational and orderly fashion was anathema to him. But he tried. When the attempt failed, he went back to the one person who had always proven reliable, Ludwig. But, in doing so, he was falling once again into the trap of hypocrisy by reverting to the exact style of patronage he had railed against as a younger man. In his essays *Artwork of the Future* and *Communication to My Friends,* essays from 1849 and 1851, Wagner had explicitly objected to the old aristocratic model whereby kings and princes would keep artists on retainer. Both Mozart and Beethoven, for example, had funded their music in this fashion. Wagner genuinely wanted to try something else. But when that attempt failed, he reverted back to what worked. It was one more example of his hypocrisy.

Now, it must be said that Nietzsche does not appear to have been bothered by any of this, mostly because he was never interested in this aspect of Wagnerism. On the contrary, what he loved about Wagner was precisely that he was an exemplar of the heroic Artist struggling against all odds to produce something great. Nevertheless, in the aftermath of Ludwig bailing out the Bayreuth project, Nietzsche sank into a deep depression. If it was not Wagner's hypocrisy that had caused this, it must have been something else, and we get a clue to what that was in the letter that we have already referenced where Nietzsche all but begged Wagner to make him "useful". The crowdfunding campaign was a brief respite in this respect because it gave Nietzsche something to do. But when Ludwig stepped in to solve the financial problem once and for all, he inadvertently removed any future need for further crowdfunding activities. Nietzsche and the other Wagnerians would no longer be required to sell patronage certificates or otherwise advocate for the premiere of the Ring Cycle. It was all taken care of. That was bad enough. But there was another, even more significant detail buried away amid the celebrations.

With the funding secure, Wagner's focus shifted entirely towards overseeing the construction of the Festspielhaus and, more importantly, engaging in the mammoth preparations for the premiere of the Ring Cycle. We have just noted that Wagner's art centred around him. That is not an exaggeration. Wagner was responsible for almost every aspect of his operas, from the set design to the costumes to the training of the singers. Everything revolved around him because every detail of the art had to be to his liking and approval. The man was about to achieve the realisation of a dream that was twenty-five years in the making, and he threw himself into the preparations with the passion and determination that had characterised his entire life. This really was the culmination of a lifetime's work.

The problem was that Wagner simply no longer needed anybody else's help. The Wagnerians had always been a loosely knit group of people with diverse interests in Wagner's art, but very few of them were involved in a practical sense. They were not conductors, singers, costume designers or whatnot. Ironically, the exception was von Bülow, who was a conductor, but Wagner had spoiled that alliance by stealing the man's wife. Nietzsche's role as court scholar was incredibly valuable to Wagner in a broader sense, but it could play no practical role in the staging of the Ring Cycle and all the multifarious tasks required to bring that epic opera to fruition.

All of that would have been bad enough, but the definitive change that would occur from this point onwards was that Nietzsche's role as the foremost authority on Wagnerism would be brought into doubt. As the saying goes, *nothing succeeds like success*. Wagner's enemies had been able to trade on the fact that the mad composer's insane fever dreams would never come to fruition. Now that it looked certain that they would, suddenly Wagner didn't seem so crazy anymore. All kinds of people who had mocked and derided him suddenly changed their tune. In a very short period of time, Wagner began to enjoy the kind of general popularity and approval of the establishment that he had lacked throughout his entire life. Wagner, the revolutionary anarchist-socialist, the mad artist who lived beyond the pale, was about to go mainstream. By the time of the Ring Cycle's premiere, seemingly the whole establishment fell into line behind the composer to the extent that Wagner's art increasingly became tied in with the growing nationalism that had accompanied the formation of Germany as a nation-state only years earlier.

All of this might look like success from Wagner's point of view (in fact, the composer had a number of reservations about it), but from Nietzsche's point of view it was a disaster. He had already been struggling to find ways to contribute to the cause, and now even the meagre tasks that he had been able to perform had disappeared. His main service had been his ability to codify Wagner's beliefs in a rigorous quasi-scholarly form and thereby to unify the Wagnerians in a kind of ideological fashion. However, Wagner's art was now being adopted by a very different type of ideology, namely, German nationalism. This cynical reversal on behalf of the mainstream press must have stung Nietzsche even worse because not only did it undermine his own efforts, it was also something he disapproved of in general. Nietzsche saw state-based nationalism, especially in its militaristic form, as the enemy of culture. For that ideology to claim Wagner as its own was not only absurd but antithetical to everything he stood for. It should also have been antithetical to Wagner, but the composer now had a very good reason to tolerate it since the deals he had made around the construction of the Festspielhaus required him to remain on good terms with the establishment. Nietzsche had been able to overlook all of Wagner's other hypocrisy, but this cut to the core of the primary beliefs of Wagnerism.

These may sound like minor quibbles that most people would set aside in the interests of a compromise required to achieve an outcome. But we must remember that we are in an Orphan Story here and the Orphan Story is not about compromise; it is about standing up for one's beliefs in the face of all odds. Let's take this opportunity to reiterate the main themes. The Orphan Story is about a prophet or other revolutionary figure during a time of political and social instability who elucidates a radical new paradigm and who is persecuted by the establishment as a result. The revolutionary figure takes on a group of disciples who will carry forward the teaching after his death. We have shown two detailed examples of this dynamic from Western history, including the New Testament story of Jesus and his disciples and the relationship between Plato and Socrates. Other famous examples from history include Julius Caesar and Brutus, Mohammed and his followers, Buddha, Luther, and more.

The Orphan Story is always told from the point of view of the disciple(s) of the revolutionary figure. Those who are familiar with the gospels may know Matthew 16:13-20. Jesus gathers the disciples together and asks what is essentially a test-of-allegiance question. "Who do people say the Son of Man is?" It is Peter who gives the correct answer, "You are the Messiah, the Son of the living God." Jesus responds:-

> *"Blessed are you, Simon son of Jonah, for this was not revealed to you by flesh and blood, but by my Father in heaven. And I tell you that you are Peter, and on this rock I will build my church, and the gates of Hades will not overcome it. I will give you the keys of the kingdom of heaven; whatever you bind on earth will be bound in heaven, and whatever you loose on earth will be loosed in heaven."*

Everybody knows that Judas was the traitorous disciple, but it has largely been forgotten, at least in the general culture, that Peter was the foremost disciple. This symbolic act of Jesus to promote Peter in front of the other disciples would also become reality after Jesus' death since the evidence suggests that Peter really did take the lead in the early Christian community. In exactly the same way, Plato would become the foremost student of Socrates, even though we know that Socrates had a number of other prominent followers, including Xenophon. The Orphan Story is therefore about the relationship between the foremost disciple and the master. It is clear from everything we have seen in our analysis that Nietzsche had become the foremost disciple of Wagner, and that is why the Orphan Story template has worked so well to summarise the relationship between them. Just as Peter had shown that he understood Jesus better than the others, Nietzsche had shown that he truly understood Wagner's art and the broader implications of it. That was why Wagner had given Nietzsche his own room at Tribschen. It was why he had pushed him to write *The Birth of Tragedy*. It was why it was Nietzsche who rode in Wagner's carriage on the momentous occasion of the laying of the foundation stone in Bayreuth.

And this is really where it all started to go wrong. The foremost disciple must be closest to the master. Nietzsche had enjoyed that physical proximity while Wagner was living in Tribschen, but the move to Bayreuth had spoiled it. His response was to literally beg Wagner to give him something to do, to make him "useful" to the cause. But the simple reality was that Wagner provided no answer because what he needed was not what Nietzsche was able to provide. Even the essays that Nietzsche had always impressed Wagner and Cosima with started to fail. Sometimes they won approval, as in the Strauss essay; more often, they fell flat. Nietzsche had always needed to balance out the expression of his own ideas against the desires of the master. Without Wagner there to guide him, he missed the mark as often as he hit.

The mild despair that had been growing in Nietzsche had been building ever since Wagner and Cosima moved to Bayreuth. The final nail in the coffin came when Ludwig stepped in to fix the financial problem. Not only was this a practical negation of the fundraising work that Nietzsche and the other Wagnerians had been doing, but it also undermined the entire basis of the Orphan Story. Jesus built his church on the rock of Peter. Although Socrates might never have foreseen it, it was Plato who would immortalise his philosophy. That is the role of the foremost disciple. Their job is to carry forward the teachings of the master. It was the role that Nietzsche had been assigned. But that role that was completely undermined when Wagner turned to Ludwig to solve the financial problem. Wagner would not build the

Festspielhaus and the premiere of the Ring Cycle on the rock of Nietzsche; he would build it on the rock of Ludwig. He would build it on the very form of aristocratic patronage he had once railed against. When Wagner chose Ludwig, he chose the disciple who did not understand his art over the one who did. He chose money and power over truth.

The Orphan Story template allows us to be very precise about what had occurred. Up until this point, we had been in Step 6 of the story: *There is a struggle between the hero, the Elder and the Shadow Elder.* Nietzsche had been struggling against the other philologists. His own mentor, Ritschl, had told him to his face he was behaving like a "teenager". Numerous newspaper articles had been written calling him a lackey of Wagner. He had been simultaneously called an *enemy of the Reich* who was in bed with the communists while also being targeted by the same communists for his elitist beliefs. Nietzsche had genuinely suffered for the cause; he had shown a willingness to endure such suffering and to do whatever it took. He did that even when the cause seemed lost. Nietzsche had played his part.

The Orphan Story template tells us what is supposed to happen next. *Step 7: The Elder dies or goes missing (usually sacrificing themselves for the hero).* When faced with the choice between making the ultimate sacrifice or giving up, the Elder chooses to sacrifice themselves. That is what makes all of the names we have mentioned great. Jesus and Socrates made the ultimate sacrifice. It is the death of the Elder which forces the foremost disciple to rise to the occasion and become the leader of the movement. Thus, Peter becomes the most important leader in the nascent Christian community, and Plato formalises the teachings of Socrates into the foundations of Western philosophy.

The Orphan Story template tells us that this is what should have happened in the case of Wagner and Nietzsche. But it didn't happen. Instead, Wagner sold out. It was Wagner who traded his integrity for the thirty pieces of silver. His hypocrisy had turned into something worse. It was betrayal. Rather than sacrifice himself for the cause, he sacrificed the cause. That is why the establishment started to adopt him as their own. That is why Wagner's art came to be associated with the militaristic nationalism of the modern nation-state. All of this was bad enough, but, as we have seen, it left his foremost disciple in limbo. Nietzsche's desperate plea for the master to make him useful was a reflection of that. In hindsight, the entire move to Bayreuth can now be seen as the preliminary action by which Wagner sold out since that had required him to do a number of deals with the leaders of the town, the exact kinds of bourgeois philistines that Nietzsche had railed against in the Strauss essay. Wagner had applauded that essay at the same time he had sold out to the very philistines that he mocked.

There is no evidence that either Wagner or Nietzsche were conscious of any of this at the time. In fact, the betrayal was something that Nietzsche would grapple with for the rest of his life. What unequivocally did happen almost immediately after Ludwig's bailout was that Nietzsche fell into a deep depression. His letters convey this very clearly. So obvious was the problem that his friends asked him point-blank what was going on. Nietzsche originally denied any issue, but by May he had acknowledged it openly. In a letter to Rohde on the 10th of that month, he wrote:-

"In Bayreuth, they were very sad and worried about my melancholy, which I may have betrayed in a letter; but at least I know this: it isn't moodiness or sullenness. One simply moves forward. Good health! And no nerves at all! Believe me. Hugging you, good friend".

Immediately afterwards, the concept of "freedom" started to appear in his letters, and it was clear that Nietzsche had some idea of where it led. As he wrote to Rohde:-

"By the way, I'm busy again making plans to become completely independent and withdraw from all official ties to the state and university into the most shameless, solitary existence, miserably simple, but dignified."

Three years earlier, Nietzsche told Rohde he was going to quit his job to devote himself full-time to the Wagner cause. Now, he had no cause at all except a "shameless, solitary existence."

All of this gives incredible weight to a letter that Wagner sent to Nietzsche in April, when news of Nietzsche's depression had reached Bayreuth. We have seen that the composer was a narcissist, a bully, and a hypocrite, and we have now accused him of being a sellout. But Wagner was never so self-absorbed as to be completely blind to others and especially to the young man that he really did love like a son. He was aware of Nietzsche's depression, and he mentions it on the first line of the letter. But what is extraordinary is the change of tone in this letter. Just as Nietzsche's tone had now become that of a depressed teenager, Wagner suddenly takes on the mien of a well-meaning uncle:-

> *"My own view is that you ought to get married, or else write an opera; the one would do you just as much good and harm as the other. But, of the two, I prefer marriage."*

Wagner goes on to also recommend that Nietzsche should consider taking some time out to travel. The rest of the letter deals with all the preparations that were going on in Bayreuth. He finishes with an admonition for Nietzsche to "eat meat" as a tonic for his problems (a reference back to their argument about vegetarianism five years earlier at the lunch table in Tribschen). If Nietzsche had been in any doubt that the master had no more tasks for him to perform, this letter made it abundantly clear. Wagner was sending him away. He was on his own.

* * *

To understand what had happened, imagine a variation of the gospel story where Jesus announces to the disciples at the Last Supper that the Pharisees and Sadducees weren't that bad after all. In fact, he's just accepted a position as head priest at the local temple and he'll be working with the authorities to implement some reforms. What would we expect the disciples to do in this scenario? Well, first of all, it wouldn't be immediately clear that this was an admission of defeat or of giving up. On the contrary, to some of them it might seem like this was the best thing possible for Jesus' teaching because he could now pursue his ideas within the existing institutional structure. Thus, it wouldn't necessarily be obvious that Jesus had betrayed the cause. Instead, he would now be incorporated into the establishment. One thing would be clear, however, and that is that he would no longer have need of disciples, and so presumably they would all have to go and find something else to do, unless Jesus also gave them positions inside the establishment. Most likely, the *fishers of men* would have to go back to being fishermen.

Something like this is exactly what happened next with Nietzsche. While we can see Wagner's betrayal in hindsight, Nietzsche had not yet processed it. But Wagner's instruction for him to get married or travel was the equivalent of telling him to find something else to do, and he appears to have understood that. Since Nietzsche still had his job at the university, what happened over the next two years was that he gradually focused his attention back on his philology work. Incredibly, Nietzsche would even make up with Ritschl during this time, as well as the other members of the faculty in Basel. He became a model teacher and even considered returning to writing scholarly papers in official philology journals. What looked to be taking place was a reversal of the Orphan Story. Nietzsche became less and less a Wagnerian and fell back to the normal life that he could have been living the whole time as a professor of philology and a teacher of ancient Greek.

As always in our story, however, something else was brewing beneath the surface, and that something appeared in the usual form of a couple of "coincidences" that happened only weeks after the fateful letter from Wagner telling Nietzsche to find something else to do. Firstly, Nietzsche received a fan letter from a certain Gonzagi who had read both *The Birth of Tragedy* and the Strauss essay and found them intriguing. In response, Nietzsche remarked that Gonzagi was the first person who had ever liked his work who was "not a Wagnerian". This was one tiny bit of evidence that perhaps Nietzsche's thinking might have an audience outside of Wagnerian circles, and Nietzsche seems to have noticed this possibility.

Then, only days later, Nietzsche received another letter from a man named

Schmeitzner who also claimed to be a fan of his writings. More importantly, however, Schmeitzner was a publisher, and he advised Nietzsche that he would be delighted to handle any future publications from the professor should the opportunity arise. What is incredible about this particular "coincidence" is that all of Nietzsche's prior work had been published through the auspices of Wagner's man, Fritzsch, with the composer's explicit or implicit approval. At just the moment that Wagner had told Nietzsche to find something else to do, "fate" had intervened and given Nietzsche the chance to publish his own work independently of the master. He immediately accepted that chance. The first work that Schmeitzner would publish was Nietzsche's essay on Schopenhauer later that year. In October 1874, Nietzsche was able for the first time to send Wagner a book that had been written and published without any involvement from the master.

Another crucial point about this is that the subject of that book was Schopenhauer and the future of German philosophy more broadly. Although this was obviously of interest to Wagner, who was still a keen exponent of the philosopher, there is nothing in the contents of the book that indicate that Nietzsche was writing it in a way to please the master. Meanwhile, the subject matter also reveals a vital change of direction for Nietzsche. Until this time, he had still been talking about a *philology of the future*. Now, he had turned his attention to the future of philosophy. We can easily see in hindsight that this was a crucial first step in Nietzsche becoming what he eventually would become: a self-published philosopher. The incredible coincidence is that it occurred almost immediately after Wagner had cut him loose, and it did so in a way that Nietzsche could never have planned or expected. Once again we see that these coincidences in the story follow major turning points which occur firstly in the esoteric, inner realm and then somehow manifest in the external world as if by magic.

Despite these seemingly positive developments, things were not going well for Nietzsche in general. His depression would soon morph into the general illnesses that would plague him for the rest of his life. No sooner had he decided to focus back on his scholarly work than his eyes began to play up, and he experienced a variety of related symptoms such as headache, nausea, and vomiting, which seemed to come in waves of differing intensity. He began to seek treatment from doctors on a regular basis. By June of 1875, the illness had reached a level of severity such that Nietzsche began visiting various health spas in search of a remedy. His sister, Elizabeth, began to join her brother in Basel for extended stays during which time she functioned as his nurse. Meanwhile, the tone of Nietzsche's letters, which had already been dark in 1874, became even more problematic. He started to talk of death or, conversely, of a desire to avoid it and live a long life. At one point, he even hinted at a suicide attempt.

In our secular scientific viewpoint, the cause of Nietzsche's illness must have a physical origin, even though Nietzsche's doctors were never able to diagnose or treat his illness and even though there is little firm evidence of a cause besides speculation such as syphilis or a genetically inherited problem. It seems clear that Nietzsche really thought he might die during this time, and so we have little reason to doubt that he was sincere about how he felt. Nevertheless, there are curious hints in the letters he sent, and also in his later philosophy, that his illness was not purely physical in nature. In a letter to Overbeck on 5th April 1876, Nietzsche writes, "...you know, of course, how my physical ailments often enough look so similar to "moral" ones; and that feeling of happiness is therefore always something more than the absence of headaches." This is an idea that pops up several times in Nietzsche's letters of this period and always to his closest friends.

What was the "moral ailment" that Nietzsche was experiencing during this time? We might answer that by way of another question: what problems did Nietzsche's illness enable him to solve? The first, and most important, was that it gave him an excuse not to have to visit Bayreuth. This was especially true of a big occasion that had been organised for the summer of 1875. All the Wagnerians, including Nietzsche's closest friends, Rohde and Gersdorff, had been invited to attend a full dress rehearsal for the premiere of the Ring Cycle, which would take place the following summer. This event had been planned as early as the middle of 1874, but we find from his letters that Nietzsche had already begun making excuses for why he wouldn't be able to attend. Contrast this with the excitement that Nietzsche had felt in 1872 with the laying of the foundation stone and his insistence that Rohde join them on that occasion, and we can see that something major had changed. We know now what that something is. It was not just that Wagner had left Nietzsche in the lurch; it was that a new prospect had opened up for him, a new dream that he had constructed: the dream of becoming a philosopher.

The major stumbling block in the way of that dream was his philological and teaching career. Although Nietzsche had now smoothed over all the earlier controversy with Ritschl and his other colleagues, he knew that these kinds of people could never understand his own work. In fact, in an earlier letter to Rohde, when Nietzsche was still angry with Ritschl, he asserts that he took a kind of joy in knowing that the old man couldn't understand what he was talking about. Nietzsche had stopped trying to fight against the system. He had simply come to terms with its shortcomings. Ironically, he was now trying to do exactly what Wilamowitz had told him to do years earlier and completely separate the new identity as a philosopher from his philological one. It was the illness that allowed him to do that by giving him time away from his day job. As he would later write in a letter to Overbeck:-

> "Now my thoughts are pushing me forward. I have such a rich year (in terms of inner achievement) behind me; it seems to me as if the old layer of moss from my daily philological emergency only needed to be lifted away—and everything stands there green and lush".

This "rich year of inner achievement" that Nietzsche mentions was one that he nominally spent in a perpetual state of serious illness. The illness and his "inner achievement" had somehow formed a symbiotic relationship to create Nietzsche the philosopher. He had created for himself the space in which to think. He had found the pattern which he would follow for the rest of his sane life, and it is perfectly fitting that the first great revelation that came to him was at the top of a mountain near Geneva, where he had been staying at a health spa.

Nietzsche's health situation had become particularly acute in the early months of 1876, and he took time off work to travel to the spa. While out walking by himself, he had some kind of epiphany. On return to Basel at the start of April, the tone of his letters was completely changed. They became manic in the way they had not been since the height of the Tribschen years. About the epiphany, he wrote to Gersdorff:-

> "My stay in Geneva came at just the right moment, as a kind of confirmation and reinforcement of what I had decided to do alone…. Not a single step toward accommodation for all the world! One can only achieve great success if one remains true to oneself."

Readers of Shakespeare will recognise here Polonius' advice to his son, *to thine own self be true*. Nietzsche had finally decided to take the bull by the horns and take control of his own life.

As evidence for his elevated mood, we have an extraordinary episode whereby Nietzsche proposed marriage (by letter!) to a woman he only met briefly just a few days prior on his return trip to Basel. The woman, named Trampendache, politely replied that she couldn't possibly entertain such an idea with a man she hardly knew, and Nietzsche wrote an equally polite reply apologising for his indiscretion.

Just a few weeks later, he wrote to his university requesting a full year's leave starting in October of 1876. This was duly granted. All of this just happened to coincide with Wagner's birthday, and Nietzsche's letter to the master this time had a distinctly new flavour to it:-

> "It is almost exactly seven years since I paid you my first visit in Tribschen, and I have nothing more to say to you on your birthday than that, since then, I have also celebrated my spiritual birthday every May. For since then, you have lived within me and have worked ceaselessly as a completely new drop of blood, which I certainly did not have within me before."

Wagner's birthday had now become Nietzsche's *spiritual birthday,* and Nietzsche no longer required orders from the master directly since he was now "within" him.

All of this may sound positive. Yet, by this stage in our analysis, we know to be wary of such seeming successes. In fact, we know quite specifically what to expect whenever the manic tone appears in Nietzsche's correspondence. It's the same tone that appeared suddenly in late 1868 when the revelation occurred to him that Wagner was the *saint of philology*. We saw the tone in early days at Tribschen and in the window of time between *The Birth of Tragedy* and the laying of the foundation stone in Tribschen. It's the same tone that occurred in the aftermath of Ludwig's bailout of the Bayreuth project. It's the tone that readers of Nietzsche's final works in the year 1888 will recognise. It's the sound of the Dionysian rising up from Nietzsche's unconscious. It is perfectly fitting that Nietzsche should have always associated that with Wagner. He was absolutely correct to now call the composer his *spiritual teacher*. It had been the discovery of Wagner which, for the first time, broke the Apollonian façade, the conscious ego, of the young man and allowed the deep, mysterious desires and thoughts to enter and take a place in his life. Those thoughts had always come to Nietzsche in the form of a combination of terror and exhilaration that threatened to overturn his psychic equilibrium. But we have also seen that these turning points almost always had a firm basis in external, objective reality too. To come back to our earlier point, this was not just all in Nietzsche's head.

Thus, it shouldn't be a surprise to find that all this was happening right before another major event that was about to take place in the real world. This event was nothing more or less than the success of the enterprise that Wagner had been involved in for twenty-five years: the premiere of the Ring Cycle in Bayreuth. It is important to note that Nietzsche had been telling the other Wagnerians that he would have to miss the occasion due to his illness. But the epiphany on the Geneva mountaintop seems also to have changed his mind in this respect. No sooner had he come down from the mountain (Zarathustra-style!) than Nietzsche set to work finishing off an essay he had been chipping away at for the past year. It was titled *Richard Wagner in Bayreuth*. Just as Nietzsche had managed to write a call to arms for the Wagnerians in advance of the laying of the foundation stone in Bayreuth, he would try to repeat the process by writing what amounted to a summary of Wagner's life and art. The book would be published on the 10th of July, just weeks before the premiere of the Ring Cycle in early August.

But just as the enthusiasm around the laying of the foundation stone in mid-1872 hid a deeper reality that the intimate personal connection between Wagner and Nietzsche had been broken, and just as the securing of the finances from Ludwig in early 1874 hid the deeper truth that Wagner had sold out in favour of the establishment, this final bright spot, which came after Nietzsche had been missing in action for almost two years, was quick to fizzle and darken.

It is because Nietzsche had been away from the real action in Bayreuth for so long that his book titled *Richard Wagner in Bayreuth* could never have been an accurate description of reality. Nietzsche had quite literally never seen the reality. He had missed the construction of the opera house and the full dress rehearsal in 1875. Gone were the days when he shared in the daily life of the Wagner family. Wagner had once told him that he would make Nietzsche the legal guardian of his son Siegfried in the event of his death. Nietzsche had missed the development of the young man and the other Wagner children. He had played almost no role in the lives of Wagner and Cosima during this time. We know that's true because there is not a single mention of him in Cosima's meticulous diary for the whole of 1875, and only sparse mentions in the years on either side.

Richard Wagner in Bayreuth was not a description of reality. Instead, it was a summation of all the Wagnerian ideals that he and Wagner had believed in over the years. In other words, it was a summation of the ideals that Wagner had betrayed. When the Wagnerians would show up to Bayreuth for the premiere, they would have a template to measure the occasion against. Nietzsche was certainly not doing this on purpose or with any ulterior motive, yet the consequences would be profound for both himself and Wagner. When he did finally show up to the premiere, the first time he had been to Bayreuth in more than two years, what was going to happen was a clash between the ideal he had created in his head and the reality on the ground. The fallout from that would usher in the final phase of our story.

Fighting the Elder

It had been the rousing manifestos that Wagner wrote in the immediate aftermath of his exile from Germany that had changed Nietzsche from a lukewarm admirer of his art to a full-blooded devotee. In the months leading up to their chance initial meeting in Leipzig, Nietzsche had written to Rohde all but demanding that his friend procure a copy of Wagner's essay "Opera and Drama" so they could discuss the contents. This was just one of several key writings that Wagner published in the period from 1849-51. They contain almost all of his core ideas about art and its connection to the future of German culture that so excited the young Nietzsche.

There are two concepts that Wagner discussed at this time that are most relevant for the analysis that we have carried out in this book. The first is his assertion that art should be connected to what he called Life and Nature. This was further related to the idea that a true art could only ever arise from a Folk, which stands in opposition to the governing elites of society precisely by being closer to Life and Nature. The trouble was that composers had relied almost exclusively on elite patronage to fund their art. Wagner had started down that path himself, but the events in Dresden and his subsequent exile seemed to have put an end to any aspirations he could have of funding his art via patronage. In any case, Wagner believed that the cloistered environment created by that funding model cut artists off from Life and Nature, leading to a sterile, pretentious, and over-intellectualised art that had lost its connection with the fundamentals of human existence. Wagner had insisted that art must be based on reality, and that is what we have shown in this book by looking at Wagner's own life as a work of art (a story).

The second idea of Wagner's that is crucial to our work was the motivation behind his preference for adapting mythological stories for his operas. He believed that myths contained timeless truths which, because they avoided contemporary debates and issues, provided an ideal way to present and explore the universals of human nature. In this, Wagner was somewhat incorrect. For example, the knight quests that were immensely popular in medieval times were very much relevant to the people of that era for the simple reason that a medieval knight was an established and respected social role that young men of the lesser nobility could strive for. Those stories were very much contemporary at the time they were written. Thus, we might define a "myth" as simply a story that is set in a society that no longer resembles our own but which, because we can compare it against ours, allows us to extrapolate what is timeless about human nature. Young men need to find a place in the world. They do that by imitating those they consider noble and honourable. That is what the medieval knight story shows us in a more abstract sense.

Wagner was wrong to say that myths were timeless and universal but correct in the implication that there is something timeless and universal about them. What is timeless and universal is both the structure of stories and what that structure implies about human nature. That has been the core assumption of our analysis in this book, although we have limited ourselves to just one kind of story: the Orphan story. We have also extended the scope of Wagner's ideas about stories beyond being merely a theory of aesthetics and into the "real world". That is why we have focused on the world-historical stories of Jesus and his disciples, Socrates and Plato, and, of course, Wagner and Nietzsche. With this, we have aimed to show that stories really are about Life and Nature since they account for real life as well as fiction.

However, just because he didn't write about it in his manifestos does not mean that Wagner was not open to the idea that stories are "real" and that the distinction between Life and Art is nowhere near as discrete as our modern culture assumes it to be. In fact, we have strong reason to believe otherwise. Remember Nietzsche's rousing line from the preface to *The Birth of Tragedy*: art is the true metaphysical task of life. That book was very much written as a partnership between Nietzsche and Wagner. It was born out of the golden days at Tribschen, and it represents a new idea that builds upon Wagner's earlier work. It was no longer simply that art should be aesthetically judged according to whether or not it reflected Life and Nature. There was a new quality to art. It had become a *metaphysical task*.

What that means is not immediately clear, but it is the theme that we will turn to in this final stage of our analysis because an incredible prospect will now open before us. Until now, we have shown how the relationship between Nietzsche and Wagner evolved in accordance with the Orphan Story structure. The structure we have used to make our analysis is what we might call the comedic or "happy path". That is, it represents stories where the Orphan successfully initiates and goes on to continue the work of the master. As we have seen, a key component of this is that the master must die in service to his beliefs in Step 7. We see this structure in countless works of fiction. More importantly, we have seen it in the two world-historical Orphan Stories of Jesus and Socrates.

However, we have also seen that there is a tragic version of the Orphan Story which involves the failure of the Orphan hero to initiate. This is achieved technically by inverting parts of the template. A prime example we analysed earlier in the book was Shakespeare's *Hamlet*. However, we can also find this pattern in the historical relationship between Julius Caesar and Brutus. Just like Wagner and Nietzsche, that relationship began by following the Orphan Story structure. Caesar was old enough to be Brutus' father. He became the Elder to Brutus, taking the young man under his wing and training him for a career in Roman public life. Thus, Caesar directly provided for Brutus' initiation. Since Caesar had numerous enemies, and since Roman society was going through a time of crisis, all the elements of the Orphan Story are present in their relationship.

But the astonishing twist in the story is that it was Brutus who later helped to kill Caesar. He did so because he believed that Caesar had betrayed the ideals of the republic. In terms of our Orphan Story, what had happened was that Step 7 of the template was not fulfilled. Caesar did not die defending the ideals he had stood for; he betrayed them. Step 8 of the template is supposed to be about defeating the Shadow Elder, but Brutus was forced instead to fight his own Elder. He went into battle against the man who had initiated him. He did so in the name of the ideals that Caesar had inculcated in him and then subsequently betrayed. In the case of both Hamlet and Brutus, these inversions in the Orphan Story led not to a successful conclusion but to a tragic one in that both men died as a result. Nevertheless, these tragic outcomes only serve to reinforce the validity of the Orphan Story structure

PART 2: THE ORPHAN STORY OF NIETZSCHE AND WAGNER

because they imply that any variation from the template results in "failure".

All this is directly relevant to the story between Nietzsche and Wagner because, as we have now established, that story deviated from the script when Wagner sold out by taking Ludwig's money in order to complete the Bayreuth project. Nietzsche's response to this was exactly what we would expect since he first fell into an intense depression, which then morphed into physical illness. During this time he had suicidal thoughts and really did seem to think that death could be near. The parallels with the story of Hamlet are direct. Just like Hamlet, Nietzsche was alone with nobody to confide in. Just like Hamlet, he considered suicide. Just like Hamlet, his depression was caused by the man who should have been his Elder but who had betrayed him.

Of course, Hamlet eventually rouses the courage to face Claudius and dies in the subsequent fight. Nietzsche would eventually go into battle against Wagner too, but their fight would not take place in the physical realm but on the ground that was familiar to both: the world of words, ideas, and books. Would Nietzsche "die" as a result of this? Well, consider that two of his last five books, all of which were written in the incredible six-month period leading up to his mental breakdown, were on the subject of Wagner. The very last work he ever wrote, which he put together just days before the end, was called *Nietzsche Contra Wagner*. A very strong argument can be made that Nietzsche went mad as a result of the split with Wagner and therefore that his story had the same ending as Hamlet and Brutus, i.e., a tragedy.

But, if we think about it a little deeper, this doesn't really make sense. In the period between the split with Wagner and when he went mad, Nietzsche blossomed into the philosopher considered to be one of the greatest in Western history. An equally solid argument could be made that this was a happy ending, but that would defy the Orphan Story as we have defined it. All the other examples we have found suggest that if the Elder betrays the cause, the Orphan must fail to initiate. Indeed, we saw that Nietzsche really was on that path as he drifted away from Wagnerism and back to his job. How do we resolve this seeming paradox?

Of course, it can easily be argued that all we have here is a new pattern, and since there is no law of the universe that says Orphan Stories must always resolve in the exact way that our template demands, then there is no problem at all. We simply add a new variation to the known list, and we say that, in the case of Nietzsche and Wagner, the Elder betrayed the cause, but the Orphan succeeded anyway. That is the correct way to think about it, but the key point to reiterate here is that the Orphan Story template that we have used is already derived from empirical evidence, including the famous stories and historical events listed towards the beginning of the book. Countless examples follow the template, and not a single one follows this particular variation. Except, that's not entirely true, and this brings us to yet another incredible coincidence in our analysis.

There is one fictional Orphan Story that follows the pattern where the Elder betrays the cause, but the Orphan succeeds anyway. Guess who wrote it? None other than Richard Wagner. That means that Wagner had written a fictional Orphan Story with a unique, seemingly unprecedented, variation that just happened to match the way in which his later relationship with Nietzsche turned out. Of all the "coincidences" in this book, this will be the most astonishing.

The story in question is none other than Wagner's magnum opus: the Ring Cycle. Wagner wrote the libretto to all four operas of the cycle in the same years that he penned his various manifestos, 1849-52. It would take him more than twenty years to complete the musical compositions for the operas, but he made no meaningful change to the story in the years after 1852. This will be a vital fact for our analysis moving forward since, while it was an incredible feat of endurance and determination for Wagner to persevere and finally stage the Ring Cycle for the first time in 1876, Wagner had become a very different man between then and when the stories were originally conceived, and because of the way in which he lived through his art, this fact would become a major turning point for both him and Nietzsche.

Entire books have been written analysing the intricate symbolism of the Ring Cycle. There are all kinds of fascinating byways that one can travel down in that respect. What concerns us, however, is the part of the cycle that is an Orphan Story and this revolves around the character who was the original inspiration for the series, Siegfried. In fact, Wagner began with the final opera of the cycle, which deals with Siegfried's death, and then wrote the story in reverse order. It is the third opera, appropriately named *Siegfried*, which is the Orphan Story that deals with Siegfried's coming of age.

Another unique innovation that Wagner makes to the Orphan Story in the Ring Cycle is that he spends the first two operas in the series outlining the backstory of Siegfried's parentage. The second opera of the cycle (*Die Walküre*) is about Siegfried's parents and how they are in an incestuous relationship since they are both children of the god Wotan. We learn at the very beginning of the third opera that Siegfried's mother died in childbirth; hence, he is an Orphan. Since Siegfried's parents were both children of Wotan, it follows that Siegfried is the grandson of the god. We know from the first opera in the series (*Das Rheingold*), that Wotan has been in a long-standing battle against the power-hungry Nibelungen. The third opera also introduces the Nibelung into the story since Siegfried has been raised by one called Mime. But Mime has not been acting out of the goodness of his heart. The reason he has kept Siegfried alive is because he plans to use him to kill the dragon Fafner and seize the ring of power that is sitting in the dragon's lair.

At the risk of doing an injustice to a wonderfully intricate and complex piece of storytelling, we can see from this brief summary how the details fit onto our Orphan Story template. Siegfried is the Orphan hero. The Shadow Elder is Mime, who represents the bad guys in the story, the Nibelungen. The question then becomes: who is the Elder? It is here that we get our first glimpse of the major innovation that Wagner made. The Elder of the story should be Wotan, who is technically Siegfried's grandfather. However, Wotan has been rendered impotent through the various treaties and obligations he has to follow, which have prevented him from exercising power. Thus, he cannot take the ring of power himself; he can only try to prevent the Nibelungen from getting it. By the time of the third opera in the series, Wotan has even given up on that idea. That is why he has allowed his own grandson, Siegfried, to be raised by a Nibelung.

By itself, this dynamic is not entirely novel because it's the same setup we see in Shakespeare's *Hamlet*. Hamlet has also been raised by corrupt Elders in Claudius and Polonius. He is also left to fend for himself without receiving any kind of initiation. Thus, Wagner's *Siegfried* could be seen as directly analogous to *Hamlet*, in which case we would expect to have a tragic ending to the story. And this is the major innovation that Wagner makes. Despite having everything against him, Siegfried will win the day. Wagner sets up all the elements of a tragic Orphan Story but flips the script by having his hero come out victorious. Siegfried still meets a tragic ending in the fourth opera of the series (*Götterdämmerung*), but that opera is not an Orphan Story. Thus, with the third opera in the cycle, Wagner had created a brand-new form of Orphan Story where the Orphan hero overcomes a corrupt Elder and wins the day.

All this might sound like intellectual hair-splitting that could only be of interest to literary critics, but we have to remember that Wagner rejected the idea that art was a frivolous luxury. He used his operas as an exploration for what he believed to be the most important questions of human existence. The Ring Cycle has all kinds of fascinating theological, philosophical, and political implications as a result. That's also why the specific innovation he made in the Orphan Story structure maps back to his larger worldview.

Remember, the Orphan Story is first and foremost about initiation. When Hamlet meets his tragic end, it's because he has had nobody to initiate him. The two men who were supposed to do the job betrayed him instead. That's exactly the situation that Siegfried is in. But Siegfried has been doubly betrayed. Hamlet's father was killed by the Shadow Elder. He had an excuse not to be there for his son. In Wagner's opera, the man who should be the Elder and protector (Wotan) has allowed the Orphan hero to fall into the hands of the Shadow Elder by deliberately not intervening. Why? Because Wotan believes that the world can only be redeemed by a child of nature who is fearless and free. To initiate the Orphan would be self-defeating. Thus, the entire premise of the Ring Cycle is actually a negation of the whole idea of initiation. This idea did not come out of nowhere. It was a core theme of the Romantic movement, which held that civilisation was inherently corrupt. Therefore, we can say that the Ring Cycle is a true expression of the Romantic ideal which Wagner and others held.

PART 2: THE ORPHAN STORY OF NIETZSCHE AND WAGNER

In relation to the Orphan Story template, two major innovations follow from this idea. The first comes in Step 7, where the Elder is normally supposed to sacrifice himself for the cause. In the Ring Cycle, Wotan will not do that because he no longer believes in the cause. He has become cynical and bitter. That's why he stayed out of the fray and left Siegfried to his own devices. What will happen in Step 7 instead is that Siegfried will defeat the Shadow Elder, Mime. That is already surprising enough, but it is what happens in Step 8 that is truly radical. The final showdown is no longer between the Orphan and the Shadow Elder but the Orphan and the Elder. Siegfried confronts Wotan and breaks his spear, signalling the end of his authority. Siegfried defeats the man who should have been his Elder but who betrayed him. It's an almost identical story to *Hamlet* except that Siegfried wins.

At the time when Wagner wrote this, he almost certainly based the story on himself and the other revolutionaries who were battling against what they saw as the corrupt and senile elite that was holding back the glorious revolution that would usher in a new era of Western culture. The young revolutionaries were in the role of Siegfried, and the corrupt old guard was Wotan. Twenty-five years later, however, the roles had changed. Wagner was no longer a revolutionary. He had become part of the establishment. That was what had been consecrated in Bayreuth, but the process had already begun a couple of years earlier when the tide suddenly changed and Wagner went from being a controversial figure to being eagerly adopted by the growing tide of German nationalism. The parallels between real life and the opera are even more direct than that, however, since Wagner, just like Wotan, had twisted himself into knots by a variety of deals and treaties in order to get the Bayreuth premiere on stage. He had needed to forge allegiances with people he despised. He really had become Wotan.

All that would be incredible enough. But something else had happened in the years leading up to this. A new Siegfried had arrived on the scene: Nietzsche. Two coincidences that occurred at the beginning of the relationship between Wagner and Nietzsche seem custom designed to reinforce this reading. What was Wagner doing when Nietzsche made his very first visit to Tribschen? He was upstairs composing the music for the opera *Siegfried*.

What happened only weeks later on Nietzsche's first overnight stay? Cosima gave birth to Wagner's first male child. His name? Siegfried. One of Wagner's most famous musical innovations was his use of the *leitmotif*, a musical theme that signified a specific character. It was as if the *leitmotif* of Siegfried was playing in the background when Nietzsche arrived in Tribschen.

Seven years after that initial meeting, after a two-and-a-half-year absence from Bayreuth, Nietzsche arrived for the premiere of the Ring Cycle. It was the first time that the opera *Siegfried* would ever be staged, the culmination of twenty-five years of determination and struggle on Wagner's part. What did Nietzsche realise? He realised that Wagner had become Wotan. Wagner was now the corrupt older man working for the establishment. He also realised what he had probably always known deep down, that Wagner had betrayed him in 1874. We have already seen that the Orphan Story of Nietzsche and Wagner had been inverted at Step 7. This exactly mirrors the inversions that Wagner wrote into the Ring Cycle twenty-five years earlier. Siegfried responds to the betrayal of Wotan in the story by going into battle against him in Step 8. That is exactly what Nietzsche would do in the aftermath of Bayreuth. He would go into battle against Wagner. In short, the inversions we have found in the Orphan Story of Nietzsche and Wagner followed the exact pattern Wagner created decades earlier when he wrote the Ring Cycle. Life was now imitating art.

* * *

Although there are clear parallels between the real-life story of Nietzsche and the fictional one of Siegfried, the equivalence is not exact. In fact, the journey Nietzsche had to go through in real life was far more difficult than that of his fictional counterpart, who, as a child of nature, simply doesn't understand the broader context of his life. He doesn't know that Wotan is his grandfather, and even when the two of them meet, Wotan is in disguise. Thus, although it's correct to say that Siegfried fights his Elder, he doesn't know that he is doing it. For Wagner, that ignorance was an important part of Siegfried's strength. It was an ignorance that would be denied to Nietzsche, however, and that is why his journey is perhaps closest to that of Brutus in that he had to realise that his own Elder had betrayed him. Just like Brutus, Nietzsche really had received an intense and profound initiation from Wagner, an initiation that was cut short before its proper end.

It took Nietzsche two years to come to terms with what had happened, and even then, we see him trying to avoid the unpleasant conclusion. That is what explains the most unique part of Nietzsche's journey, which is the fact that he wrote a hagiography of Wagner before Wagner was even dead. This has no precedent in any of the other Orphan Stories we have covered, either fictional or real. The disciples of Jesus created the story of his life (which would later be put down in written form in the New Testament) after he had died. Similarly, all of Plato's writings came after the death of Socrates. It's an interesting question whether the Platonic dialogues count as hagiographies. However, it is clear that Socrates is heavily idealised in that he represents an almost omniscient figure who always carries the day against his interlocutors. There is not a single Platonic dialogue where Socrates turns to one of the others and says something like, "That's a good point, Thrasymachus. I'd never thought about it that way." Both Socrates and Jesus are presented as perfect figures. Their stories were written by the disciple(s) as idealised accounts of the master.

Nietzsche had already dabbled in this form of idealisation in his earlier writings, but it would reach a peak of perfection with *Richard Wagner in Bayreuth*. The work is both a summation of Wagner's life and a glistening reflection on the meaning of his work and the artistic achievements he had engendered. It is a brilliant and highly polished piece of writing. Nietzsche would later take up the aphoristic style for which he is best known, but, in his earlier writings, we see the skills of the man who was one of the most promising scholars of his day. He knew perfectly well how to write a reasoned, logical argument. *Richard Wagner in Bayreuth* has a beautiful symmetry and proportion in its presentation. It flows swiftly and makes its points effortlessly and eloquently.

What makes the book a hagiography is the fact that there is not a single word spoken against Wagner or the Wagnerian cause. The minor criticisms that are made are not even framed as such. For example, of Wagner's notoriously poor prose style, Nietzsche politely notes it but says that it comes from an excess of feeling, something which was notably lacking in the scholarship of the day. Thus, he manages to turn even Wagner's vices into virtues. What Nietzsche achieves with *Richard Wagner in Bayreuth* is to present an overview of Wagner's own beliefs and arguments back to him in the form of a beautifully proportioned piece of writing. He smooths over the contradictions in Wagner's ideas, including that between the artist-as-genius and the notion that art can only ever come from a *Volk*. As Nietzsche explains it, both the genius and the Volk are required. Without an educated and understanding group to bear witness, whatever a great man does cannot be great because it cannot be understood. Not only is this a true observation in itself, but it is especially poignant when we consider that Nietzsche would spend most of the rest of his life without an audience and would suffer greatly from the fact.

As of 1876, however, Nietzsche still had the Wagnerians as an audience, and it is clear that the hagiography is just as much dedicated to them as to the master. In this respect, the constant use of religious terminology throughout the work is noteworthy. For example, "And as for us, the disciples of this revived art, we shall have time and inclination for thoughtfulness, deep thoughtfulness." Meanwhile, Wagner himself is characterised as being guided and watched over by a quasi-religious spirit: "It seems as if from that time forward the spirit of music spoke to him with an unprecedented spiritual charm." Nietzsche finishes the book by noting that Wagner's art will only be truly understood by the next generation, which is perfectly in keeping with the idea of *Zukunftsmusik* (future music).

One of the main purposes of a hagiography is to convey the teachings of the master in their most ideal form. That is what Plato does for Socrates and what the disciples did for Jesus. Even though it seems certain that Nietzsche was writing *Richard Wagner in Bayreuth* with the best of intentions and probably in order to boost his own morale during an incredibly despairing time in his life, it is quite fitting that he would write the hagiography at the time he did because it would create a separation from Wagner, albeit in a highly spiritualised sense. Wagner was not actually dead, but the ideal form of Wagner was, the one who could still pretend to uphold the beliefs he had advocated for without rampant hypocrisy. Of course, if Nietzsche had paid more attention, he would have seen that Wagner had always been a raging hypocrite. One of the most difficult realisations Nietzsche would have to make in the years ahead is how blind he had been about realities that were right in front of his nose in the preceding seven years.

In the lead-up to Bayreuth, however, we see once again the pattern that has repeated time and again throughout our story, which is that Nietzsche knew something big was happening; he felt it in the Dionysian sense, but he had not yet understood it consciously. At some level, he knew that it was highly inappropriate to write a hagiography of somebody who was still alive. When he sent the finished book to Wagner and Cosima, he wrote three separate letters in the space of two days trying to clarify what it was all about. In the first of them, he writes:-

> *"Here, most beloved master, is a kind of Bayreuth festival sermon. I couldn't keep my mouth shut and had to say more. For those who are rejoicing now, I will certainly have increased the joy—that is my pride and my confidence today. How you yourselves will receive these confessions, I cannot guess at this time."*

"Confessions", "sermons", ""rejoicing"—the religious terminology is all perfectly fitting and reveals that Nietzsche knew the work was somewhat unseemly. He acknowledges this more directly in the next letter:-

> *"This time, all I can do is ask you: read this work as if it were not about you and as if it were not about me. Actually, it is not good to speak among the living about this work in the manner I have dared to do: it is something for the underworld."*

"It is something for the underworld." In Jungian terms, we might say it is something for the unconscious. In terms of our Orphan Story template, we say that it is an inversion. The hagiography is supposed to follow the death of the master. Step 7 is supposed to come before Step 8. In reality, however, Nietzsche had already begun to separate himself from Wagner. When he wrote the book, he hadn't met Wagner in person for two years. They would only ever meet twice more in their lives, once in Bayreuth and then again in Italy later in the year. Wagner had not actually died, but he was symbolically dead to Nietzsche, and the act of writing the hagiography can be seen as Nietzsche separating the ideal Wagner from the real one, the one who had become corrupt. And that is actually the role of the foremost disciple, namely, to set down for posterity the best possible version of the master's beliefs.

We should be clear, however, that the ideal that Nietzsche had built up around Wagner and Wagnerian art in the preceding years had not been done alone. It was co-created with Wagner through a direct personal relationship of the most intimate kind that lasted almost three years and which took place entirely at Tribschen. It should not be in the least surprising to find that Nietzsche understood that ideal better than Wagner because Wagner was living it out, and Nietzsche, although involved, was mostly an observer. Again, that is the role of the disciple. He is the audience to the great man. The foremost disciple is the one who understands best. Nietzsche really did understand best. No other Wagnerian could have written *Richard Wagner in Bayreuth*, not even Cosima.

But the reason that the death of the Elder is such a crucial part of the Orphan Story is because it requires the disciple to no longer be a member of the audience but to become the lead character. If that does not happen, the disciple is forever stuck in a subordinate role. It was this that was pressing on Nietzsche, not in his conscious mind, but in the "underworld". What Nietzsche was going to do in Bayreuth was to be part of the audience. That is the role of the disciple. But the story should now have been at the point where the disciple steps up to a leadership position. Nietzsche was not doing that. If anything, he had been demoted since the size of the audience now included seemingly the entire establishment of the German Reich, and Nietzsche was no longer in a lead role but just one of the mob.

Wagner's betrayal was partly about his own ego. Rather than hand over the reins to the next generation, he stayed on to fulfil his own desires and his own program. He was still the leader. In fact, he had become even more of a leader since he had needed to take on the monumental task of organising almost everything for the premiere. In doing so, he had left Nietzsche with nothing to do except show up and be just another member of an audience which was not even the educated audience that Nietzsche had dreamed of in *Richard Wagner in Bayreuth*; rather, it was full of people who would never understand the true meaning of Wagner's art and who, until a couple of years beforehand, would never have dreamed of attending a Wagner opera in the first place.

By his own admission, the happiest days of Nietzsche's life were spent in Tribschen with just him, Wagner, and Cosima. But this intimate, personal connection had been slowly falling apart ever since Wagner had moved to Bayreuth in 1872. It deteriorated further in 1874 with Wagner's betrayal and then Nietzsche's more than two-year absence. Nietzsche might have hoped that things could be patched up when he arrived in Bayreuth, like the prodigal son returning from exile. Perhaps that was another reason he wrote the hagiography, so that nobody could accuse him of not contributing anything to the occasion. But any dreams that it was going to be alright quickly evaporated when the extreme idealism of *Richard Wagner in Bayreuth* met the actual reality of Richard Wagner in Bayreuth.

Nietzsche arrived in the final week of July, just in time for the last rehearsals ahead of the premiere. What did he find? It was the exact opposite of the idyllic solitude of Lake Lucerne with the majestic Swiss Alps in the distance. There were people everywhere. The whole town was abuzz at the news that King Ludwig would be arriving shortly. Meanwhile, the Emperor of the new German Reich, Wilhelm I, would also be there in time for the premiere. We need only imagine how the local dignitaries and townsfolk of Bayreuth were scurrying around all over the place organising the appropriate fanfare for the arrival of the leaders of the country. Meanwhile, at the *Festspielhaus* itself, people without the slightest interest or understanding of Wagner's art were hovering around waiting for their chance to spot the king or shake hands with the emperor and his retinue.

For his part, Wagner was furiously preoccupied with ironing out the last kinks in the show during the rehearsals, and Cosima was run off her feet with hostess duties. Even assuming that she was not harbouring a great deal of resentment towards the man who had been absent for so long (she certainly was), she could only have given the most cursory attention to Nietzsche. With neither Wagner nor Cosima available, Nietzsche might still have found solace in the two men with whom he had shared so many of his intimate thoughts about Wagnerism over the preceding years. But even here, he was out of luck. Both Rohde and Gersdorff had fallen in love and brought their sweethearts with them to Bayreuth. They were talking about marriage, which could only have reminded Nietzsche of his absurdly clumsy proposal to a woman he barely knew just months earlier. Nietzsche's sister could have been his final consolation, but she wasn't due to arrive until just before the main show. As if all that wasn't bad enough, there were the rehearsals themselves, which revealed all of the shortcomings in the sets and props, the inevitable mistakes, an apparent mismatch between the singers and the orchestra, and so on. Among a throng of people, Nietzsche somehow found himself completely alone, the only person who knew the difference between what should have been and what was.

Another guest who was present during this time commented that Nietzsche carried a strange look about him, something resembling melancholy. Nietzsche's version of events is that he was overcome by nausea. At first, he tried retiring to his accommodation and using illness as an excuse to avoid the festivities. Word got back to him that Wagner had noted his absence and believed that he was deliberately making himself scarce. The master had never tolerated such anomalies in the past, and he certainly wasn't going to put up with them on this grand occasion. At that point, Nietzsche made the decision to leave Bayreuth altogether. Crucially, he did not tell the master directly. He did not say goodbye to anybody in person. He sent a telegram saying that he was too ill to stay and then disappeared.

* * *

PART 2: THE ORPHAN STORY OF NIETZSCHE AND WAGNER

For once, we no longer need to rely on Nietzsche's private correspondence to understand what he was feeling during his short stay in Bayreuth. In *Ecce Homo* (published in 1888), he remembers it as follows:-

> "This book was begun during the first musical festival at Bayreuth; a feeling of profound strangeness towards everything that surrounded me there is one of its first conditions. He who has any notion of the visions which even at that time had flitted across my path will be able to guess what I felt when one day I came to my senses in Bayreuth. It was just as if I had been dreaming. Where on earth was I? I recognised nothing that I saw; I scarcely recognised Wagner. It was in vain that I called up reminiscences. Tribschen—remote island of bliss: not the shadow of a resemblance! The incomparable days devoted to the laying of the first stone, the small group of the initiated who celebrated them, and who were far from lacking fingers for the handling of delicate things: not the shadow of a resemblance!"

Note here Nietzsche's references to Tribschen and the laying of the foundation stone and also the "small group of the initiated" that he remembered in that connection. This passage confirms that Nietzsche had no idea what was coming when he arrived in Bayreuth for the first time in more than two years. The shock between the ideal he had so eloquently described in *Richard Wagner in Bayreuth* and what he saw with his own eyes became one of the main themes in Nietzsche's subsequent philosophy as he railed against "idealism". We also shouldn't discount the extent to which this episode really did form the basis of his philosophy. If we accept that all philosophy begins with the realisation of error, then the size and magnitude of the "error" that Nietzsche confronted in Bayreuth was truly enormous. He now needed to revaluate the entire previous seven years of his life, the whole relationship with Wagner, and the whole nature of Wagnerian art.

The extraordinary thing is that this revaluation began immediately in a very literal sense. Nietzsche left Bayreuth and took up lodgings in a remote cabin in the Bavarian forest. We know from his notebooks that have been retained for posterity that he then began writing the set of ideas that would later appear in what is considered his first book of mature philosophy, *Human, All Too Human*. The poetic symbolism of this is something even as great a storyteller as Wagner would have admired. When Nietzsche first visited Tribschen, Wagner was composing the music for the opera Siegfried. Now, while that very same music was being performed in public for the first time in Bayreuth, Nietzsche was not there to enjoy it but was sitting alone in the Bavarian forest doing exactly what Siegfried does in the third opera of the Ring Cycle: going into battle against his Elder. The inversion that Wagner made in the Orphan Story twenty-five years prior was now playing out in his own life. His public triumph mirrored but also hid the private reality.

Another poetic aspect of this was that Nietzsche really was inverting many of the ideas that he had so beautifully enunciated just months earlier. To take just some of the more obvious examples, Nietzsche had always believed in the idea that Wagner's was the music of the future, and he had ended *Richard Wagner in Bayreuth* on exactly that theme. Now, he began to describe Wagner as an end, not a beginning. Music, he said, is always the final development in cultural movements. It arrives as their overripe fruit (a favourite metaphor in Nietzsche's mature philosophy). Wagner no longer symbolised a bright future for German culture but the end of an era. A second inversion that Nietzsche was now formulating was on the question of gender. He had always described Wagner's music as "manly". Now, it had become feminised. Related to this were other qualities such as softness, moodiness, and over-sensitivity. Wagner's music had previously been for the brave and strong-spirited. Now, it was for the weak and decadent seeking escape from a world that they did not have the energy to face directly. Nietzsche had once lionised the Artist-as-genius and placed them above the scholars and scientists as the true leaders of culture. Now, Nietzsche brought into question both the existence of genius and the position of the artist, who becomes nothing more than a peddler of illusions as opposed to the clear truths of science. It was these ideas that Nietzsche was writing down in his notebooks at the exact same time that the premiere of the Ring Cycle was taking place. While Siegfried was going into battle against Wotan on the stage of the Festspielhaus, Nietzsche was sharpening his own sword to later wield against the master.

For analysts who have not grasped the true meaning of the Nietzsche-Wagner relationship, and especially its importance in the creation of Nietzsche as a philosopher, all of this presents a huge problem. If you stick to the published works and take them at face value, how could you explain the complete inversions that suddenly occur in Nietzsche's position? One of the most common explanations to solve the paradox is one we alluded to at the start of the book. You simply say that, to use the phrase of Hollingdale, Nietzsche's earlier writings were a "false start". With this rhetorical trick, the analyst has full licence to simply ignore the early works and therefore the contradictions they contain. Any inconsistencies that emerge are perfectly acceptable and can be explained away by the fact that Nietzsche simply didn't know what he was doing. The source of truth then becomes the later works, and since they present a consistent critique of Wagner, all inconsistencies are squared away nicely.

The trouble with this trick is that it glosses over what should be a major question in any Nietzsche analysis. How could it be that he completely changed his viewpoint between early 1876 and later the same year? What exactly happened to bring this about? From a third-person objective point of view, there is no explanation. There were no harsh words said between him and Wagner. There was no argument or public falling out of any kind. Even their correspondence showed no animosity. If we want to say that Nietzsche simply changed his mind about Wagner's art, fine, but on what basis did he do that? After all, Wagner's art had not changed one little bit. There was nothing radical about the performances in Bayreuth. They were a true representation of Wagner's vision for opera. Nietzsche is perfectly entitled to change his opinion, but aren't we entitled to know on what basis that opinion was formed and therefore why it changed? All of these fundamental questions are just washed away by the idea that all of Nietzsche's beliefs prior to and including 1876 were simply wrong; he realised the error of his ways and went on to correct the record without bothering to explain why.

Of course, Nietzsche never explained his positions in the first place; he just asserted them. In this respect, he really was the student of Wagner since that is the approach that the composer had always taken in his life. The reason why Nietzsche had such a falling out with the philological community in the aftermath of *The Birth of Tragedy* was precisely because he had borrowed Wagner's approach of asserting things rather than proving them via evidence and argumentation. All of his published works follow this style, both early and late. One of the results is that when Nietzsche stops asserting X and instead asserts the opposite of X, it is never clear on what grounds he is doing so, and we are left to try and figure it out for ourselves. The "false start" explanation is one attempt to try and explain the inversions in Nietzsche's thinking. It is one way to erase contradictions that seem otherwise incommensurable.

Because we have now found the true reason for Nietzsche's change of heart, we understand those contradictions. More importantly, though, this also allows us to see the continuity that exists between his earlier and later writings. One of these properties is the one we just mentioned, where Nietzsche simply asserts things to be true. Related to this is the bombastic and belligerent tone he always favoured. There was nothing in Nietzsche's formal education that taught him this. He learned it from Wagner. Thus, several of the core features of Nietzsche's mature writing style arose directly from the Orphan-Elder relationship he was in with the composer.

This was achieved because all of Nietzsche's writing prior to and including 1876 was born out of the Orphan-Elder relationship with Wagner. Nietzsche was not just writing the earlier works for himself; he was also writing them for Wagner and the Wagnerians. Right from the beginning of the Tribschen days, he had presented his ideas and lectures to Wagner and Cosima. He gave them as Christmas and birthday presents, and he eagerly awaited the feedback he received. This was Nietzsche's initiation into a new way of thinking and writing. That is what he meant when he wrote in his letters that he was "learning many things" from Wagner.

The initiation first came to public fruition when Wagner provided both the moral and logistical support to have *The Birth of Tragedy* published. It is absolutely clear that, without Wagner, that work would never have seen the light of day. Even assuming Nietzsche could have written it without Wagner's intellectual support, the professional philologists, including and especially Ritschl, would never have allowed it to be printed through scholarly publishing houses because it simply didn't follow the rules of the discipline. Instead, it followed the rules of Wagner, i.e., a style of thinking and writing based on asserting things in a creative fashion. It is impossible to write off these early years as a "false start" because, without them, Nietzsche would never have become the philosopher we know. Instead, he might have been hanging around in Paris with Rohde, studying chemistry, getting married, or doing anything else. It should now be clear that it was Wagner who guided him to the path, and therefore it was Wagner who educated and mentored the philosopher that Western history regards as one of its greatest.

In return, Nietzsche had to alter his work to serve the interests of the master. That is a perfectly normal part of the Orphan-Elder relationship. Nietzsche had become a Wagnerian, and it is only natural that he should support the cause. Thus, for all of the books that he wrote during the *Wagner years*, we find a mixture of motivations. He was partly exploring his own ideas, partly writing to please the master, and partly writing to glorify the Wagnerian cause. Some of the works had a more specific purpose. For example, the David Strauss essay was written during the darkest days of the financial crisis in Bayreuth when it seemed like all was lost. Nietzsche wrote the work to lift Wagner's spirits, and the minor controversy it caused in the public discourse also helped Wagnerism to a small degree. Similarly, the later essay on Schopenhauer was obviously tailored to the master's interests, even though the content of the essay foreshadowed the more personal writing style that Nietzsche would adopt later. Finally, it is clear that *Richard Wagner in Bayreuth* was written to appeal to the master and the Wagnerians who were about to gather for the momentous event that was the premiere of the Ring Cycle. Nietzsche was not just writing for himself; he was writing for an audience.

And this is another key point: Nietzsche had an audience in the first place due to Wagner's influence. Wagner told his printer to publish Nietzsche's works. He then actively promoted them to his friends and acquaintances.

When we consider the kinds of people that Wagner knew, it should not surprise us that this made a real difference to Nietzsche's prospects. He was receiving praise and acclaim from an influential and accomplished group of people. This earned him a public reputation, which later opened the door for him to become a philosopher because he could trade on the notoriety he had gained from his association with Wagner. In all of these ways, Wagner lifted Nietzsche up and made it possible for him to become the great philosopher who is still widely read to this day.

All of this needs to be reiterated because Nietzsche's overt criticism of Wagner, which became more and more vehement in his later philosophy, has led seemingly all commentators and readers astray. It's not hard to see why. It has taken us an entire book to lay out the groundwork for understanding the relationship between him and Wagner, and even then, we have seen that the Orphan Story between the two men took on a unique form. To grasp all of this, we have had to understand the Orphan Story as a structure. We have had to accept the possibility that this structure exists in the real world and not just the fictional one. We have had to see that the relationship between Nietzsche and Wagner fitted that structure perfectly. And, finally, we have had to see both how Wagner's betrayal inverted the structure and how Nietzsche responded in an identical fashion to Siegfried in the Ring Cycle by going into battle against the corrupt Elder.

Step 8 of the Orphan Story is normally: *The hero faces the Shadow Elder alone.* The meaning of this step is that the Orphan hero is now on their own, and they must make the courageous effort to live up to the example that has been set for them by the master. In the case where the master has died, this is relatively straightforward since the Orphan can fill the space left behind and continue the work in a direct fashion. That is what Plato did as he took over from Socrates. It is also what the disciples of Jesus did. In the story of Nietzsche, we have two problems in this respect. Firstly, Wagner was not dead. Secondly, even if he was, Nietzsche could never have filled his shoes anyway since he was not an opera composer (even though Wagner had once jokingly suggested that he write an opera). However, it should now be clear that what Nietzsche had learned from Wagner was a style of writing and thinking, and it was this style which Nietzsche now manifested to the fullest extent. More importantly, he could do that whether Wagner was dead or not. Thus, Nietzsche would turn the bombastic, belligerent, and rebellious style of writing against Wagner himself. He would go into battle, only it was against the Elder.

The other property of Step 8 of the Orphan Story is encapsulated in that little word "alone". Only when there is nobody else to rely on can the hero truly prove what they are capable of. But this is also the sternest test of character there is. Nietzsche received an extra bitter dose of this medicine because he found himself alone right in the middle of the promised land in Bayreuth. At what should have been the moment of triumph, he was thrown into despair. This would set the tone for the rest of his life. If Nietzsche was going to go into battle against the master, then it followed that he was also going to have to fight the Wagnerians. All of the people he had considered his closest friends would now become his enemies. Unlike Brutus, he would not even have co-conspirators to share the workload with. The pathway he would now have to walk led directly to the point where we know that he ended up, i.e., as a philosopher-hermit. That was the choice that Nietzsche made by going into battle against Wagner.

The irony of it is that, whereas modern readers begin with Nietzsche's mature writing and, through them, completely misunderstand his earlier works, it was the exact other way around for his contemporaries. What they could never understand is how the man who was Wagner's favourite and who had sung the composer's praises to the heavens more eloquently than anybody else could suddenly and inexplicably become an outspoken critic. Not only that, Nietzsche did this at just the same time that the rest of Germany had decided that Wagner was the bee's knees. For modern readers, Nietzsche went insane in 1889. For his contemporaries, he went mad in 1878, and many wondered whether his "illness" wasn't more mental than physical in nature.

Of course, there were other explanations that people found to explain Nietzsche's sudden about-face. What most of the Wagnerians saw was that Nietzsche had betrayed the cause. That is a final bitter irony that he had to deal with because he was the only one who had grasped that Wagner was the real betrayer. When he pointed this out, all that happened was that he was accused of the same. Is it any wonder that Nietzsche's critique of Wagnerism would become more and more shrill in his later writings as the cult of Wagner continued to grow and morph into something even more unrecognisable than it was in Bayreuth? Nietzsche had to sit back and watch that happen while his own writings fell on deaf ears. He may have become a philosopher-hermit, but Nietzsche still deeply cared about art, culture, and truth, and he hoped that people would read his works and understand. But very few did, and most completely misunderstood. This gives new poignancy to the famous scene in Zarathustra where the "madman" runs around the marketplace declaring "God is dead," and all the people can do is point and laugh. Nietzsche would fight the final battle against Wagner with the weapons that he knew best: words, ideas, and books. But, of course, almost nobody read them during his sane years, and it was only when he went insane that his popularity started to rise. It's an irony that Nietzsche would have appreciated that he had to go mad before people would finally take him seriously.

* * *

As with every other major turning point in our story, the manifestation of Step 8 occurred entirely in the esoteric realm in the first instance and only gradually made its presence felt in the exoteric world. The official story about Nietzsche and Bayreuth was that he had suffered the same kind of illness that had been plaguing him for years, and, given most of the Wagnerians knew about his troubles, this made sense to them, and they thought no more about the matter. Similarly, there are no entries in Cosima's diary to indicate that she had taken offence. She had been too busy trying to manage the chaos around her to worry about Nietzsche and perhaps even felt relieved that the sight of his melancholic visage was no longer there to darken an otherwise successful occasion. Of all the people who had an excuse not to have paid much attention to Nietzsche's absence, Wagner had to be at the top of the list given the intense workload he was under in the lead-up to the premiere. But, as we will see shortly, just as Nietzsche was the only one who understood Wagner's betrayal, Wagner was the only one who understood the true meaning behind Nietzsche's need to flee the premiere. Still, as far as the external, objective world was concerned, nothing had changed in the relationship between the two men. On the contrary, the publication of *Richard Wagner in Bayreuth* had re-established Nietzsche as the most eloquent public voice on the nature of Wagner and his art.

The first sign we have of a changed relationship between the two is one that is so subtle that almost nobody would have been able to see it. In any case, it was a private matter because it came in the form of a letter. We have already noted several times that Nietzsche had always referred to Wagner as "Meister" in his correspondence. A prime example of that comes from the letter he sent in July 1876, just before the Bayreuth festival, where he addresses Wagner as "most beloved master". That is the form in which Nietzsche had written to Wagner for seven straight years. Now, the very first time he wrote to him after Bayreuth, Nietzsche would address Wagner as "friend" (specifically, in German, *Hochverehrter Freund*). If Wagner had not yet managed to understand what Nietzsche's absence from Bayreuth entailed, this was his second big clue as to what was brewing inside the younger man. The irony was one that Nietzsche would have appreciated. The first time he ever called Wagner his friend was when he now considered him his enemy.

It shouldn't surprise us by now that the next important event in the relationship would take the form of a coincidence. Earlier in the year, Nietzsche had petitioned his employer at the University of Basel to allow him a twelve-month absence so that he might do some travelling. The letter itself is interesting because Nietzsche references the early age at which he started his professorship and connects this with his recent bouts of illness, suggesting that he had been overworked and that a long trip away would help to restore his health. In any case, the leave was granted, and Nietzsche wrote to one of his closest fellow Wagnerians, Malwida von Meysenbug, to confirm that he would stay at her villa in Sorrento, Italy.

Little did Meysenbug or anybody else know that what Nietzsche would end up doing with this time was to turn the notebooks that he had started writing while the Bayreuth Festival was in full swing into his first work of philosophy,

Human, All Too Human. When it was published in early 1878, it would be this book which signalled to the world that Nietzsche had broken with Wagner. He wrote it while staying at the villa of one of the most devoted Wagnerians. As if that wasn't enough, Wagner and Cosima had decided to take a trip to Italy in the aftermath of Bayreuth, and where else should they decide to make a stop except the home of one of their closest friends.

In the end, their visit lasted just a few short days, and there is no indication of any overt unpleasantness. On the contrary, Wagner and Nietzsche took several long walks together. It was the first time Wagner gave the younger man details about his latest project, which would turn into his final opera, *Parsifal*. Although Wagner had been toying with the concept for decades, he had begun work on what would become the final version of the libretto in the immediate aftermath of the Bayreuth festivities. He told Nietzsche he was doing it for the money. The Bayreuth premiere had been a financial failure, and Wagner had promised to deliver *Parsifal* to Ludwig as a way to ease the king's anger over the situation. All of this could only have played to Nietzsche's new conclusion that Wagner had sold out and given up his artistic integrity. But, as we will see shortly, *Parsifal* was perhaps his most brilliant work. It's fitting that, in their final meeting together, both men had a secret project underway that directly related to the other. We know what *Human, All Too Human* meant for Nietzsche. *Parsifal* contained something equally important for Wagner. The old master storyteller still had a few tricks up his sleeve and one more lesson to teach his disciple.

There is one other occurrence from the Sorrento meeting that is worth relating. It is found in a letter of Cosima's to Malwida von Meysenbug a month or so after she and Wagner had returned to Bayreuth from Italy. Nietzsche's contrarian tendencies, which had always been present to some extent, had shown themselves as a now dominant feature of his personality in Sorrento. With his newfound independence, he had found occasion to speak against some of Wagner's most heartfelt heroes, including Shakespeare. Cosima noted to Malwida:-

> "*I believe there is in Nietzsche a dark productive substratum of which*

> *he himself is unconscious; it is from this that whatever is significant in him springs, but then it alarms him, whereas all he thinks and says, which is brilliantly lit up, is actually of no great value. It is the tellurian element in him that is of importance; the solar element is insignificant and rendered even alarming and unedifying by its conflict with the tellurian."*

This is a brilliant observation and one that Nietzsche probably would not have disagreed with. After all, he was the philosopher who would later associate himself with the Antichrist. But Cosima's astute remark also fits perfectly within our Orphan Story framing and specifically Wagner's betrayal. What had led Nietzsche to embrace the tellurian element? Wagner. Wagner had left him in the lurch back in 1874. Let's remember that Nietzsche had written to Wagner begging him to give him something meaningful to do, and Wagner had responded by saying, essentially, *You're on your own, kid.*

Put into Cosima's terms, Wagner had been the *solar element* which had lit Nietzsche's way for the past seven years. He was the Socrates to Nietzsche's Plato, the Jesus to Nietzsche's Peter. But by not providing a pathway to complete the Orphan Story and allow Nietzsche to graduate into his own solar element, Wagner had ensured that the young man was left in the tellurian. Nietzsche had spent two whole years in the tellurian battling suicidal depression. He had needed to lift himself up out of this miasma. He did so by embracing the tellurian to the fullest extent. And that would be his strategy from that point onwards. Now, there was nothing that he would not criticise: not Shakespeare, not Socrates, not Jesus, and certainly not Wagner. It became the defining feature of his entire philosophy from that point onwards. As he himself put it, he philosophised with a hammer, his weapon of choice in his battle with the Elder.

* * *

In the year or so after the meeting in Italy, Wagner would put the finishing touches on the libretto for *Parsifal* while Nietzsche would do the same with

Human, All Too Human. Nothing further had changed in the public sphere or in the increasingly less frequent letters that were now exchanged between them. It was the calm before the storm, and it may now be getting tedious if we must once again point out that the manner in which the split between the two would become public was consecrated by yet another set of improbable coincidences.

It is clear that Nietzsche had decided that 1878 would be the year to turn over a new leaf. He had completed *Human, All Too Human* while on leave in Italy and had sent it to the printer in late 1877. On the 1st of January 1878, he had the first copies in his hand. On that day, he carried out two highly symbolic acts. We know that he, Wagner, and Cosima had, from the very early days of their relationship, gifted each other their works on major occasions such as birthdays, Easter, and Christmas. The very first people that Nietzsche had sent every one of his published works to thus far in his life had been Wagner and Cosima. It is against this backdrop that we must understand the significance of the fact that, on the 1st of January 1878, Nietzsche gave away two of his personalised scores of Wagner operas, one to Heinrich Köselitz and the other to Paul Wiedemann. The text of the letter to Köselitz gives us some idea of the meaning of the gesture:-

> "This score will be more fruitful in your hands, my dear friend Köselitz, than in mine: it has certainly longed for a more worthy owner and disciple of art than I am, in case something of the soul of the great man who gave it to me remains in it."

The man Nietzsche is referencing in the letter is clearly Wagner, and we barely need to point out that the implication here is that Nietzsche no longer considered himself a "disciple" of Wagner's art and, by extension, Wagner himself. The letter to Wiedemann conveyed a similar sentiment and included a personally signed score of *Die Meistersinger* that Wagner had gifted Nietzsche for Christmas back in the golden days at Tribschen. These symbolic actions were the preliminaries to the major event of the day, which was that Nietzsche sent a copy of *Human, All Too Human* to Wagner. It was to be the very last letter he ever sent to the old master. The first lines read as follows:-

> *"By sending this, I entrust my secret into your and your noble wife's hands and assume that it is now also your secret. This book is mine: I have brought to light my innermost feelings about human affairs in it and, for the first time, explored the periphery of my own thoughts."*

Although Wagner is not mentioned by name at all in the first volume of *Human, All Too Human*, Nietzsche knew there was no chance that both he and Cosima would not understand who and what was meant by the ideas contained therein. To the extent that there was a "secret" involved, it was because only the two of them could have understood the depth of Nietzsche's renunciation. We have to remember, these were people who had spent many a long evening in the Tribschen drawing room discussing all manner of philosophy, art, and whatever else took their fancy. They were people who lived in the realm of ideas and took them with the utmost seriousness. Nietzsche had thrived in an environment where small details and oversights had been picked up and corrected for him. He was taught that nothing in a work should be arbitrary or accidental. This attention to detail was another skill he learned from the master.

Human, All Too Human follows the pattern of contrarian thought that Nietzsche had begun writing in the Bavarian forest in August 1876. Among other things, it contains a renunciation of the idea of the artistic genius, of the hero in general, and of the notion that art could be redemptive in nature. Nietzsche even managed to slip in some mildly derogatory references to Wagner's musical hero, Beethoven. There could be no doubt what all this meant in terms of Nietzsche's continued adherence to Wagnerism. He was now going his own way, and apparently that way involved refuting many of the ideas he and Wagner used to share. As if he already knew what was coming, Wagner declined to read the book initially. The task fell to Cosima, who did not hold back her opinion, writing a scathing indictment of the work to Nietzsche's sister, Elizabeth.

It didn't take long for the other Wagnerians to find out what had happened. Almost immediately, Nietzsche began receiving angry letters from former allies accusing him of being an "ingrate" and worse. Gersdorff and Rohde were among those who shunned him during this time (although they would reconnect many years later). In a letter, Nietzsche wrote of the backlash, "It cannot be helped: I must cause distress to all my friends—precisely by finally speaking out what helped me out of my distress." Later in the same letter, he says, "Now I shake off what doesn't belong to me: people, as friends and enemies, habits, conveniences, and books; I live in solitude for years to come, until I can (and then probably must) interact again, mature and complete, as a philosopher of life." This was incredibly prescient given the lifestyle that Nietzsche would end up leading as a result of his break with Wagnerism.

Wagner would finally get around to reading *Human, All Too Human,* and he poured out his displeasure in an article in a publication called the Bayreuther Blätter. This was a journal that he himself had founded and which was intended to be the preeminent repository of Wagnerian thought. Curiously, the first issue of the paper appeared in February 1878, just one month after he had received Nietzsche's book. It seems highly probable that Wagner had launched the project at the exact time that he knew for sure that he had lost his main intellectual ally. It's not surprising then that the journal would then be used to target Nietzsche later in the year. Nietzsche was not named in Wagner's article, but an obvious pun was made at the title of *Human, All Too Human* lest anybody miss the target of the diatribe. Step 8 of our amended Orphan Story—*the hero battles the Elder*—had finally gone public. Siegfried and Wotan were now at loggerheads.

It's clear that Nietzsche knew that all this was coming, just as he had known what was coming from the philologists six years earlier when *The Birth of Tragedy* was first published. Nevertheless, he could not help but be affected by the vitriol. As he put it in a letter to Overbeck in September 1878:-

> "Much is going on inside me. I have almost only to fend off what is coming from outside. Horrid letters. I've now also read Wagner's bitter, unfortunate polemic against me in the August issue of the Bayreuther

PART 2: THE ORPHAN STORY OF NIETZSCHE AND WAGNER

Blätter: it hurt me, but not where W. wanted it to."

Despite the difficulties, he upped the ante the following year. In the second volume of *Human, All Too Human*, Nietzsche criticised Wagner by name for the first time in print. Wagner would be a mainstay of Nietzsche's cultural critique for the rest of his philosophical career. His battle with the Elder would last for the next ten years before finally ending with his mental breakdown at the start of 1889.

All of this public intellectual brawling was something that Nietzsche had been involved in for a long time and would not have come as a surprise. What must have been a surprise was yet another coincidence that had happened at the start of the year. Just two days after he had posted *Human, All Too Human* to Wagner on the 1st of January, Nietzsche received a package from Wagner in turn. It was clear that the two parcels must have passed each other in transit, and, therefore, there could be no question that Wagner had known about *Human, All Too Human* when he sent his parcel to Nietzsche.

Enclosed with Wagner's letter was the finished libretto to what would become Wagner's final opera, *Parsifal*. In one sense, this would not have been too surprising for Nietzsche since he knew that Wagner had been working on it for more than a year. But Wagner had told him that he was doing it for the money and, as always, to please Ludwig, who was a devoted Christian and was eagerly looking forward to the religious themes that were contained in the medieval version of the story. As if to reinforce this expectation, Wagner signed off the letter containing the libretto "Church Councillor".

As we are about to see, this was only the beginning of a diversionary tactic that Wagner had been using for more than a year. *Parsifal* has almost nothing to do with Christianity, nothing to do with money, and even nothing to do with the original medieval myth from which it is nominally derived. When it was eventually premiered in 1882, the general response from the audience was mystification. Nobody knew what it was about. To this day, it is the most obscure of Wagner's works, and many commentators write it off as a story without a plot that needs to be understood symbolically.

We should know by now that none of this is accidental. Wagner was a master storyteller, and his final opera is perhaps his most brilliant work, even if only from a technical point of view. Overtly, it is his answer to the Ring Cycle and his solution to the weakness which finally brought down his great hero, Siegfried. But this exoteric meaning derives from a stunning depth of esoteric meaning, which was targeted directly at the one man who would be able to understand, the man who had just become his public enemy. *Parsifal* would be Wagner's final lesson to Nietzsche, delivered in the very last piece of correspondence that was ever exchanged between the two men, which, incredibly, it seems that they both placed in the mail on exactly the same day. We have allowed Nietzsche's voice to dominate in this book. To complete our analysis, let's now allow Wagner to speak.

Wagner's Apology

We have not shied away from Wagner's vices in this book. We have called him a narcissist, a bully, and a hypocrite. We have noted that his non-fiction writings were expressed in an infuriatingly cavalier fashion. We have seen multiple examples of his hypocrisy, and we have briefly touched on the fact that Wagner spent most of his life living beyond his means and then doing whatever it took to wriggle out of the consequences. Of course, with such a long list of vices, Wagner must have had an equally impressive number of virtues. Undoubtedly, he had the ability to charm and to inspire. But it was his art that people loved him for, and they forgave him everything else because of it.

This was not just because of the magnificence of Wagner's creations but because he had dedicated his life to art and suffered significantly in its service. In fact, we might even say that all of the vices listed above were in service to art. Even Wagner's proclivity for luxury can be explained this way. Once he had lost his official position in Dresden, he became a kind of freelance artist. But in order to pass himself off as an opera composer, there was a certain archetype he needed to manifest, and that required an appearance of wealth. At a time when opera audiences were drawn entirely from the middle and upper classes of society, who viewed poverty as a symptom of moral failure, it was simply not possible for Wagner to pass as a composer without the right kinds of clothing and accommodation. Similarly, Wagner's bullying and narcissism were also in service to his art, for which he would not tolerate the slightest imperfection.

Therein lies the secret to understanding the man and his appeal because Wagner's art was as good as flawless. We may object to it on aesthetic or intellectual grounds, but almost never on technical ones. Furthermore, what set Wagner apart from every other composer was that his technical mastery was not limited to the domain of music. He was also a master storyteller. His talents extended into all the other peripheral aspects of staging opera, including architecture. The *Festspielhaus* was built to Wagner's specification and was predicated on detailed knowledge of both acoustics and the visual aspects of opera, not to mention the technical aspects of performance such as stage management, prop movements, etc. For Wagner, all these technical questions were subordinate to the unifying meaning of the artwork itself. Since he was the one who determined that meaning, he was also the only one who could truly understand what was required. For some people, that made Wagner a bully and a narcissist. For others, it made him a visionary. What is not in doubt is that Wagner dedicated his life to his craft and was uncompromising in relation to it.

It is Wagner's complete dedication to a form of art where the story was the supreme source of meaning that makes the relationship between him and Nietzsche uniquely relevant for the theme of this book. What we have been doing is interrogating the relationship between Art and Life. The central assumption of our analysis is that there is no difference. We have shown that the structure of a story seems to mirror the structure of reality. Wagner and Nietzsche's relationship was always a story. All we have done in this book is to tell it properly. If we think about this in terms of *cause and effect*, we might say that reality creates stories, and then the storyteller's job is to observe and capture reality in the correct form. That is certainly not the way we are used to thinking about stories in the modern West, but it is implied by our analysis.

A far more challenging possibility that goes against our modern secular materialism is that the causation can be the other way around and stories can create reality. That is the mind-bending idea that follows from the incredible "coincidences" in the relationship between Nietzsche and Wagner and the fact that they map directly to the specific Orphan Story structure that Wagner wrote in the Ring Cycle. Wagner's innovation was to have the Orphan hero go into battle against a corrupt Elder and win. Twenty-five years later, the man who had become an Orphan to Wagner in real life went into battle against Wagner, who was now in the role of corrupt Elder. It's an extraordinary coincidence, but it's the kind of coincidence we have seen time and time again throughout our analysis.

Even more extraordinary is that there is *prima facie* evidence that it was not the first time in Wagner's life that this had happened. For example, Wagner had said that what he was trying to do with his opera *Tristan and Isolde* was to write the most glorious love story he could imagine. He claimed at the time that he had never been in love (the fact that he was married is no necessary contradiction to that assertion). He wrote *Tristan and Isolde* in the late 1850s. Just years later, his affair with Cosima would begin and would be based around the exact same dynamic as the opera, i.e., illicit love between a man and a married woman. There were a number of other coincidences in this respect, such as the fact that Cosima would name the daughter she conceived with Wagner "Isolde" and that her husband, Hans von Bülow, would shortly thereafter be the conductor for the premiere of *Tristan and Isolde*. It would be fascinating to do an in-depth study of the relationship between Wagner and Cosima to see whether these smaller coincidences are part of larger ones, as we have seen in our analysis of the Nietzsche-Wagner relationship.

It is against this backdrop that we must understand the meaning of Nietzsche's somewhat cryptic line from the preface to *The Birth of Tragedy* that art was the supreme metaphysical task of life. Setting aside questions of causality, what Wagner's life seems to show is the boundaries between Art and Life are much less distinct than we assume and maybe don't even exist at all. We have focused on the Apollonian aspects of the matter by basing our work on a structural analysis of the Orphan Story. This has yielded significant insights, but we must also acknowledge the other side of the coin, the esoteric, Dionysian realm. In Wagner's language, this is Feeling (we have also used the concept of the *sacred*).

From the very first, Wagner had demanded that art should incorporate the part of human existence that had been ignored not just by opera but by Western philosophy and culture in general. He asserted that only an art that contained Feeling could be connected to Life and Nature. That was a specifically German idea that had arisen first in the philosophy of Herder and Goethe and the thinkers that followed them, including Wagner. Wagner's art incorporated Feeling, but so did his life. That is why his foremost enemies were always the academics, philistines, and other upstanding members of society who demanded that the rules be followed and the correct behaviour observed at all times. Wagner put as much Feeling into his art as he put into his life, and that is another reason why he won such dedicated support from those who were closest to him.

It follows that Wagner's art always had a personal dimension to it, which he was able to abstract away from by using mythological characters from another age who could not be mistaken for real people in the 19th century. That was another part of the magic because Wagner's use of these archetypes to symbolically represent individuals also meant that he had needed to look beyond the individual and see what was universal and timeless in himself and in those around him. That is why he was able to simultaneously represent issues that were directly relevant to 19th-century Germany even though he was presenting them in forms that came from a different era. This combination of the personal and the universal sits at the heart of the brilliance of his artwork.

Thought about in the terms that Nietzsche would later use, Wagner's art utilised the "mask". It created surface forms that were exotic and enormous and which spanned centuries of Western culture. Nevertheless, he imbued these forms with the most intimate personal details. This is one of the most important things that Nietzsche learned from Wagner. It is an approach he would use brilliantly in his mature philosophy, where he places outrageous claims that he has no right to make alongside the most poignant and intimate revelations. But Nietzsche learned that from Wagner not just in a theoretical but in an empirical fashion because he could contrast the intimate discussions that took place in the Tribschen drawing room against the interpretations published in the press. It became a favourite game for Nietzsche, Wagner, and Cosima to find the most ridiculous things that were written about Wagner and have a good laugh about them. Wagner's life and character were misunderstood just as much as his art. It is this that we must bear in mind as we turn to what is certainly Wagner's most misunderstood piece of art, his final opera, *Parsifal*. As we will see, Wagner invited that misunderstanding very much on purpose.

On the surface, *Parsifal* was the same kind of thing Wagner had been doing for his whole career: adapting a famous medieval myth. The character of Parsifal belongs to the larger collection of stories about the knights of the Holy Grail. The best-known version of the story in Germany was the 12th-century epic written by Wolfram von Eschenbach called *Parzival*. Wagner had already adapted one of the Arthurian tales for his earlier opera *Lohengrin*. Nominally, he was retreading old ground. But it should now be clear that Wagner had always used the medieval stories as a quarry for his own purposes and had taken whatever liberties he needed with the source material to convey a new set of meanings. Having said that, *Parsifal* would be his most radical departure from the source material. In fact, for all intents and purposes, we can treat Wagner's *Parsifal* as an entirely original story that just happens to use the characters from the medieval tale. More specifically, Wagner chose to focus in on just one part of Eschenbach's sprawling epic, and it should be no surprise to us that the part of the myth he borrowed was the relationship between the young hero and the older man who initiates him as a knight of the Grail. Yet again, Wagner had chosen to write an Orphan Story.

It is our first major clue as to what Wagner was doing with *Parsifal* that he uses the same unique inversion he made in *Siegfried* whereby the hero defeats the Shadow Elder in Step 7 of the story instead of Step 8. But there are numerous other correspondences which make the comparison with the third opera of the Ring Cycle clear. Firstly, just like Siegfried, Parsifal is a child of nature, raised in the forest, who will come of age into a society that cannot offer him a positive initiation but one that is corrupted in various ways. For Siegfried, the corruption was inherent in his parents and in the man who had raised him, Mime. For Parsifal, it will be the knights of the Grail who are corrupt. Another correspondence is that Siegfried's mother died during childbirth, while Parsifal's mother dies when he leaves her to become a knight. Wotan carries a spear in *Siegfried*. The action in *Parsifal* revolves around a holy spear that has been stolen from the knights of the Grail and must be retrieved. Siegfried forges his own sword. Parsifal makes his own bow and arrow. From these observations it should be clear that Wagner was inviting a direct comparison between *Siegfried* and *Parsifal*. This makes sense when we consider that he wrote the latter opera in the immediate aftermath of the premiere of *Siegfried* in Bayreuth.

For those who are not used to this kind of symbolic and structural analysis of stories, these details may seem trivial or unnecessarily cryptic. The first thing to note is that all high art has this level of intricacy, and it substantially increases our appreciation once we learn how to identify and understand these deeper meanings. The second thing is that educated art fans of the 19th century expected this as a matter of course, and Nietzsche was at the forefront of the category of people who knew how to make such interpretations. However, none of this was done for trivial or egotistical reasons. It was done because art was expected to deal with the biggest questions of life, and those questions don't have easy answers. That's what Nietzsche meant when he said that art should be taken seriously.

That's also why Nietzsche was the first person to whom Wagner sent the libretto for *Parsifal*. He believed he had captured something new and important with the opera, and he wanted Nietzsche to understand. That is true in the abstract, but what we are about to see is that *Parsifal* took Wagner's proclivity for inserting personal meanings into operas to a new level. The crucial fact to understand is this: *Parsifal* was the first and only libretto Wagner wrote after the beginning of his relationship with Nietzsche. All of his other stories predated that relationship. When they first met, Wagner was busy finishing the musical score for the Ring Cycle, which would take him several more years, after which he needed to put all his energy into organising the premiere in Bayreuth. Wagner had always put his own relationships into his art, and it was natural that he would do so with the person who had become, in his own words, the most important in his life after Cosima. That is why *Parsifal* is directly about Nietzsche. In fact, we might go a step further and say that Wagner wrote it for Nietzsche. It is his last lesson for the man who had unexpectedly become his disciple.

We should remember here that, for all of the bombastic, belligerent seeming egotism of the two men and their work, their relationship had been formed in the most intimate surroundings in Tribschen. Both men loved each other, and that is why the Father-Son paradigm has often been invoked to understand their relationship. However, this level of intimacy is a core feature of the most intense Orphan-Elder relationships. It is implied in the bond between Socrates and Plato, Jesus and the disciples, Caesar and Brutus, and, to use a more contemporary example, that between Freud and Jung. Just as Nietzsche referred to Wagner as his *Pater Seraphicus*, Jung referred to Freud as his second father. The fact that Wagner was harder on Nietzsche than on anybody else follows naturally from this fact since he always demanded the best from that which he cared about the most.

When we understand that the story of *Parsifal* is about Nietzsche, the fact that Wagner was drawing a direct correlation with the character of Siegfried takes on new importance since we also know that it was at exactly this time that Nietzsche had mirrored Siegfried by getting ready to battle his own Elder. That is why it is no coincidence that the main difference between the two operas lies in Step 8. Siegfried battles Wotan, but Parsifal will not be called upon to fight his Elder, instead, he will redeem him. That is the twist that Wagner inserted into his final opera, and it was directed at Nietzsche.

But this twist also represents a major development in Wagner's self-understanding. He wrote the Ring Cycle in the immediate aftermath of Dresden, and there is no doubt that the character of Siegfried was meant to represent himself and the other revolutionaries fighting against a corrupt establishment. As we will see shortly, in *Parsifal*, Wagner is not represented by the hero of the story but by the Elders. That means that Wagner knew, at some level, that he had become an Elder to Nietzsche. The story therefore represents his understanding of their relationship. We have spent this whole book describing that relationship in our terms. We will now get an insight into how Wagner thought about it through the meanings he inserted into *Parsifal*. What we will see is that the opera is Wagner's apology to Nietzsche. He knew that he had done his disciple wrong, and he dedicated his final work of art to setting the record straight.

* * *

Since we know already that *Parsifal* is an Orphan Story, identifying the roles of the main characters is almost second nature to us by this stage of the book. Parsifal is obviously the Orphan hero. Gurnemanz is an older Grail knight who is clearly the Elder. The Shadow Elder is Klingsor. In the medieval myth, he is an evil magician. In Wagner's story, he is a former Grail knight who has turned bad. That fact will become important shortly. Although we haven't focused too much on the romantic love interest in our analysis, another very common character in a male Orphan Story is the virtuous maiden. In the original Parzival, this role was filled by Queen Condwiramurs, who becomes the wife of the hero. In Wagner's *Siegfried*, the role belongs to Brünnhilde, although she is anything but a side character, since the second opera of the Ring Cycle, *Die Walküre*, is about her. All of Wagner's mature operas contain such a love interest. *Parsifal* is the notable exception. Wagner explicitly excludes this theme from the story and replaces it with the character of Kundry, who is a shapeshifter that appears both as an old crone and a beautiful young woman. More on that shortly, too.

Now that we know the main characters, let's walk through the opening moves of the story.

The opera begins with the Elder. Wagner makes this reading extra clear because he shows us Gurnemanz giving instruction to a group of young squires, i.e., conducting their initiation into knighthood. Just as in *Siegfried*, however, this initiation looks problematic. The Grail knights have a major issue to contend with. Their king, Amfortas, has been wounded by the holy spear, and the wound will not heal. We see Amfortas being carried back to the seat of the Grail clearly in great pain. The squires ask Gurnemanz to tell the story of what happened to the king. He explains that Amfortas was bewitched by a woman of fearsome beauty. This allowed Klingsor to steal the holy spear. Amfortas was wounded in the process. Gurnemanz also relates the reason why Klingsor has turned bad. Grail Knights must be pure of heart, but Klingsor succumbed to sin and then castrated himself in a mad desire for purification. He now lures prospective knights to their doom using beautiful women as an enchantment. His ultimate goal is to take the Grail itself.

It scarcely needs to be said that all of these themes map to the Orphan Story template. The Elder, Gurnemanz, represents the institution of the knights of the Grail. The Shadow Elder, Klingsor, has become their enemy (note that the character of Klingsor is almost identical to Darth Vader, who is a Jedi Knight gone bad). All the story needs now is the Orphan hero. Wagner sets our expectations by having Gurnemanz tell the squires about a prophecy that a "pure fool", enlightened through compassion, will arrive to save Amfortas. Sure enough, the very next thing that happens is that Parsifal accidentally stumbles into the scene. Gurnemanz interrogates him. We find that he doesn't know where he came from. In fact, he doesn't even know his own name. Here we have the classic *child of nature*, almost identical to Siegfried. Gurnemanz wonders whether Parsifal could be the "pure fool" described in the prophecy. All of this fulfils Step 3 of the Orphan Story template.

The template tells us that what will happen next is that the Elder will offer initiation to the Orphan. Wagner again satisfies our expectations by having Gurnemanz invite Parsifal to witness a ceremony that is about to take place. The wounded king, Amfortas, is going to uncover the Grail and release its immortality-conferring power on the other knights who have gathered for the occasion. However, we see that the ceremony causes immense pain to the king due to his wound. He cries out and asks to be spared, but the knights demand that he proceed. Amfortas forces himself through the pain to complete the ceremony, and the Grail knights who have gathered eat the holy bread and drink the holy wine.

At this point, we are approaching the end of Act 1. Wagner has expertly set up all the elements of the Orphan Story. All that remains is for the Elder to offer the Orphan initiation. Sure enough, after the ceremony is completed, Gurnemanz approaches Parsifal and asks him to explain what he has just witnessed. Remember, Parsifal does not know where he came from. He doesn't even know his own name. He was raised alone in the forest, away from civilisation. What chance can he have of understanding the elaborate ceremony that has been performed before him? Unsurprisingly, he tells Gurnemanz that he doesn't know the meaning. That's fine. This gives the Elder the perfect opportunity to begin his initiation. Everything we have seen so far sets up that expectation. And then Wagner pulls the rug out from under us. Gurnemanz flies into a rage. He tells Parsifal he is not a *pure fool*, just a garden-variety village idiot. He sends him away with the stinging rebuke, "A gander should look for a goose".

The disorienting nature of this is hard to understate. What Wagner had done at the end of Act 1 was to call into question the entire basis of the plot. Having set up all the elements of the Orphan Story, he negates what is, in fact, the central theme of that story, which is that the Orphan will receive initiation. This is unprecedented in Wagner's operas. Despite the innovations and inversions in *Siegfried*, that story is still very much about initiation. At the end of Act 1 of that opera, we know what the story is about, what the stakes are, and what is coming next. Siegfried will fight the dragon, and Mime intends to try and poison him afterwards so he can steal the dragon's treasure, which includes the ring of power. That is a normal part of storytelling in general. The purpose of Act 1 is to clarify the main stakes and set up the action ahead. Wagner had subverted not just the Orphan Story template but the structure of stories more generally.

As a result, we reach the end of Act 1 not knowing any more what sort of story we are watching. Nothing in Wagner's operas is accidental, so we can be sure that whatever Wagner is doing, he is doing it on purpose. In fact, he reinforces the disorientation in the musical score by making extensive use of the technique of chromaticism, which was always present in his earlier works but which is far more prominent in *Parsifal*. The result is that, as we go into Act 2, we have no idea what is going to happen next because we no longer know what kind of story we are in.

THE INITIATION OF NIETZSCHE

Despite all this, there are a number of clues in Act 1 that allow us to figure out what Wagner might be doing. Our starting point to solve the mystery is the dramatic ending where Wagner overturns our expectations. Having set up all the elements of the Orphan Story, Wagner subverts that reading by having the Elder (Gurnemanz) send the Orphan (Parsifal) away without initiation. But we can start to understand the meaning of this by examining the words that Gurnemanz sends Parsifal away with: "A gander should look for a goose". What does this mean?

Well, first of all, Gurnemanz is calling Parsifal a goose, i.e., an idiot. But, since he is sending Parsifal away without initiation, he is telling him to go and find a wife. He is saying, *You're not Grail material, boy, and we're not going to train you. Go and get married instead.* Remembering that Wagner's operas always contained personal meanings, let's think back to the letter that Wagner sent to Nietzsche in April 1874 when Ludwig had bailed out the Bayreuth project. We know that Nietzsche had fallen into a depression. He wrote a letter begging the master to give him a task and make him useful. Wagner responded by telling him to get married. That moment represented the time in Wagner's and Nietzsche's own Orphan Story where the Elder sent the Orphan away. Now Wagner just happens to put the same line into the exact part of the story of *Parsifal* where Gurnemanz sends the hero away. Coincidence? Not a chance.

Thus, we can formulate a hypothesis. Wagner has written the story of *Parsifal* to mimic his own relationship with Nietzsche. That means that the character of Parsifal represents Nietzsche, and the character of Gurnemanz represents Wagner. Is there any other evidence from Act 1 to back up this theory? The answer is yes. The line about the gander looking for a goose is preceded by another one that relates to the event that introduces Parsifal into the story. Gurnemanz tells the young man, "In the future, leave the swans here in peace". This follows from the fact that Parsifal had entered the scene by killing a swan.

We said earlier that Parsifal accidentally stumbles into the seat of the Grail. More specifically, what happens is that the young man shoots and kills a swan that was flying overhead. The swan falls to the ground and catches the attention of Gurnemanz and the squires. Remember, nothing in a Wagner opera is accidental. Parsifal could have shot a rabbit, a chicken, or any other animal. He shoots a swan. The question we must answer is, what is Wagner communicating with the symbolism of the swan, and especially the death of a swan?

Almost everybody will have heard of the concept of the *swan song*, which is a figure of speech that denotes the farewell performance of a well-known artist, musician, actor, sportsman, etc. The metaphor has deep roots in a number of mythological traditions where swans are said to sing before they die. In Plato's *Phaedo*, which is the story about Socrates' trial and death sentence, before Socrates drinks the hemlock, he makes the point that swans sing for joy before they die, not despair as was commonly believed. This is part of the larger theme of the dialogue, which makes clear that Socrates is not afraid to die. Since *Parsifal* is an opera, the characters are literally singing when the swan is discovered. Thus, the swan song reading is implied. But the swan in the story has not died naturally. Parsifal has killed it. Therefore, Parsifal has prevented the swan from singing. He has ruined the swan song.

If Parsifal represents Nietzsche, then it is Nietzsche who has spoiled the swan song. Whose swan song are we talking about? Clearly, it must be Wagner's. What was Wagner's swan song? The Bayreuth premiere. We know that Nietzsche ran away from the premiere. Therefore, he spoiled Wagner's swan song. But it's even more specific than that. Nietzsche fled during the rehearsal of the second opera of the cycle, which is called *Die Walküre* (The Valkyrie). In the mythical tradition, Valkyries can transform into swans. But there is yet another symbolic resonance that ties swans to Nietzsche. In Greek mythology, swans are associated with the god Apollo. All the way back in his very first book, *The Birth of Tragedy,* Nietzsche had criticised Greek culture at the time of Socrates (who talked about the swan song in the *Phaedo*!) as being excessively Apollonian. He had metaphorically killed Apollo, i.e., the swan.

At this point, it should be crystal clear that Parsifal represents Nietzsche. This makes perfect sense since we know that Wagner wrote the libretto for Parsifal in the immediate aftermath of Bayreuth, which is when Nietzsche spoiled Wagner's swan song. The reading is further reinforced by the fact that Parsifal is reproached by Gurnemanz for killing the swan. The knight asks why the young man did it, and Parsifal says he doesn't know. Nietzsche had never provided Wagner with a real explanation for why he fled Bayreuth. He sent a telegram saying he was ill, and that was all. If we think about how close the two men were and how much they must have talked and dreamed about the premiere of the Ring Cycle over the years, this excuse was simply not good enough. After all they had been through together, for Nietzsche simply to run away without at least giving a face-to-face explanation was unacceptable. That is what Wagner is implying in the scene.

This sets the context for what happens next in the opera. Having established Parsifal's (Nietzsche's) ignorance, Gurnemanz invites him to the elaborate ceremony where the Grail will be opened. What does the ceremony show us? A number of Grail knights are standing around demanding that the wounded Amfortas put on the show, i.e., open the Grail. He gives them what they want, and then they leave. What event does that sound like? It sounds an awful lot like the Bayreuth premiere.

Let's remember the background to that event. Wagner had tried and failed to raise the money for the festival himself. Ultimately, he relied on King Ludwig. But that was not a new dynamic. In one form or another, Ludwig had been financially supporting Wagner for more than a decade. The house in Tribschen had been paid for by Ludwig, for example. However, Ludwig's generosity came with strings attached. The king wanted to watch performances of the first two operas of the Ring Cycle. Wagner vehemently objected because the whole cycle was supposed to be performed in one go at the premiere. However, since he was financially dependent on Ludwig, he had no choice but to give in and allow the operas to be performed. *Das Rheingold* and *Die Walküre* were performed in 1869 and 1870 in Munich.

All this adds an extra layer of symbolism to the first act of *Parsifal*. The character of Amfortas is also a symbol of Wagner, more specifically, Wagner's pain at having to put on a show against his will for the Grail knights. When Gurnemanz leads Parsifal to watch that ceremony and witness the pain, we must understand this as Wagner leading Nietzsche to witness his pain. When

PART 2: THE ORPHAN STORY OF NIETZSCHE AND WAGNER

Gurnemanz asks Parsifal to explain what he has seen and he does not know the answer, this is Wagner telling Nietzsche that he was ignorant, a "pure fool", as to what was really going on. Nietzsche had not understood the suffering that Wagner had gone through in order to perform his art. That is the meaning of Act 1, and it will become the meaning of the larger story. Thus, even though Wagner has subverted the Orphan Story format, the meaning of Act 1 is clear. Wagner is educating Nietzsche about how he had suffered for his art and specifically the suffering he had gone through in Bayreuth, which Nietzsche did not know about because he ran away.

Note that this reading is completely in accordance with the broader facts about the relationship between Nietzsche and Wagner. Cosima had complained in her diary that Nietzsche did not understand the sacrifices that Wagner needed to make. We must remember that Nietzsche, Rohde, and Gersdorff really did view Wagner as a godlike omnipotent force, and Wagner had encouraged that reading indirectly because he never expressed the pain and suffering he went through. That would have gone against his pride. It was also against his interests. He needed to project the image of power. It was a huge part of his success over the long run.

All of this incredible depth of meaning is communicated in Act 1 of the opera. Gurnemanz is sending Parsifal away both because that is what Wagner did to Nietzsche in real life and also because it represents the fact that initiation is over, i.e., Nietzsche's initiation with Wagner is over. That is why Wagner pulls the rug on the Orphan Story reading. However, it is also implied that the rest of the opera will be about Nietzsche finally coming to understand the truth. He must no longer view Wagner as an all-powerful king but as a wounded one (Amfortas).

This theme is continued immediately at the start of Act 2, where we meet Klingsor in his lair. Because Klingsor is plotting to bring about Parsifal's downfall, Wagner manages to instantly recreate the Orphan Story reading because we know that the hero is going to battle the Shadow Elder. Furthermore, this establishes a parallel with the Ring Cycle because Klingsor is going to use the exact kind of deception that Alberich, Mime, and Hagen use against Siegfried. We know that Siegfried was brought down by this kind of deception at the end of the Ring Cycle, and now we are going to see if Parsifal can avoid the same fate. Therefore, we are not just back in the Orphan Story reading; we are back in the specific variation of the template that Wagner had used in the Ring Cycle. It's a brilliant piece of storytelling that Wagner both undermines the Orphan Story and then re-creates it so effortlessly.

Klingsor is the caster of illusions, and he has cast a spell on Kundry, who is now transformed into a beautiful young woman who will seduce Parsifal and thereby corrupt him. In Act 1, Kundry was introduced to us as an old crone who was striving to help the knights of the Grail by applying a healing potion to Amfortas. Now, she is working for the Shadow Elder. In Kundry we have a strange kind of character who appears to be supporting both sides in the struggle. How can we explain this fact?

If Parsifal represents Nietzsche and the Grail knights represent Wagner, then Kundry would have to be Cosima. That reading makes perfect sense because Kundry is tending to Amfortas' wounds in Act 1, and that is metaphorically what Cosima did for Wagner in real life, primarily in an emotional and logistical sense. Cosima had devoted her life to Wagner, even sacrificing her own children in order to live with him in Tribschen. The manic character of Kundry in Act 1 represents this. Furthermore, Kundry is also present when Parsifal arrives on the scene, which, of course, is how it was in real life when Nietzsche and Wagner first met.

If Kundry represents Cosima, then her appearance in Act 2 alongside Klingsor leads to the conclusion that Klingsor is also a representation of Wagner. That would make sense because one of the modifications Wagner made to the character was that he is an ex-Grail knight and therefore somebody who was once on the same team. That also explains why Kundry appears to be supporting both teams. What we learn at the beginning of Act 2, therefore, is that both Klingsor (Wagner) and Kundry (Cosima) are plotting to seduce Parsifal (Nietzsche). Wagner has now upped the ante significantly. He is now revaluating the entire relationship with Nietzsche and revealing that his and Cosima's underlying intentions were not entirely wholesome when they welcomed Nietzsche into Tribschen. Again, that accords with the facts since it does seem that the two of them wanted Nietzsche to the extent that he could further Wagner's influence.

Is there any further evidence for this reading? Yes. Once again, Wagner places a symbol at the beginning of Act 2 that Nietzsche could not have misunderstood.

One of the more notorious episodes in Wagner's life was when he was forced into using ballet dancers in his opera Tannhäuser in Paris in 1861. It may sound absurd, but, at the time, it was expected that every opera should include a ballet performance. What's more, the ballet had to be staged at the beginning of Act 2 of the opera because large sections of the audience preferred to spend Act 1 eating and drinking at the bar. Remember, Wagner had written entire treatises upholding the virtues of art as a sacred form of culture and specifically demanding that every aspect of an opera serve the greater unity of the story. Inserting a random ballet performance was the exact kind of nonsense that Wagner had been railing against his whole life. It trivialised the art form.

Wagner used all his methods of persuasion to try to convince the theatre managers not to make him include the ballet. He was told in no uncertain terms that if he wanted Tannhäuser performed at all, there must be dancers. That's what the audience demanded, and that's what drove ticket sales. In the end, he managed to extract a compromise. The ballet dancers would be included, but they would be placed towards the end of Act 1, where Wagner could make it seem that they belonged in the story. The problem was, nobody told the audience. On the opening night premiere, a large section of the crowd did what they always did and spent Act 1 at the bar. When they stumbled into the theatre at the beginning of Act 2, they learned that they had missed the ballet and proceeded to tear up the place up in a riot. Despite this disaster, Wagner still refused to relocate the ballet dancers to the normal position at the beginning of Act 2. As a result, Tannhäuser was only performed three times before theatre management pulled the pin. Wagner was so angry at the debacle that he spent the rest of his life hating the French.

It is this real-life episode that is symbolised at the beginning of Act 2 of *Parsifal* when the hero wanders into Klingsor's lair and is greeted by a group of flower maidens who offer him every pleasure a young man can desire. But

Parsifal is completely immune to their charms, and the seduction doesn't work. For most commentators, this is evidence of Parsifal's chastity and the theme of "purity" that runs through the opera, etc. But we know that Parsifal represents Nietzsche, and so what Wagner is showing us is that Nietzsche was not interested in opera because of pretty ballet dancers. He was actually interested in art for its own sake.

That is one meaning. A second meaning is a reference to the very first scene of the Ring Cycle, where the Nibelung dwarf Alberich stumbles across the Rhinemaidens. He tries to seduce them, and they laugh in his face. This sets off the dynamic that motivates the entire story as Alberich tries to make up with power what he lacks in love. The implication is that Nietzsche is not like Alberich in that he desires the higher things in life. The third and most direct meaning is that all this happens immediately after Gurnemanz has told Parsifal that he should look for a wife. Parsifal then wanders into a group of women but is immune to their charms. That's exactly how it was with Nietzsche in his own life. It didn't mean that Nietzsche was not interested in women but only that he had no interest in physical pleasure for its own sake. He was a "pure fool," not in the sense of chastity but in wanting meaning and purpose. In that respect, he was different from Wagner since, at least earlier in his life, Wagner was quite the womaniser.

In *Parsifal*, all of this is happening at the behest of Klingsor, who is trying to seduce and therefore corrupt the hero. The implication is that Wagner was trying to corrupt Nietzsche. What is Klingsor's backstory? We learned in Act 1 that he was a Grail knight who strove for a purity that he could not achieve. As a result, he castrated himself. But that is exactly the meaning of the story of the ballet dancers. Wagner attempted to preserve the purity of his opera by putting the dancers in Act 1. As a result, the opera was a disaster, and his career in Paris was all but over. Metaphorically, he had castrated himself. We must remember that Wagner was still living in exile at that time, and so this was an enormous setback to him in real life. Furthermore, it was because of this commercial failure that Wagner would later need to turn to Ludwig for money. Thus, Wagner is symbolising the fact that he had become Klingsor through his uncompromising desire for purity. It was that desire that had turned him into a caster of illusions, and he had become an evil Grail knight as a result.

The further implication of this is that Wagner had also set out to corrupt Nietzsche with his illusions but that Nietzsche had been protected by his own innocent foolishness. That also matches the facts in real life. The reason Nietzsche had become a disciple of Wagner in the first place was because he fervently believed in the ideals that Wagner proclaimed in his early writings. He did so in the face of all the obvious real-world corruption of Wagner's art. Nietzsche never blamed Wagner for that corruption. He blamed everybody else, including the king, the Kaiser, and the German public. Let's remember that Nietzsche had written the hagiography of Wagner in the lead-up to the premiere in 1876. Even as late as that, he had absolved Wagner of all blame for the things that had gone wrong. Wagner was now telling him that this was not true. He was to blame for the debacle in Paris. He was to blame for selling out to Ludwig. He was to blame for the Bayreuth circus. All this was the result of striving for purity. He was taking responsibility for having become the caster of illusions.

Let's take stock of the ground we have covered. We have seen that Wagner sets up a perfect Orphan Story and then subverts it in exactly the same way he subverted the relationship with Nietzsche in real life (telling the hero to "get married"). As a result, he creates a story whose purpose is to educate the foolish Orphan hero (Nietzsche) in all the things he does not know. He does not know that Wagner suffered immensely to put the Ring Cycle on stage. He does not know that the Bayreuth premiere was just the latest in a series of debacles that Wagner had been putting up with his entire life. Most importantly, he does not know that Wagner himself is now taking responsibility for turning into Klingsor, the caster of illusions. In short, Wagner is signalling to Nietzsche that he was fully well aware that Bayreuth had turned into a sham but that he had to go through with it anyway.

The two things going on here are Wagner taking responsibility while also pointing out Nietzsche's own failings. There were all kinds of real-world problems that Nietzsche had ignored. Again, this fits with the facts. There is no evidence in any of Nietzsche's letters or notebooks that he had been aware of the difficulties that Wagner faced. This follows from the simple reality that he had never been involved with the practical side of Wagner's work. He had no idea about conducting, about training singers, about choosing costumes, or about any of the countless other tasks that were required. It took two years of full-time preparation to put the Ring Cycle on stage, including the construction of the *Festspielhaus*. Nietzsche was absent from Bayreuth for the entire time. When Wagner characterises Nietzsche as a "pure fool" by associating him with Parsifal, he means that in both a good and a bad way. The bad side of it is that Nietzsche was ignorant of the practical difficulties that Wagner had to work through and had provided no meaningful assistance in that respect. (In fairness to Nietzsche, his request that Wagner make him "useful" was an invitation for Wagner to give him some of the workload. Why Wagner did not do so was because he was a perfectionist and control freak).

Now we are ready to understand the dramatic event that takes place in the middle of Act 2 of *Parsifal*, and which forms the central meaning of the entire opera. With the flower maidens failing to seduce Parsifal, Kundry arrives to try to achieve the same outcome. She manages to win his trust and then kisses him. But things do not go according to plan. With the kiss, Parsifal suddenly experiences the pain of Amfortas, not as a third-party witness, which he had been in Act 1, but as a direct subjective experience. What is extraordinary about this is that it is one of the earliest representations in art of a concept that is now widespread in our culture but which originated in 19th-century German thought. In English, we call the concept *'empathy,'* but it comes from the German word *'Einfühlung'*.

What Parsifal is able to do is to put himself in the shoes of Amfortas, to experience his pain directly, not as an abstraction. Wagner explicitly shows us the process by which empathy can occur. In Act 1, Parsifal witnesses the pain of Amfortas but doesn't understand it. Why? Firstly, because that pain is wrapped up in a complex and mysterious ritual that includes the needs and desires of the other Grail knights. All these distract attention from the emotional state of the king. Furthermore, it is clear that nobody else is empathising with Amfortas because they want something from him. The implication is that empathy can only occur in a state of "purity". Secondly, when Parsifal first witnesses Amfortas' pain, he is looking on as an objective, third-party observer. Even if he understands that the king is suffering, this is a rational, logical form of understanding. It is a completely different thing from the feeling of pain. Only by getting into a subjective frame of mind and feeling the pain as if it were his own can Parsifal experience true empathy.

All of this is interesting in relation to our broader understanding of empathy, but Wagner was not just making an objective or rational point here. This was a direct invitation to Nietzsche to do what Parsifal does and really empathise with Wagner's pain and suffering. In other words, *Parsifal* is an apology by Wagner to Nietzsche. It is an admission of guilt and regret. But it is also a request for forgiveness, not in the form of a public statement but a private experience. This act of empathising and forgiveness also leads to truth. That is what is signified by what happens after Parsifal's epiphany. Once he has learned to subjectively understand Amfortas' pain, the illusions of Klingsor simply melt away. Since both Amfortas and Klingsor represent Wagner, this means that Nietzsche can redeem Wagner by understanding him. He will no longer be a caster of illusions because truth will have taken the place of deception.

This sets up another direct parallel with the Ring Cycle because in the fourth opera of that epic, Siegfried is brought undone by deception and illusion. Siegfried was the hero who knew no fear. He was able to forge his own sword and defeat gods and dragons with it. But his sword could not defeat deception and illusion. By contrast, Parsifal holds no sword at all. Nevertheless, he defeats the Shadow Elder through empathy—*Einfühlung*. Empathy is the defence against deception. But Wagner does not mean that empathy can bring about world peace or prevent the need for bravery, strength, and all the other virtues of Siegfried. Parsifal still requires those. Thus, at the beginning of Act 3, when the hero stumbles back to the seat of the Grail, we learn that he is bloody and bruised after years of fighting various battles. Parsifal still needs to fight.

At the conclusion of the Ring Cycle, Siegfried is stabbed in the back by the wielder of illusions, Hagen. It is because Parsifal has learned to see through those illusions that he escapes the same fate. It doesn't mean that he has no enemies; it just means he is not deceived by them into thinking they are friends. That was Siegfried's failing. Crucially, Parsifal's enemies are elsewhere. He must leave the Grail in order to fight them. When he returns at the beginning of Act 3, he has the Holy Spear with him, which he won from Klingsor, but he tells us that he has not used it in any of the fighting, as he wanted to retain its purity. Wagner is implying that empathy must not be used as a weapon. If it is, it becomes a weapon of deceit and illusion. The hero must either develop empathy or be destroyed by it.

The more personal message that Wagner was sending to Nietzsche was that he too would have to go off and fight battles but only after learning how to empathise. Otherwise, he would end up just like Klingsor, brought undone by his own obsessive desire for purity. We have to remember that Wagner wrote *Parsifal* in response not just to the Bayreuth debacle but also to the book of Nietzsche's that came just prior to it. It was Nietzsche's hagiography that led Wagner to conclude that he was still the "pure fool" who had created for himself an ideal that no longer had anything to do with reality. With *Parsifal*, Wagner set out to put the record straight. He did so by admitting his own failings.

But this warning was not an instruction to give up on the ideals, only to incorporate them with real-world experience. At no point in the story does *Parsifal* lose his *pure foolishness*. His empathy with the Knights and their failings does not negate the ideal that he holds. That is why he still goes off to fight. He is battling on behalf of the ideal. Nietzsche had already built up an ideal of Wagner before the two ever met, but we must understand that this ideal was not a falsehood. He *had* understood the ideals that even Wagner himself was only scarcely conscious of. He was able to see the best version of Wagner because he was a pure fool. Wagner is saying that it is this quality of the Orphan which is able to redeem the wounded king (i.e., the Elder).

But Nietzsche had done more than just understand intellectually. He believed. This is another schism that we have opened up for ourselves in the modern West: the one between intellect and feeling. Why should there be a necessary difference between the two? Why can't we both understand something intellectually and feel it at the same time? It was precisely that which drew Nietzsche to Wagner in the first place. He felt something in relation to Wagner's idea, something which was lacking in the philological study of the ancient world. Philology cared only for an intellectual understanding. Wagner wanted to put the feeling back. He did that in his art, his life, and his ideas.

Nietzsche had both intellect and feeling. He understood the ideals and passionately believed in them. The final thing he was lacking was experience. He had spent his whole life in the cloistered environment of academia. Even the golden days of Tribschen had taken place in a fairy-tale setting on the banks of Lake Lucerne, all funded by the King of Bavaria. Whatever that was, it was not the "real world". Now we are able to understand why Wagner had pushed Nietzsche to publish *The Birth of Tragedy*. It wasn't just that this would glorify Wagner's own work; it would force Nietzsche into the real world. For the first time, he would enter public life advocating for something that he actually believed in. The job in Basel didn't count. That was handed to him on a platter while he was thinking about giving up philology altogether. *The Birth of Tragedy* was his real entry into society, and Wagner was the Elder who pushed him to make it happen.

Thus, although *Parsifal* is an apology on Wagner's behalf, it also implies a subtle criticism of Nietzsche. Gurnemanz gets angry at Parsifal in Act 1 and sends him away because he doesn't understand. That is what Wagner had done in real life. He sent Nietzsche away. Why did he do that? Because what Nietzsche needed was to do exactly what Parsifal does in the opera and go off into the real world to fight his own battles. He must leave the implied safety of the seat of the Grail, leave the Elder, and go off and experience life for himself. Wagner had sent Nietzsche away, telling him to get married, travel, or write an opera. What had Nietzsche done instead? He wrote a hagiography. He took refuge in idealism.

The irony is that it is almost certainly that hagiography that forced Wagner to confront the fact that he had become a corrupt Elder. At the time of what should have been Wagner's greatest triumph, when all the dignitaries of the German establishment showed up to Bayreuth to pay homage to him, Nietzsche held up an idealistic mirror that proved that it was not a triumph at all and that Wagner had betrayed his ideals. Only Nietzsche's pure foolishness, only his one-eyed devotion to those ideals, could have allowed this to happen, and the result was that it forced Wagner to see the difference between what he had once believed in and what he had become. Yet another incredible coincidence in our story is that both Nietzsche and Wagner realised at the exact same time what the meaning of Bayreuth was. Wagner was forced to confront Nietzsche's hagiography. Nietzsche was forced to confront the reality in Bayreuth. It was a shock for both men. In the aftermath, Wagner immediately began writing the libretto to *Parsifal*, and Nietzsche immediately began writing *Human, All Too Human*. Nietzsche's disillusionment caused him to go to war not just against Wagner but against all the idols of the world. Wagner wrote an apology.

The fact that Wagner would write an apology in the form of an opera is not surprising when we remember the point made earlier that he had always made art his life, and this entailed putting intimate personal meanings into his works. The *Gesamtkunstwerk* was not just a unification of different forms of art such as story, poetry, and music; it was also the unification of the individual and the collective through the artwork. As noted earlier, Wagner's use of mythology facilitated a union of the individual and the universal, and that is why he could use Parsifal as the Orphan to represent Nietzsche and the Elders in the story to represent himself. Although he almost certainly didn't think about them using the names of the archetypes as we have, his choice of mythical character reveals that he understood what was really going on between him and Nietzsche.

It should not surprise us that Wagner would apologise through his art. Neither should it surprise us that his apology included some criticisms of Nietzsche. All of this is part of the Orphan Story, and we may turn to our template one final time to understand the meaning of what had happened. For simplicity's sake, we did not include it in our original analysis; however, the apology of the Elder is a core feature of the Orphan Story in that it is the prelude to the death of the Elder that occurs in Step 7. Therefore, that Wagner should make an apology is also perfectly in keeping with the Orphan Story between him and Nietzsche. But the nature of that apology reflects the modern Western culture of which the two men were a part and in which we still live.

To understand Wagner's apology, we first need to refer back to the two world-historical stories that have been our main comparison point through the book.

It is fitting that the word "apology" comes from the Greek. In ancient Greece, an *apologia* had nothing to do with an expression or emotion of regret. Rather, it was a speech given in defence in a legal proceeding. The Greek legal system required the individual who was charged to speak in their own defence. Nobody was allowed to speak on their behalf. There were no lawyers in ancient Greece. Since Socrates was brought to trial for the charge of corrupting the youth, it is no surprise to find that he needed to give an *apologia*, and that is exactly the name of the Platonic dialogue that deals with the trial, although, again, the modern translation given to that dialogue, "The Apology," is misleading because the meaning of the word has changed in our time. A better modern translation would be "The Defence".

Thus, Socrates was not apologising in the sense that we mean it; he was publicly defending himself against accusations made against him, and he was doing so in the way that Greek culture required by making a reasoned argument. It follows that Socrates did not express regret at all. On the contrary, he denied the validity of his trial and said that Athens would be the one to regret his wrongful death. Of course, Socrates was found guilty, and so his death came almost immediately after his "apology" (Step 7 of the Orphan Story template).

The exact same thing happens in the gospels, and it happens at exactly the same time in the story, i.e., right before the death of Jesus. The gospel story is slightly more complex, however, because it is the Jewish religious leadership which is trying to have Jesus found guilty under Roman law rather than under Jewish law. The implied reason is because Jesus had not actually broken any Jewish laws and therefore could not be tried under them. That is why Jesus is hauled before Pontius Pilate and subjected to almost the identical legal proceedings that Socrates had to face centuries earlier, including the expectation that he would need to make an *apologia*, a legal defence of himself.

Of course, the charges laid against Jesus are invalid, as were the charges laid against Socrates. Pontius Pilate notes this fact and tells the mob that he can see no case against Jesus. He invites Jesus to make an *apologia*, but, unlike Socrates, Jesus refuses. He remains completely silent. Pilate is stunned at this because in Greek and Roman culture to remain silent was a very bad tactic. Pilate still attempts to avoid a wrongful conviction but quickly gives up and literally washes his hands at the miscarriage of justice that has occurred. Jesus is then taken away to be crucified.

Socrates had made an *apologia* and had stated that his trial and sentence were unjust. Jesus had shown that his trial and sentence were unjust precisely by refusing to make an *apologia*. In both cases, the apology or lack thereof leads to the next step of the Elder being killed. However, note that both of the apologies are consonant with the teachings of the Elder. Socrates was a true Greek citizen in that he carried out both his philosophy and his apology in public forums. Jesus' refusal to make a public apology was also in accordance with his teaching since he held that the highest arbiter of truth and virtue was spiritual in nature. His "apology" would not be to the Roman state but to God, and that is how it would be for Christians thereafter.

Wagner's use of art to make his own apology was perfectly consonant with his own belief that art was the highest metaphysical task of life. But there are several properties of Wagner's apology which distinguish it from the historical examples of Socrates and Jesus. The first is that it comes not in answer to a public legal charge but in answer to an essentially invisible private charge. At the time that Wagner wrote *Parsifal*, Nietzsche had never said or written a word in accusation against him. The unspoken accusation was implied by his fleeing from Bayreuth, his address of Wagner as "friend" for the first time, and the contrarian nature of his behaviour in Italy in late 1876. All of these, together with the hagiography published just before Bayreuth, would have been enough for Wagner to figure out what was going on. But nobody else could have pieced this puzzle together. Therefore, the accusation and the apology were an entirely private affair between the two men.

Of course, what this implies is that the accuser of Wagner is Nietzsche. That is a radical departure from the stories of Socrates and Jesus, who are accused by their enemies. But this inversion makes sense to us now because we know that Wagner had sold Nietzsche out. Therefore, Wagner became the enemy, but only when Nietzsche realised the betrayal, and that only happened at Bayreuth. Because Nietzsche is the only accuser, it follows that the meanings in Parsifal are almost entirely directed at him. That is also why the opera contains criticism of Nietzsche because Wagner is defending himself, and one way to do that is to attack the accuser and point out the ways in which they contributed to the problem.

The final, and perhaps most important, twist in Wagner's apology is that it is a genuine expression of regret. That is in stark contrast to Socrates and Jesus, who were defiant until the end. Wagner's pride would have prevented him from ever apologising in public, and so he hid the apology away in the deepest layers of an opera, where he knew that only Nietzsche could find it. There is something in this that reflects modern Western culture more broadly, which is that, to a very large extent, it is esoteric in nature. Socrates and Jesus acted in the exoteric, public world. But the meaning of Wagner's opera is entirely esoteric since it relies on an interpretation that can only be carried out privately. The only way to figure it out at all is to get to the deeper meanings. It is an empirical fact about *Parsifal* that almost nobody was able to do that, and still to this day the opera is not understood.

We have said that the apology of the Elder normally comes just before their death. The final incredible coincidence in our story is that Wagner died in early 1883, only months after the premiere performance of Parsifal. But the far more important "death" occurred in early 1878 when Nietzsche gave away his personal copies of Wagner's operas and then placed *Human, All Too Human* in the post. The 1st of January 1878 was Wagner's symbolic death from Nietzsche's point of view. Just months later, he would begin to accuse Wagner in public and not just in private. In that respect, the incredible coincidence of him receiving Wagner's apology only days later becomes even more incredible since it arrives at the exact time in the story when our template would expect it. But we should not be surprised by such coincidences anymore.

There is no chance that Nietzsche did not understand all of the meanings of the *Parsifal* libretto that we have outlined and many more. Given that we know that he would spend the rest of his sane life railing against Wagner in his philosophical works, it follows that he did not accept the apology. The main reason why this was the case can be found in a seemingly minor detail. But, of course, for either Nietzsche or Wagner, nothing was minor when it came to art because art was the expression of the most serious business of life. To say it one last time, the *Gesamtkunstwerk* was holistic not just in its techniques but also in its assumption that the meanings contained in art were the highest meanings about human existence. Another way in which Wagner's art and his worldview were holistic is that he wanted to achieve the fullest expression of what it meant to be human, including and especially those parts of human nature that had been suppressed in Western culture, namely, feelings, emotions, and passion. Wagner emphasised these not because they are an end in themselves but because he believed Western culture had tilted far too much towards the intellectual, Apollonian aspects of existence. Thus, the *Gesamtkunstwerk* really did aim to encompass the sum total of all aspects of human nature, including the individual, the collective, the unconscious and conscious mind, the emotions and passions, male and female, young and old, and all other properties. The word that Wagner would have used to describe this holistic state in his earlier life would have been "love". That is why love forms the central motif in all his mature operas.

Parsifal has a different central motif. The concept of empathy is relevant. But the word Wagner used explicitly was "compassion", although the German *Mitleid* can also be rendered into English as "pity," and this is the thing that Nietzsche most objected to about the message of the opera and the change it represented in Wagner's worldview. It was this that led Nietzsche to condemn *Parsifal* as a work of resignation and decadence in contrast to the grand passion of all the preceding operas.

Whether that is actually true of the meaning of *Parsifal* is not a question we need to answer here; arguments can be made both ways. But it certainly is true of the relationship between Nietzsche and Wagner. *Parsifal* was Wagner's final message to his disciple, but it was sent in written form through the post. Of course, Nietzsche had done exactly the same in response by sending

Human, All Too Human on the same day. But therein lay the whole problem. The golden days of the relationship were over, and we must remember that in those golden days the two men really had loved one another. It must have seemed to Nietzsche that Wagner was now suggesting that compassion and pity could fill the gap left by love. Nietzsche was correct in saying that this idea goes against the teachings of Wagner's earlier operas, most of which are tragedies where the hero sacrifices everything in the name of love. That is why Nietzsche could not accept Wagner's apology, and that is why he would spend the rest of his sane life being Wagner's accuser.

* * *

To close out this book, we might ask a fairly obvious question: couldn't all this have been done in private? Nietzsche and Wagner met in person in Italy in late 1876. They'd both had enough time to digest what had happened in Bayreuth. Wagner was already writing *Parsifal*, and Nietzsche was already writing *Human, All Too Human*. The ideas communicated in both those books could have been shared directly. Why weren't they? Why didn't Nietzsche tell Wagner about his disappointment and feelings of betrayal? Why didn't Wagner ask for forgiveness as he had done symbolically in *Parsifal*?

Our answer to these questions relates back to the issue with which we began this book: what was the nature of the Nietzsche-Wagner relationship? If we believe, along with the majority of commentators, that Nietzsche and Wagner were friends, then perhaps a mutual exchange of the kind just described would have been desirable. But we know that Nietzsche and Wagner were never friends. They were in an Orphan-Elder relationship, one that, due to the socio-cultural dynamic of 19th-century Germany, was religious in nature, which means it revolved around the biggest questions of life. The point of the *Gesamtkunstwerk* was to combine these highest questions of life with the most personal issues, the individual with the collective, culture, philosophy, music, and everything else. That is why the issues could not be reduced down to a merely personal disagreement. The personal was a vehicle for the collective and the universal.

It follows from this that the feelings and emotions the two men felt were always in service to the higher ideals that they were exploring. The disputes between the two were never merely domestic matters. Nietzsche's vegetarianism early on in the relationship was not a problem because it caused an inconvenience in the arrangements for lunch but because of the larger worldview that it implied. It was that worldview which Wagner attacked at the time. That's how it was for everything in the Wagner household, and that's why Nietzsche loved it there. Everything was important. Everything had meaning. Just as everything in a Wagner opera had to have a higher meaning that served the overall vision for the work, so did everything in Wagner's life, including the dietary requirements of a lunch guest.

We might argue that this is all far too severe, but the fact that we don't take this kind of thing seriously reveals something about the state of our culture. Part of the reason why the Wagner-Nietzsche relationship is valuable to us is as a point of comparison with our times. We would never dream of taking art as seriously as Nietzsche and Wagner. But what do we take seriously instead? The GDP. The inflation rate. The sports results from the weekend. Are these the real issues of life? Are they worthy of our highest attention? Are they capable of raising us up as humans, of understanding more about ourselves and the world in which we live? Are they able to inspire love and grand passion?

Another comparison point with our time comes via the concept of empathy or compassion that Wagner explored in his final opera. Nominally, both of these are important concepts in modern Western culture. But it is clear that we use empathy in a reduced sense compared to the way that Wagner did. Empathy has now come to mean something equivalent to a sharing of emotions and feelings as an end in itself. That may have validity in personal relationships, but when it is applied to a culture, it serves mostly as a smokescreen for the real issues. Empathy then quickly devolves into the form of emotional manipulation which dominates modern public discourse. The result is that ideas and ideals are almost never discussed anymore. Perhaps ironically, we have swung to the other extreme from that of the 19th-century, which was excessively intellectual and paid almost no attention to feelings. Our age is excessively emotional and pays almost no attention to intellect. Both of these lead to degraded forms of culture.

An argument could be made that both Nietzsche and Wagner were somewhat responsible for our current state of affairs because they included in their written works a great deal that could be seen as excessively emotional at the expense of intellectual rigour. But that is a misunderstanding of what the two were trying to achieve. Over and above the dichotomy between intellect and feeling lie ideals, meaning, and purpose. The ideals of a culture can never be proven by intellect or by emotion. Culture is not rational because life is not rational, but that doesn't mean that we should jettison reason and logic altogether, and it certainly doesn't mean that feelings should dominate. Wagner was not proposing that. He wanted a holistic solution that combined intellect, emotion, and ideals. Once upon a time, religion served that purpose. For Wagner, Nietzsche, and many others in the 19th century, art would need to fill the void left by the collapse in religious faith.

Of course, art can be just as illusory and deceptive as religion. Wagner demonstrated that with the character of Klingsor in *Parsifal*. What is it that saves art from illusion? It is not simply emotion. The character of Kundry provides plenty of that in the opera. Neither is it the idealism of the *pure fool* who is able to present ideals in an abstract, intellectual form. Nietzsche had been able to do that very well. The unity which redeems Kundry, Parsifal, and Amfortas is an art which can express the ideal and also manifest it. That is why it is only through art that Wagner could express what needed to be expressed. Until the artwork is created, there can be no unification of ideal, intellect, and emotion. That is why Wagner and Nietzsche couldn't have simply discussed their problems over a cup of tea in Italy, because their problems were larger than themselves; they were part of culture. The ideals of a culture must be made manifest. Only in that way can they be communicated, debated, and discussed. Since a culture is what unifies individuals into a collective, it also follows that a purely private exchange does not contribute to culture. It is through art and culture that individuals become a collective.

More than that, though, an artwork is also a process of becoming. Every artwork done with full conviction and commitment is a journey into the sacred to the extent that the creators themselves can never be fully aware of what will manifest at the other end of the process. In that way, art is an exploratory medium that reveals ourselves to ourselves. Something that was hidden now comes to light. Something unknown becomes known. Something that was not manifest is now made manifest. To practice art the way Wagner and Nietzsche practiced it requires discipline, determination, and devotion. It requires seriousness, but it also requires play. Perhaps it requires everything that we find in life itself. If, as Wagner had always demanded, we incorporate all of life into art, then the boundaries really do break down, and life becomes art as art becomes life.

Although it ended up taking a very different form, something like this idea was always present in Nietzsche's mature philosophy in the notion of self-creation, not in an egotistic or narcissistic sense but in the sense of exploration and play that strives always to incorporate something new and interesting via bold conjecture and grand passion. In that respect, he carried on what Wagner had taught him, and, in the final words of his final book, even though the book was titled *Nietzsche Contra Wagner,* he still paid homage to the ideal of the artist which had drawn him to Wagner in the first place:-

> *Are we not precisely in this respect— Greeks? Worshippers of form, of tones, of words? Precisely on that account— artists?*

About the Author

For more information on upcoming releases and a weekly blog, check out my website at https://simonsheridan.me

You can connect with me on:
🌐 https://simonsheridan.me

Also by Simon Sheridan

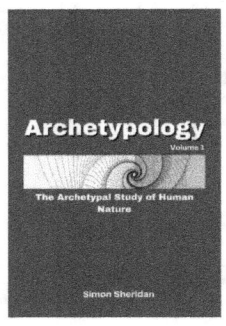

Archetypology: The Archetypal Study of Human Nature
An introductory volume that outlines a framework for understanding human nature that places the concept of the archetype at the centre of analysis. The model revolves around four primary archetypes inspired by the psychology of Carl Jung – the Child, the Orphan, the Adult, and the Elder. With these and just a few other core concepts, archetypology provides a succinct but powerful framework that expands the archetype concept beyond the psychological to integrate nominally discrete domains such as biology, anthropology, history, and literature. The result is a holistic account of human development centred around the pattern of the cycle-ending-in-transcendence.

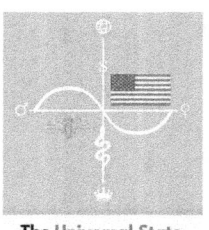

The Universal State of America: An Archetypal Calculus of Western Civilisation
Drawing on the work of the great comparative scholars Joseph Campbell, Arnold van Gennep, Oswald Spengler, and Arnold Toynbee, this book expands the concept of the archetype beyond the domain of psychology to integrate biology, anthropology, literature, and, especially, history. The result is a unique synthesis that posits that the unfolding of civilisation proceeds according to the same pattern as an individual human life: a cyclical process punctuated by dramatic periods of transcendence.

The Devouring Mother: The Collective Unconscious in the Time of Corona

Those who fail to incorporate the shadow are doomed to project it. In the modern materialist West, we don't merely fail to incorporate our shadow, we deny its existence. In The Devouring Mother, author Simon Sheridan takes a journey into the other half of the psyche looking for an archetypal explanation for the social ructions in western society over the last several years beginning with the Trump and Brexit votes and reaching earthquake proportions with the corona event.

The Plague Story and Other Essays: Re-evaluating the Coronavirus Narrative

The Plague Story is a work that draws inspiration from the systems thinking and cybernetics movements of the 20th century. It is a multi-disciplinary series of essays that aims to place the corona event in the broader cultural and philosophical context of modern society. If you have the feeling that the story of corona is not quite right, this book aims to provide a framework for understanding and a guide to meaningful re-evaluation.